business solutions

Microsoft® Office Access VBA 2007

Scott B. Diamond

with Brent Spaulding

800 E. 96th Street
Indianapolis, Indiana 46240

D1359381

Microsoft® Office Access 2007 VBA

Copyright © 2008 by Que Publishing

ISBN-13: 978-0-7897-3731-1
ISBN-10: 0-7897-3731-0

Library of Congress Cataloging-in-Publication Data

Diamond, Scott B.

Microsoft Office Access 2007 VBA / Scott B. Diamond with Brent Spaulding.

p. cm.

ISBN 0-7897-3731-0

1. Microsoft Access. 2. Microsoft Visual Basic for applications. 3. Database management. I. Spaulding, Brent. II. Title.

QA76.9.D3D493 2008

005.75'65—dc22

2007044041

Printed in the United States of America

First Printing: November 2007

Trademarks

Warning and Disclaimer

Bulk Sales

Que Publishing offers excellent discounts on this book when ordered in quantity for bulk purchases or special sales. For more information, please contact

U.S. Corporate and Government Sales
1-800-382-3419
corpsales@pearsontechgroup.com

For sales outside the United States, please contact

International Sales
international@pearsoned.com

This Book Is Safari Enabled

The Safari® Enabled icon on the cover of your favorite technology book means the book is available through Safari Bookshelf. When you buy this book, you get free access to the online edition for 45 days.

Safari Bookshelf is an electronic reference library that lets you easily search thousands of technical books, find code samples, download chapters, and access technical information whenever and wherever you need it.

To gain 45-day Safari Enabled access to this book:

- Go to http://www.quepublishing.com/safarienabled
- Complete the brief registration form
- Enter the coupon code SUJ2-L9NK-HUBD-WHKU-HCC6

If you have difficulty registering on Safari Bookshelf or accessing the online edition, please email customer-service@safaribooksonline.com.

Associate Publisher
Greg Wiegand

Acquisitions Editor
Loretta Yates

Development Editor
Todd Brakke

Managing Editor
Patrick Kanouse

Senior Project Editor
Tonya Simpson

Copy Editor
Geneil Breeze

Indexer
Tim Wright

Proofreader
Paula Lowell

Technical Editor
Truitt L. Bradly

Publishing Coordinator
Cindy Teeters

Book Designer
Anne Jones

Contents

About the Authors

Scott B. Diamond has been an information technology geek for more than 20 years. He has spent much of that time designing databases on various platforms. He started using Microsoft Access with Office 97 and has mastered all the subsequent versions. Besides developing database applications for the company where he's employed as an applications administrator, Scott also does freelance work, developing Access applications and consulting. He has always maintained that he's lucky his vocation is also his avocation, so he spends some of his free time helping people on web-based Q&A boards such as utteraccess.com (the premier support site for Access). He recently received Microsoft's MVP award for Access in acknowledgment of his contribution to the Access community. Scott, an avid bicyclist, lives on Long Island, New York, with his wife and daughter. You can reach Scott at AccessVBA@diamondassoc.com or visit his website, www.diamondassoc.com.

Brent Spaulding started writing applications about 20 years ago, generally focusing on data and data analysis. He has designed systems that have a wide range of focus: gymnastics class management, product assembly analysis, equipment fault logging, and manufacturing management systems. He has used Microsoft Access since version 2.0 and looks forward to using Access well into the future. In July 2007 Brent, who is employed in the automotive industry, received the Microsoft MVP award for Access, which recognizes his talent and contribution to the Access community. He spends much of his personal time learning and helping others on websites such as utteraccess.com, where he is known as datAdrenaline. Brent lives in southern Indiana with his wife and children.

Dedication

To my wife and daughter, who have helped me realize one of my dreams.

—*Scott B. Diamond*

To my wife and our seven children who have loved me, encouraged me, and prayed with me throughout the entirety of this adventure.

—*Brent Spaulding*

Acknowledgments

A number of people contribute to a book like this, and this section is where I can reward their efforts by acknowledging them. First, thank you to Loretta Yates, who believed in me and gave me the opportunity to fulfill a longtime dream of mine. I also want to acknowledge the contributions of the editorial team: Todd Brakke and Geneil Breeze and technical editor, Truitt L. Bradly. Todd and Geneil made a major contribution to making sure my prose made sense to the reader. Truitt's contributions helped make this book possible as an editor and a friend. A special thanks also goes to Crystal Long for her encouragement and input.

Another thank you goes to my collaborator on this book, Brent Spaulding, who filled in some of the gaps in my knowledge and experience.

And finally, many thanks to my wife and daughter, who gave me support and, more importantly, put up with my hours of sitting in front of the computer to produce this book.

Personal note from Scott: I hope you enjoy using this book as much as I have enjoyed writing it. I truly believe that by following these lessons you will become an accomplished Access developer.

Personal note from Brent: Working with talented people like Scott and Truitt while I wrote Part III has been an incredible experience. The practical tips, advice, and code samples will provide a strong foundation as your knowledge and ability expand. With that said, grab a soda and a snack and start programming!

We Want to Hear from You!

As the reader of this book, *you* are our most important critic and commentator. We value your opinion and want to know what we're doing right, what we could do better, what areas you'd like to see us publish in, and any other words of wisdom you're willing to pass our way.

As an associate publisher for Que Publishing, I welcome your comments. You can email or write me directly to let me know what you did or didn't like about this book—as well as what we can do to make our books better.

Please note that I cannot help you with technical problems related to the topic of this book. We do have a User Services group, however, where I will forward specific technical questions related to the book.

When you write, please be sure to include this book's title and author as well as your name, email address, and phone number. I will carefully review your comments and share them with the author and editors who worked on the book.

Email: feedback@quepublishing.com

Mail: Greg Wiegand
Associate Publisher
Que Publishing
800 East 96th Street
Indianapolis, IN 46240 USA

Reader Services

Visit our website and register this book at www.quepublishing.com/register for convenient access to any updates, downloads, or errata that might be available for this book.

Introduction

So, you've been using Access for a little while. Now that you have used Access to build databases for yourself, and maybe some friends and/or colleagues, you are ready for the next step: developing automated database applications. If you want quicker, easier, and more accurate data entry; faster searching; better reporting; the ability to manipulate data behind the scenes; and much more, this book is for you.

With *Microsoft Office Access 2007 VBA* we show you how to unleash the power of Access using Visual Basic for Applications (VBA). VBA is a superset of the Visual Basic programming language that combines Visual Basic command syntax and a rich assortment of functions with the capability to control objects in your application (hence the "A" in "VBA").

This book shows you VBA in action with real-world examples. We introduce you to programming and its use within Access and hold your hand every step of the way. With the information provided in this book you will explore commands, functions, properties, and methods and how to use them to make your applications dance to your tune and jump through hoops.

What's in the Book

This book isn't meant to be read from cover to cover, although you may find that you can't put it down! Instead, most of the chapters are set up as self-contained units that you can dip into and extract whatever nuggets of information you need at will. If you're a relatively new Access user, I suggest starting with the first one or two chapters in each of the book's four main parts to ensure you have a solid foundation in the fundamentals of working with data in Access tables by using queries, forms, and reports.

The book is divided into four main parts. To give you the big picture before diving in, here's a summary of what you find in each part:

- **Part I, "The Building Blocks"**—The nine chapters in Part I introduce you to the building blocks you use to build VBA modules. We start by explaining the advantages of using VBA. From there we introduce you to the Visual Basic Editor (VBE). This is where you enter, edit, and test all your code. In Chapter 3, "Using Variables, Constants, and Data Types," we talk about the various ways you assign and identify data. And Chapter 4, "Using Built-in Functions," moves on to a discussion of the many functions that Access and VBA provide. In Chapter 5, "Building Procedures," the topic is procedures in their various forms and modules, the containers for your code. Chapter 6, "Conditional and Looping Statements," gets into the meat of coding as we go over important syntax for branching using conditions and repeating code with looping. We follow that with a chapter on using arrays. And then Chapter 8, "Object and Event-Driven Coding," explains how to launch your programs using object and event-driven coding. Part I closes with a chapter on scope, which covers lifetime and visibility of variables and procedures.

- **Part II, "Working Within the User Interface"**—This part shows you how to use VBA to create a great user interface. You learn to work with form and report design and understand their components such as controls and sections. We introduce you to the wide variety of different controls available and show you how to use them. You learn what events are and how they are triggered and discover how to create different menus and use VBA to navigate through your application. Part II ends with a discussion of collections and how to reference Access objects.

- **Part III, "Working with Data"**—This part of the book deals with working directly with data. You will learn the two main ways to get at data: Data Access Objects (DAO) and ActiveX Data Objects (ADO). DAO and ADO are presented in a comparative fashion. We cover these object models as they apply to the Access Connectivity Engine (ACE), the database engine under the hood of Access. ACE is the successor to the Joint Engine Technology (JET) database engine, so you will see JET and ACE terminology where appropriate. You will learn not only how to find, add, edit, and remove data, but also how to create and modify the structure of how data is organized (the shema). With DAO, ActiveX Data Objects eXtentsion (ADOX), and Data Definition Language (a subset of SQL), you can modify and create databases, tables, fields, indexes, relationships, and queries. This section also touches on some of the more advanced topics of database analysis, such as retrieving a list of all the relationships in your database or discovering all the computers that are connected to your database.

- **Part IV, "Advanced VBA"**—In this final section, you encounter working with other types of data files such as Excel spreadsheets, Word documents, and flat files. You also learn the basics of automation with other Office applications. Finally, we show you how to call on the Windows Application Programming Interface (API).

- **Appendix**—This includes a great reference on Structured Query Language (SQL) in its many different flavors and shows how to integrate SQL into your applications.

This Book's Special Features

Microsoft Office Access 2007 VBA is organized to give you a firm foundation for using VBA in a logical manner that builds your knowledge step by step. We have also made the book a functional reference for VBA techniques.

- **Steps**—Throughout the book, each Access task is summarized in step-by-step procedures.
- **Code lines**—Lines of VBA code, commands, and statements appear in a `monospace` typeface.
- **Required Text**—Any text you need to enter will be **boldfaced**.
- **Italics**—Technical terms being defined appear in italic, such as *RecordSet Property*.
- **Syntax**—Within code statements certain arguments will be *italicized* to denote where you will need to substitute values relevant to your task. Brackets ([]) are used to indicate optional arguments.

This book also uses the following elements to draw your attention to important (or merely interesting) information.

> **NOTE**
> Notes are used to provide sidebar information about the topic being discussed. They provide extra insights that help you understand the concepts being covered.

> **TIP**
> Tips tell you about Access methods that we have found to make coding with Access easier, faster, or more efficient.

> **CAUTION**
> Caution elements warn you about potential pitfalls waiting to trap your code, such as common errors that might occur, and how to avoid or fix them.

→ Cross-reference elements point you to related material elsewhere in the book.

CASE STUDY

You'll find case studies throughout the book based on an Inventory Tracking application. They are designed to show you how to apply what you've learned.

The Examples Used in the Book

All the tables, objects, and code samples referred to in this book can be found at http://www.quepublishing.com. There will be a folder for each chapter. The files build on the examples from the previous chapters. The Introduction file will be pretty bare bones and just have the objects that don't pertain to specific lessons we cover. You can build on the Introduction files or use the files that already have the examples coded for you.

The Building Blocks

Advantages of Access and VBA

Understanding Where Access Fits in Office

Access is the database management tool for the Office suite. Access comes with Office Professional and higher versions. Although other tools included in Office (specifically Excel and One Note) also provide some capability to manage data, their functionality is severely limited. Only Access offers a full set of functions to manage relational tables, create robust data entry forms, build complex queries to analyze data, and design comprehensive reports to present your data.

Access comes with VBA, the core automation language provided with many applications developed by Microsoft. Other companies have also licensed VBA to use in their apps and allow integration with Office products. Beyond the base commands and functions within VBA, application-specific mechanisms allow you to manipulate the current environment.

Within Office 2007, however, Access stands a little on the side. Access is a self-contained development platform. Although it can integrate with the rest of the Office suite and other applications, those applications can also function with Microsoft's .Net Framework. Access, because of its nature, has limited capability to integrate with .Net. What Access does give you is a much easier and robust platform for developing database-centric applications of varying complexity and scope. The ease of using Access along with its power, makes it the best tool for rapidly developing database applications.

1

Understanding Access Programming Choices

Access provides three methods for automating itself. Naturally, the primary method we deal with in this book is Visual Basic for Applications (VBA). Besides VBA, however, there are also macros and SQL statements. Each of these choices has advantages and disadvantages. Neither of them is mutually exclusive, meaning you can use VBA, macros, and SQL together in the same application.

Macros

If you're a regular user of Microsoft Word or Excel you're probably familiar with the concept of macros. Macros were originally put into the early versions of Access to provide an easy way to provide some automation. As VBA became more powerful, the limitations of macros caused most developers to move to VBA. Macros started life simply as recorded keystrokes that could be played back in a sequence. Applications included a macro recorder that read each keystroke and converted them into commands that could then be executed as a batch. Then macros evolved and added programming-type commands such as conditionals and loops, which gave developers more control over the flow of the application.

Within Access macros are a set of actions that can be selected from a form. Many of these commands have arguments that can be assigned through the form.

In Access 2007, Microsoft has revived macros to a certain extent. In previous versions, macros were a standalone object. With Access 2007, Microsoft introduces *embedded macros*, which are macros specifically attached to a form or report event. They exist only within the form or report object. In addition, Microsoft has also added error trapping commands within the macro language.

You can name a macro AutoExec, and it will run when Access first loads. This is useful when you're doing some setup. Figure 1.1 shows an AutoExec macro that runs a report showing items that have fallen below reorder levels. The action selected from the pulldown is the OpenReport action. The arguments available are Report Name, View, Filter Name, Where Condition, and Window Mode.

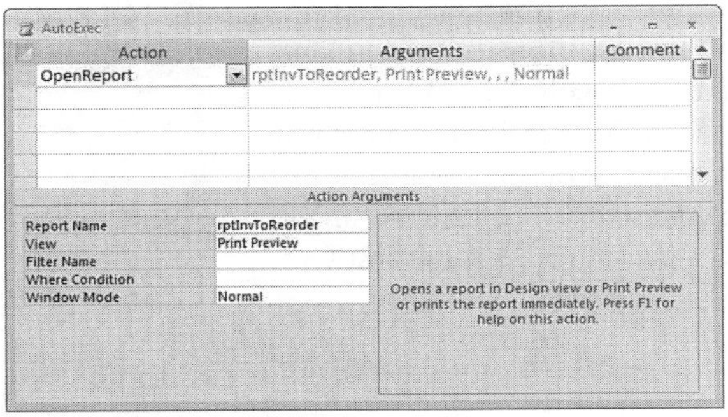

Figure 1.1
One of the most common uses for a macro is to run a set of instructions at startup. This AutoExec macro runs a report.

Using SQL

SQL stands for Structured Query Language. Although not a programming language per se, it's a standard syntax used by relational databases for more than 30 years to add and retrieve data and to manage tables. Although there are different dialects of SQL, the base language is pretty much the same.

Any queries you develop are saved as a single SQL statement. You can build your SQL queries using Query Design mode or enter the SQL code directly into SQL view. Figure 1.2 shows the query used to find the items that have fallen below reorder levels. Following is the SQL code for that query:

```
SELECT qryInventoryStockLevels.*
FROM qryInventoryStockLevels
WHERE (((qryInventoryStockLevels.CurrentStock)< Nz([ReorderLevel],0)));
```

Figure 1.2
The query shown in Design mode.

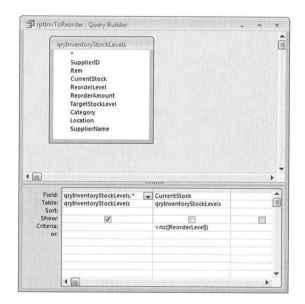

CAUTION

The preceding code snippet uses the wildcard asterisk (*) in place of a field list, which returns all the fields in the table. However, in most of your queries you should add only the fields that the query needs to display.

SQL and VBA are not mutually exclusive. You will frequently use SQL statements within your VBA modules to filter and manipulate data from tables. SQL often is your best choice for retrieving data, especially when multiple tables are being accessed.

→ To learn more about SQL, see the Appendix, "Review of Access SQL."

Using VBA

This brings us back to VBA. Built on the highly successful Visual Basic programming language, VBA provides a superset of that language. As a full-featured procedural programming language, VBA provides the capability to do just about anything within Access. Add the capability to control Access and other VBA-compliant applications, and you have a powerful environment. Yet this environment is not difficult to learn. Microsoft provides a myriad of wizards and other tools to help you generate code.

VBA includes conditional and looping commands that are not included in macros and SQL. These commands give the developer full-fledged programming tools to test for values and act, depending on the value, to process sets of values, all without user intervention.

This book shows you how to make the most of those tools, it teaches you programming techniques so you understand how to build your own code, and it provides some tips and tricks to speed and ease the development process. In short, it will help you become an Access developer!

Using the Visual Basic Editor

First Look at the Visual Basic Editor

The Visual Basic Editor (VBE) is the environment you use to manage your VBA code. The VBE provides tools to enter, test, and organize your code. There are several ways to access the VBE. Pressing Ctrl+G or Alt+F11 opens it. You can also press the Visual Basic button on the Tools Ribbon. Another method is to click the ellipsis next to any event property and choose the Code Builder. In addition, if a code error occurs, you might be presented with a Debug option that also loads the VBE.

This chapter reveals how to use the VBE and its various components. You learn an overview of the environment that will help you follow along in the rest of the book's chapters. As you move through this book, you learn certain techniques in greater detail. So, at this point, just get acquainted with the environment and its tools so you can deal with the rest of the lessons.

When you first open the VBE, you see six areas (going counterclockwise from the top, and shown in Figure 2.1):

- **Toolbars/menu bar**—Along the top are the menu bar and toolbars.
- **Project Explorer window**—Lists all the objects that use VBA within the current application.
- **Properties window**—Shows the properties for the object selected in the Project Explorer.
- **Immediate window**—Allows you to see the results of test or running code.

2

- **Locals window**—Displays the values of variables in the currently running code.
- **Code window**—The largest window that contains the actual code; each object that contains code is displayed in its own window.

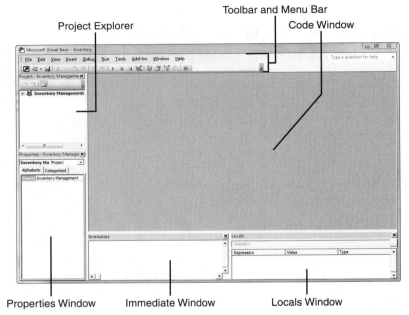

Figure 2.1
This is how the VBE looks on a new database with no objects.

Project Explorer
Toolbar and Menu Bar
Code Window

Properties Window   Immediate Window   Locals Window

> **TIP**
> You can dock or float the various windows within the VBE by double-clicking the title bar of the window.

The VBE is a separate window that exists outside the Access window. You can switch back and forth between the VBE and the main Access window. Table 2.1 presents a list of the options on the VBE's menu bar and an explanation of each.

Table 2.1   The VBE Menu

Name	Purpose
File	Enables you to save the database, import/export code, remove modules, print modules, and return to Access.
Edit	Standard Edit menu allowing Undo, Copy, Cut, Paste, and Find and Replace. It also includes options to Indent/Outdent code, list properties and methods of a command, list constants available for a parameter, list Intellisense info about a command, show the values of a parameter, complete typing of a recognized word, and work with bookmarks.

Name	Purpose
View	Options for viewing Code, Objects, Definition, Last Position, and Object Browser. Controls the display of the different panes within the VBE. Controls the display of the VBE toolbars.
Insert	Enables you to insert a procedure, module, or class module, or import code from a file.
Debug	Enables you to "compile" the application, debug specific code modules, and manage break points and watch points. Set and show the next statement. (Note: All these are also available from the Debug toolbar.)
Run	Run or stop code.
Tools	Manage references added to the application, deal with macros, set options for the VBE, and manage properties and digital signatures for the application.
Add-Ins	Access the Add-In manager.
Window	Manage the windows with the Code pane.
Help	Access VBA Help.

Below the menu bar is the Standard toolbar, which offers quick access to frequently used options from different menus. You can see the Standard toolbar in Figure 2.1. Table 2.2 lists the tools on the Standard toolbar and what they are used for.

Table 2.2   Standard Toolbar in VBE

Icon	Name	Purpose	Keyboard Shortcut
	View Access	Returns to the main Access window leaving the VBE Open	Alt+F11
	Insert Module	Select from a drop-down of module types to insert a new, blank module	
	Save	Saves the application	Ctrl+S
	Cut, Copy, Paste	Icons to perform the Cut, Copy, and Paste actions	Ctrl+X, Ctrl+C, Ctrl+V
	Find	Finds a specific text string within the active module	Ctrl+F
	Undo	Cancels the previous operation (either a keystroke or mouse click) when possible	Ctrl+Z
	Redo	Reverses the last Undo	

continues

2

Table 2.2 Continued

Icon	Name	Purpose	Keyboard Shortcut
	Run Sub/user form	Executes or continues execution of the current procedure, if a break occurred	F5
	Break	Pauses the current procedure	Ctrl+Break
	Reset	Ends the current procedure; resets all variables to default values	Shift+F5
	Design Mode	Toggles between the edit and forms Design modes	
	Project Explorer	Moves control to the Project Explorer window (the window opens if it's currently closed)	Ctrl+R
	Properties Window	Moves control to the Properties window (the window opens if it's currently closed)	F4
	Object Browser	Moves control to the Object Browser window (the window opens if it's currently closed)	F2
	Toolbox	Displays the toolbox	
	VBA Help	Opens the VBA Help window	F1

In addition to the Standard toolbar, three other toolbars are offered for the VBE. This book covers the two more useful ones: the Edit and Debug toolbars. The third, UserForms, isn't used within Access (see the following note). Figures 2.2 and 2.3 show the Edit and Debug toolbars. Those toolbars are used more later in this book, so we will go into more detail at that time.

> **NOTE**
> Access forms are much more powerful than Userforms, so there is no reason to use them within Access. Because the VBE is a shared component, it includes some features that are more useful in other software packages. Userforms are an example of that.

Figure 2.2
The Edit toolbar gives options to make your code more readable.

Figure 2.3
The Debug toolbar
enables you to control
execution to find coding
errors.

Viewing or hiding toolbars can be done in two ways. You can either right-click on a blank area of the toolbar and then click the toolbar you want to show or hide, or select View, Toolbars. Visible toolbars are indicated by a check mark.

Explaining VBA Modules

All VBA code is contained within modules. These modules fall into one of three categories:

- **Standard**—Contains procedures and/or functions that are not part of another database object.

- **Access object class**—Contains code snippets specific to a form or a report. Each form or report can have an object module attached to it. When you create event procedures, they are part of an object module.

- **Custom class**—Contains code snippets that describe user-defined objects. Chapter 8, "Object and Event-Driven Coding," covers class modules more in depth.

To create a global or class module from within the VBE, you can use the Insert menu or the Insert Module icon on the toolbar. Then select either Module (for Global Modules) or Class Module.

When inserting a module, the Project Explorer is updated with the addition of a new module, and the Properties window reflects this added module. Finally, a code window opens with the line Option Compare Database. Figure 2.4 shows the VBE with a new module added.

Figure 2.4
A new module has been
added to the VBE.

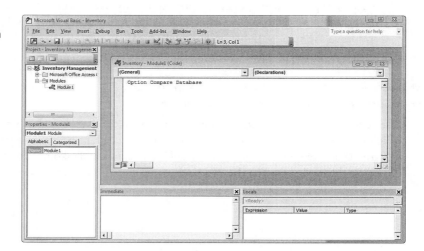

Form and report objects have modules attached. Most code snippets in object modules are attached to events that are part of the object or controls on that object. The code snippets you enter into object modules respond to these events. However, object modules can also contain code snippets that are not linked to an event.

Entering and Running Code

To start writing code, use the Insert Procedures dialog box to initiate a new procedure. Follow these steps to create a new procedure:

➔ A *procedure* is a snippet of code that performs one or more tasks; **see** "Types of Procedures," **p. 67**.

1. Select Insert, Module from the menu or click the Insert Module icon to open the Add Procedure dialog (see Figure 2.5). (We assume you have a code module open.)

Figure 2.5
The Add Procedure dialog is set to add your new procedure.

2. Enter a name for the procedure. In this example use **OpenSupplierForm**.

➔ For recommended naming conventions, **see** "Using a Naming Convention," **p. 21**.

3. Select a Type and a Scope for the procedure. If you are creating static variables, uncheck the All Local Variables as Statics option. In this example, select Sub, Public, and leave the static variable option unchecked.

4. Click OK to create the procedure.

➔ You learn more about procedure types in Chapter 5, "Building Procedures."

➔ You learn more about scope in Chapter 9, "Understanding Scope."

After clicking OK, a *stub* is inserted in the code window. A stub includes the opening line, which indicates the scope, type of procedure, and procedure name. The stub also adds the required End statement for the procedure. In between is a blank line. Your task is to enter the executable code between the two lines of the stub. Figure 2.6 shows the inserted stub.

Figure 2.6
A stub for the procedure has been inserted into the module.

This book teaches you the code to enter within the stub, so let's get started with a simple procedure to open an Access form. You complete the procedure by entering the following additional code:

```
Public Sub OpenSupplierForm()
    'Open the Supplier form
    DoCmd.OpenForm "frmSupplierDetails"
    Debug.Print "The form is open!"
End Sub
```

Make sure the Immediate window is open by selecting View, Immediate Window from the menu (or pressing Ctrl+G). To run the code, position the cursor anywhere within the procedure code, and then press F5 (or click the Run icon on the toolbar). Access then opens the form within the Access window, returns to the VBE, and displays the text, "The form is open!" in the Immediate window.

Of course, in the real use of this code, you wouldn't display anything in the Immediate window. The Debug.Print command is very useful, however, in debugging code. This leads us to the next section.

Debugging Code

No one writes pristine code that works perfectly the first time, unless it's simple code, and even then it's not uncommon for typos or small errors to crop up. So debugging is an important skill to learn. Therefore, you need to test your code before you start using it.

Figure 2.3 showed you the Debug toolbar. This essential tool enables you to step through a code snippet, line by line. You can also run, pause, or restart a module.

Using Run and Break Modes

The first step in testing code is to execute it within the VBE. The quickest and simplest way to do that is to position your cursor within the code snippet and press the F5 key or click the Run button on the Debug toolbar. If no errors occur, you are fine.

If an error does occur, you need to determine its cause and repair it. To help make this determination, you should temporarily suspend execution of the code. This is referred to as *Break mode*. There are a few ways to switch between Run mode and Break mode:

- Insert a breakpoint within the code, the point where execution halts.

> **TIP**
>
> To set a breakpoint, click in the left margin next to the line where you want to pause, or highlight the line and press F9. Do the same to remove a breakpoint.

- Insert a `Stop` statement at the point you want to pause the code execution.
- Insert a watch expression. Watch expressions are variables or formulas whose values you want to monitor. While in break mode, the values of these expressions are displayed in the watch window. This differs from the locals window in that you can use full expressions; the locals window just shows variables.
- Press the Ctrl and Break keys during execution. (I don't recommend using this unless you need to halt runaway code, because you can't control where the code halts.)
- Select the Debug button on the runtime error dialog box if and when it pops open.
- Click the Break button on the toolbar.

When execution is paused, you can edit the code. When completed, test the changes by pressing F5 again. At times, you will want to just continue instead of restarting. Click the Reset toolbar icon, in that case.

> **CAUTION**
>
> Editing code while execution is paused could result in database corruption.

Figure 2.7 shows a code module with a breakpoint and `Stop` statement inserted.

Figure 2.7
A breakpoint has been set for the `OpenForm` method with a `Stop` statement inserted afterward.

Breakpoint

Stop Statement

Single Step Through Code

Frequently, you have to step through the code, line by line, to catch bugs in your code. After execution has been paused, the Debug toolbar, shown previously in Figure 2.3, becomes valuable. You can click the Step Into icon to execute the next line of code. The executing line is then highlighted.

As you step through the code, you need to check the value of variables to make sure they are representing the correct values. You can do this either by hovering the cursor over the variable or checking the Locals window. Not all variables, however, appear in the Locals window. Specifically, values of controls referenced by the code are not shown in the Locals window.

> **TIP**
>
> Sometimes it's easier to assign a control to a declared variable within the code so that it appears in the Locals window.

Other tools that you can use during single stepping are as follows:

- **Step Over** (Shift+F8, Step Over icon, or Debug, StepOver)—Skips the next statement.
- **Step Out** (Ctrl+Shift+F8, Step Out icon, or Debug, Step Out)—Skips the procedure. This is useful if you need to skip a called procedure and return to the buggy code.
- **Run to Cursor** (Ctrl+F8 or Debug, Run to Cursor)—Executes all the code from the current line to the line that contains the cursor. This allows you to execute several lines at once.

Saving Code

When entering code into a new module or making changes to an existing module, you need to save the code before closing the VBE. You can do this by clicking the Save icon on the Standard toolbar or selecting File, Save from the menu. If you are working in a new module you are prompted to supply a name for the module. Modules should not be given the same name as any procedure within the module or any other object.

→ For recommended naming conventions, **see** "Using a Naming Convention," **p. 21**.

Getting Help on Code

With the complexity of VBA, it would be an unusual coder who has the entire coding structure and syntax memorized. Most developers need to refer to a reference to refresh their memory about syntax and available commands. The VBE includes a comprehensive Help reference apart from the Access Help. You can open the Help reference by pressing F1 or selecting Help, Microsoft Visual Basic Help from the VBE menu. Figure 2.8 shows the opening screen.

You can enter a search string to bring a list of matching links both on your system and on the Web. Another, quicker alternative is to place the cursor within a keyword in your code and press F1. This brings up Help for that command.

VBE help includes details of the syntax for each command. Frequently there are coding examples to help you understand how to use the command.

Figure 2.8
The opening screen for the Help facility lists some broad topics.

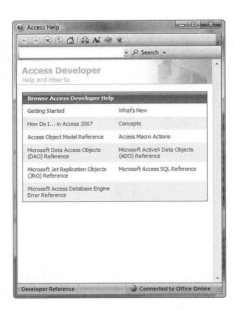

Coding Shortcuts

Another type of Help the VBE provides is Intellisense. As you type in a command, the VBE offers advice on completing that command. Figures 2.9 and 2.10 show examples of how Intellisense helps you fill in code. Figure 2.9 shows how, when you click the period after DoCmd, you get a list of the methods applicable to the DoCmd object. Figure 2.10 shows the parameters for the selected method (in this case OpenReport); as you enter these parameters, the current one is highlighted. Some parameters present a list of constants in a drop-down list for you to choose from. Intellisense makes it easy to enter code correctly. Intellisense even fills in the remainder of declared variables available to your procedure. As you are typing, at any time you can press the Ctrl+spacebar keys, and the Intellisense list drops down.

Figure 2.9
Some methods displayed for the DoCmd command.

Figure 2.10
Intellisense shows the parameters for the OpenReport method.

Good Coding Habits

Even if you are writing code just for yourself, you might often have to go back to code after a time; therefore, it becomes important that you write code that you or another coder can easily follow. The following are some points to keep in mind as you enter your code:

- Use a naming convention so that variables and object names are easily and consistently identifiable.
- Use indenting to show the flow of your structure.
- Document your code with comments to remind you what the code does. Believe me, you *will* forget.

Each of these points is detailed in the following sections.

Using a Naming Convention

As you enter code, you use variables and objects that need to be named. There is no requirement about what names you use; however, most developers use some convention that allows for identifying these items. Many Access developers use a standard naming convention based on a naming style called the Hungarian style for its inventor, Charles Simonyi. Your organization may use its own convention that you should follow. It doesn't matter what you use, as long as you use something to make sure names are consistent.

Some other considerations in naming are not to use spaces or special characters in your names. If you need to use multiple words in a name, either use title case, where the first character of each word is uppercase, or use an underscore to separate the words. An example of title case is LastName. An example of using an underscore is Last_Name.

It's also recommended that you use prefixes to identify the purpose of the object being named. Tables 2.3 and 2.4 list some of the more common prefixes used by the Hungarian convention.

Table 2.3   Object Tags

Access Object	Prefix
Table	tbl
Query	qry
Form	frm
Report	rpt
Check box	chk
Command button	cmd
Label	lbl
List box	lst

continues

Table 2.3   Continued

Access Object	Prefix
Option button	opt
Subform/Subreport	sfrm/srpt
Text box	txt

Table 2.4   Variable Tags

Data Type	Tag
Byte	byt
Integer	int
Single	sgl
Long Integer	lng
Double	dbl
Text	str
Currency	cur
Date/Time	dte
Boolean	boo

This might seem like more work than necessary, but I guarantee that as you write more code, you will come to appreciate having a consistent naming convention in your code.

Indenting

Indenting your code is another good habit to start off with. Much of your coding will use looping or conditionals. Following the flow of the code structure is much easier when you set off the code within each loop or condition.

The VBE indents blocks of code for you. Select the lines you want to indent, and then select Edit, Indent (Outdent) from the menu. The Tab (which, by default, is four spaces) or spacebar keys perform your indentation on individual lines while creating your code. Figure 2.11 shows the same code snippet side by side with one version indented and the other not indented. As you can see, the indented version is more readable because the indents show the code flow more easily.

Another way to indicate the flow is to use blank lines around blocks of related code.

Figure 2.11
A code sample shown side by side, indented and not.

Documenting

Comments are another good idea that you should get in the habit of using. Although code is often self-explanatory, it frequently helps to add comments that explain the task that each group of lines performs. You can easily add comments by preceding the comment with an apostrophe. Any text following an apostrophe (not within quotes) is considered a comment and is ignored during execution. Recall the code snippet you entered earlier in this chapter:

```
Public Sub OpenSupplierForm()
    'Open the Supplier form
    DoCmd.OpenForm "frmSupplierDetails"
    Debug.Print "The form is open!"
End Sub
```

A good style to follow is to place an introductory comment describing the procedure's purpose after the first line. From there, the structure and complexity of the code dictates further commenting. Comments need not occupy a separate line; they can follow the code line itself. For example:

```
Me.txtUnitPrice = Me.cboItem.Column(2)   'Assign unit price for selected item
```

The VBE formats any comments in a green font.

The following are some guidelines for commenting:

- Be brief.
- Be descriptive.
- Be grammatically complete.
- Use punctuation as appropriate.
- No need to comment self-explanatory code.
- Comment revisions.
- Write your comments within the code when they are fresh in your mind.

The Edit toolbar has an icon to set a line or block of lines as a comment. Just highlight the lines you want to convert to comments and click the Comment Block icon. There is also an

Uncomment Block icon to reverse the process. This is useful when you need to temporarily skip lines during execution of the procedure without removing the code from the module. This frequently occurs during debugging and testing—you find a code snippet that doesn't work right and you need to use a different set of code lines but you don't want to lose the original lines in case you find the fix for it.

2

Using Variables, Constants, and Data Types

3

Declaring Variables and Constants

VBA is a programming language and, like all programming languages (even like any spoken language), VBA has its rules of grammar. These rules are generally called *syntax*. As in any programming language, though somewhat unlike spoken languages, you must be precise in following the syntax and using the language's components. Computers are actually pretty dumb machines; they can do only what they are told to do. The instructions they are given must be ones they have been taught to understand. If you aren't precise in your use of syntax, you will encounter errors in your code.

Like most programming languages, VBA uses variables and constants to substitute for values. In pure terms, a *variable* refers to a piece of data that is stored in memory; a *constant* is similar in that it's a name used to represent stored data. Where the two differ is that a constant's value doesn't change, whereas a variable can have its value reassigned during processing and be based on the code being processed.

Declaring Variables

Variables represent a value or an object. The coder chooses a name that describes the value being stored according to the naming convention in use, and a data type is declared for the variable. The variable can then be used and reused or have its value reassigned throughout your code processing.

A variable must be declared before it can be used. The Dim (short for Dimension) statement is used to make the declaration. The following is the syntax for the Dim statement:

```
Dim variablename As datatype
```

The components are *variablename*, which is the descriptive name of the variable, and *datatype*, which identifies what type of data is stored in the variable.

➔ For more on data types, **see** "VBA Data Types," **p. 28**.

You can leave off the data type and Access defaults it to the Variant data type, which is a catch-all. I highly recommend that you explicitly declare your data types and that you do so using a naming convention. A Variant data type is not efficient because it uses more memory and performs less speedily than other variable types. The advantage is that you can assign different types of data to a Variant data type. This becomes valuable when you aren't sure what data you will be assigning. It's especially valuable if you might have to store a null value. However, such instances are rare, and explicit declarations are the norm.

> **TIP**
>
> Most developers declare their variables at the top of the module, grouping them all together. Although this isn't required, it makes finding your variables easier.

It's also possible to declare several variables on one line of code. This would look as follows:

```
Dim variable_a As datatype, variable_b As datatype
```

You still need to identify the datatype for each variable individually; what is saved is repeating the Dim statement.

The Dim statement supports Intellisense, which is talked about in Chapter 2, "Using the Visual Basic Editor." After typing the As keyword, a drop-down list appears with a listing of data types from which you can choose.

> **TIP**
>
> When declaring multiple variables on one line, I usually use the same data type for all variables on that line. Although not necessary, it just makes more logical sense to me.

Using Option Explicit

Option Explicit requires that variables be declared before they can be used. This prevents situations where a misspelling or typo can cause a procedure to not work properly. In an odd departure from the usual hand-holding Access does for you, it does not require that variables be specifically declared. It's the function of the Option Explicit statement to force that requirement.

You can set Access to automatically insert the Option Explicit statement whenever you create a new module. To do so, and I highly recommend that you do, follow these instructions:

1. Select Tools, Options from the VBE menu.
2. Select the Editor tab.
3. Uncheck the Require Variable Declaration check box (see Figure 3.1).

Figure 3.1
Check the Require
Variable Declaration box
on the Editor tab of the
VBE Options dialog.

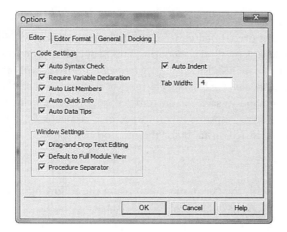

Naming Variables

Review the section on naming conventions in Chapter 2. Variables should be named according to whatever convention you are using. You should also be aware of a few other rules regarding naming variables:

- The first character of a variable name must be a letter.
- The characters ., !, @, #, $, and % should not be used in variable names.
- Variable names must be declared uniquely within the module. Although variables can be reused within the module, you can declare it only once.
- A variable name can consist of up to 255 characters, but you would be well advised to keep names as short as possible.

→ For more on naming conventions, see "Using a Naming Convention" **p. 21**.

Constants

A constant symbolizes a literal value to Access, similar to the way a variable symbolizes a value or object. Where they are different is that a constant cannot be changed during code processing. Access includes *system-defined* and *intrinsic constants* that you can use in your code. You can also create your own constants.

System-Defined Constants

Access provides four system-defined constants: Yes, No, On, and Off. These constants can be used within any database object except modules. Three additional constants can also be used in modules: True, False, and Null.

Intrinsic Constants

VBA includes a variety of predefined constants called *intrinsic constants*. Such constants are used as values within Access methods, functions, and properties (more on what they are can be found in subsequent chapters). Intrinsic constants are prefaced with ac or vb; some examples are acForm, acCmdSaveRecord, acPreview, vbCrLf, and vbYes. They indicate a form object, executing a command to save the current record, display a Print Preview, adding a new line, and returning a yes response in a message box, respectively. Intellisense will give you a list of available intrinsic constants for the method being used.

Declaring Constants

Constants are declared with the Const statement using the following syntax:

```
[Public ¦ Private] Const constantname As datatype = expression
```

The square brackets indicate optional arguments. Arguments separated by the vertical bar represent choices for the argument. Constants are given a name to identify them in your code. You must specify the data type of the constant, which is assigned a value using an expression. The expression can be a value or a formula; however, an expression cannot include a variable or the result of a built-in or custom function.

Constants are used for values that are either static and/or may be referred to many times during a procedure or group of procedures. The following are some examples of constants:

- A subfolder that stores product image files

  ```
  Const conPath As String = "\imagefiles"
  ```
- The name of your company

  ```
  Const conCo As String = "Acme Builders, Inc."
  ```
- A MAC address for the machine the app will run on

  ```
  Const conMAC As String = "12CD3E4A22B1"
  ```
- A value to be used in a formula

  ```
  Const comPi As Double = 3.14
  ```
- A starting date for all calculations

  ```
  Const con74 As Date = #7/4/1776#
  ```

By using constants you can provide one point to set a value. By changing the value in the Const statement, you change it wherever the constant is used in processing.

VBA Data Types

Each variable or constant is assigned a data type with the declaration statement. When you create tables in your applications you assign data types to fields in the table. You use the same data types to define your variables and constants in VBA.

The purpose of a data type is to validate the data being stored in the variable or constant. You won't be allowed to enter an invalid type; Access issues a data type mismatch error. You can omit the data type, and Access defaults to the Variant type. Table 3.1 lists and compares data types.

Table 3.1   VBA Data Type Comparison

Data Type or Subtype	Required Memory	Default Value	VBA Constant	Range
Integer	2 bytes	0	vbInteger	–32,768 to 32767
Long Integer	4 bytes	0	vbLong	–2,147,483,648 to 2,147,486,647
Single	4 bytes	0	vbSingle	–3.402823E38 to –1.401298E-45 or 1.401298E-45 to 3.402823E38
Double	8 bytes	0	vbDouble	–1.79769313486232E308 to –4.94065645841247E-324 or 1.79769313486232E308 to 4.94065645841247E-324
Currency	8 bytes	0	vbCurrency	–922,337,203,477.5808 to 922,337,203,685,477.5807
Date	8 bytes	00:00:00	vbDate	January 1, 100 to December 31, 9999
Fixed String	String's length	Number of spaces to accommo-date string	vbString	1 to 65,400 characters
Variable String	10 bytes plus the number of characters	Zero-length string ("")	vbString	0 to 2 billion characters
Object	4 bytes	Nothing (vbNothing)	vbObject	Any Access object, ActiveX component, or class object
Boolean	2 bytes	False	vbBoolean	–1 or 0
Variant	16 bytes	Empty (vbEmpty)	vbVariant	Same as Double
Decimal	14 bytes	0	vbDecimal	–79,228,162,514,264,337,593,543,950,335 to 79,228,162,514,264,337,593,543,950,335 or –7.9228162514264337593543950335 to 7.9228162514264337593543950335
Byte	1 byte	0	vbByte	0 to 255

3

The following list explains the purpose of each of these datatypes in more detail:

- **Boolean**—The Boolean data type is used to store data used in a logical comparison that has only two values that can be expressed as true and false, yes and no, on and off, and so on. The system-defined constants True and False can be used to represent the actual values of –1 and 0, respectively.

- **Byte**—The Byte data type takes the least amount of memory, holding a decimal value of between 0 and 255. It cannot hold negative numbers.

- **Currency**—The Currency data type is used primarily to store monetary values. It is accurate to 15 places to the left of the decimal and 4 places to the right. It's used to avoid rounding problems when precision is absolutely necessary.

- **Date**—The Date data type stores a Double value that represents both the date and the time. The date is stored as the number of days from 12/30/1899. The time is stored as a decimal representing a fraction of a day—for example, 6 a.m. (or 6 hours) = .25.

- **Decimal**—The Decimal data type is not a true data type but a subtype of the Variant data type. Its values can range from –79,228,162,514,264,337,593,543,950,335 to 79,228,162,514,264,337,593,543,950,335, if there are no decimal places in the value. It can be precise up to 28 decimal places for values from 7.9228162514264337593543950335 to 7.9228162514264337593543950335.

- **Double**—The Double data type is used to store precision floating point numbers in a range from –1.79769313486232E308 to –4.94065645841247E-324 or 1.79769313486232E308 to –4.94065645841247E-324.

- **Integer**–The Integer data type stores whole numbers in a range from –32,768 to 32,767. After strings, the Integer is the most widely used data type.

- **Long**—The Long data type is an expanded form of Integer but with a much larger range. It can store values from –2,147,483,648 to 2,147,483,647.

- **Object**—The Object data type is used to store an Access object, such as a form, report, or control. It can also reference an ActiveX object or class module.

→   We go into more detail about object variables in Chapter 8, "Object and Event-Driven Coding."

- **Single**—The Single data type is used to store precision numbers—fractional numbers or ones with decimals. It's the same as the Double data type with a smaller range from –3402823E38 to –1.401298E-45 or from 1.401298E-45 to 3.402823E38.

- **String**—The String data type is used to store any character-based value as a text string. It can store letters, numbers, punctuation, and other special characters. String data types come in two flavors: variable and fixed. The variable string can shrink or grow to accommodate its contents. This is the default type of string.

  The fixed string is limited to 1 to 65,400 characters. Because the variable string is the default, a fixed string must be explicitly declared using the following syntax:

  ```
  Dim variablename As String * stringlength
  ```

- **Variant**—The Variant data type stores both numeric and non-numeric values. This makes the Variant the most adaptable of the data types. However, it should be used only when you are unsure of the data type you will be storing. It's always better to explicitly declare data types because Access processes this data type more slowly than others because it must first determine the actual data type. The Variant is the default type, so the following statement defaults to Variant:

```
Dim varMyVariable
```

Referencing Syntax

As you code your procedures you will often reference Access objects. Usually these will be controls on the form for which you are writing code. How to refer to these objects is one of the core skills you need to learn. Let's define a few terms to get you going:

- **Identifier**—Identifies the value of a control, property, or expression.
- **Operator**—In the context of references, the operator separates different components of the reference. An identifier can have several components that represent a layer of reference. Two symbols are used as operators within an identifier; the dot and the bang—a period or an exclamation character, respectively. The bang is included with Access 2007 for backward compatibility.

> **TIP**
> The advantage of using the dot over the bang is that the dot kicks off the Intellisense lists, whereas the bang doesn't.

> **NOTE**
> In the past, the bang was used to identify user-created objects, whereas the dot preceded built-in properties. For example, in the following reference:
>
> ```
> Forms!frmSuppliers!txtAddress.Enabled
> ```
>
> frmSupplier is the name of the form, and txtAddress is the name of the control, so they are preceded by the bang. Enabled is a property of a control, so it's preceded by a dot.
>
> In Access 2007, you can use the dot exclusively, but many developers still use the bang because it identifies user-defined objects.

→ The dot operator is discussed further in "Reading and Setting Object Properties," **p. 104**.

- **Qualifier**—Identifies the collection to which an object belongs.

The goal of referencing an object is to let VBA know what object to reference, where the object is, and what kind of object it is. The sample database we've included for you currently has many objects, forms, reports, and tables as well as many controls within them.

The basic format for referencing an object is

```
qualifier![objectname]
```

where *qualifier* names the collection to which the object belongs and *objectname* represents the object. We've used the bang operator to separate the two components. So, to refer to the Inventory Details form (frmInvDetails) in Inventory3.accdb, in the following, Forms refers to the Forms Collection, and frmInvDetails is the name given to the form:

```
Forms!frminvDetails
```

To refer to the Reorder report you enter the following expression:

```
Reports!rptInvtoReorder
```

You reference controls similarly, but controls are a part of a collection within a collection. This means you must use two identifiers to refer to each layer to which the control belongs:

```
qualifier![objectname]![controlname]
```

where *qualifier* refers to the Object class (either Forms or Reports).

CAUTION

Many Access users think there are fields on a form (or report). Actually, *controls* are on the form. Controls are objects that may or may not be bound to a field in a table. This is a subtle but important distinction. It's unfortunate that Access automatically names controls the same as the bound field when you use the wizard to create forms. Most developers use their naming conventions to name controls with a prefix that identifies the type of control or the data stored by the control. For example, txtItem would be used to store the Item field from the Inventory table.

CASE STUDY

Case Study: Using Form References

To demonstrate how to code your references we will look at a case study that demonstrates using a form to set a range of dates to include in a report. This is a technique you will frequently use to supply parameters that filter a report.

1. From the Create Ribbon, select Blank Form.
2. Add a text box to the form and set the Name property to **txtStart**.
3. Add a second text box and set the Name property to **txtEnd**.
4. Save the form as **frmDateRange**.
5. Make a copy of the query qryInventoryTransactionsExtended and name it **qryInvTransByDate**.
6. Add a column for CreatedDate from tblTransactions.
7. Uncheck the Show box because the column is already included.
8. In the Criteria cell type **Between [Forms]![frmDateRange].[txtStart] And [Forms]![frmDateRange]![txtEnd]** (see Figure 3.2).

Figure 3.2
Your query with the criteria entered.

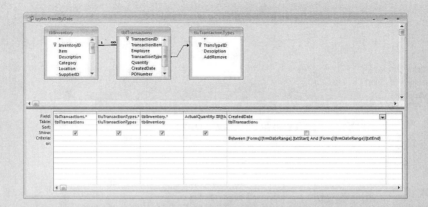

9. Save the query.

10. From the Create Ribbon select Report Wizard.

11. Select `qryInvTransByDate` as the source and add `CreatedDate, Item, Quantity,` and `tluTransactionTypes.Description` fields.

12. Follow the prompts to create your report.

13. At the final screen select Modify to open the report in Design mode.

14. Add a text box to the Report Header, set the Label to From, and set the ControlSource to `Forms![frmDateRange]![txtStart]`

15. Add another text box, set the label to To, and set the ControlSource to `Forms![frmDateRange]![txtEnd]`

16. Close and save the report as `rptInvTransByDate`.

17. Return to `frmDateRange` in Design mode.

18. Use the Command Button Wizard to create a button that runs the report.

The Date Range form shown in Figure 3.3 shows the completed form with dates filled in.

Figure 3.3
The Date Range form with a range covering the month of March 2006.

When you click the button on the form, the report runs and opens in Print Preview mode. Figure 3.4 shows the completed report.

Figure 3.4
The finished report showing the dates.

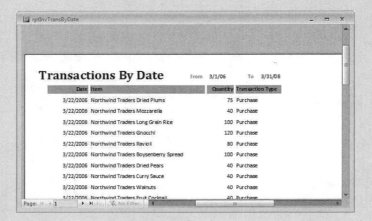

One type of control you can place on a form is a *subform*. This is a separate form, embedded on the main form and linked to the record on the main form. At times you might need to refer to controls that are on a subform. Because a subform is, in itself a control, it adds another layer that needs to be referenced. The syntax for referencing a control on a subform is

```
qualifier!identifer![objectname].qualifier![objectname]
```

The first qualifier indicates the main object, either Forms or Reports; the second identifier is the name of the form or report. This is followed by the subform/subreport name. The second qualifier indicates the type of subobject, either Form or Report. Finally, you indicate the name of the control whose value you want.

Figure 3.5 shows a text box to display the total quantity from the subform. The control source for that text box is

```
=[Forms]![frmInvDetails]![sfrmInventoryDetailsTransactions].[Form]![txtTotalQty]
```

As you can see, it displays the Total Quantity for the records shown.

Figure 3.5
The Inventory Details form showing the Total Quantity displayed under the subform.

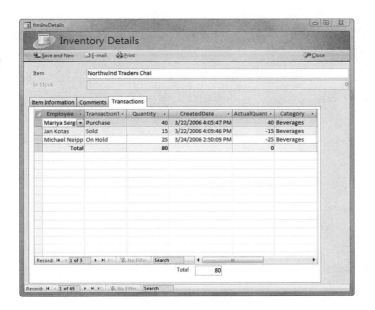

Using Built-In Functions

What Are Functions?

Built-in functions are commands provided by Access and VBA that return a value. The value returned is dependent on the purpose of the function and the arguments, if any, passed to it. VBA is rich in functions that perform a variety of tasks and calculations for you. There are functions to convert data types, perform calculations on dates, perform simple to complex mathematics, make financial calculations, manage text strings, format values, and retrieve data from tables, among others.

Functions return a value, and most accept arguments to act on. A lot of your code will use functions to make calculations and manipulate data. You should familiarize yourself with the functions that VBA makes available to you, but don't expect to memorize their syntax. Between Intellisense and the VBA Help screens you can't go far off course, especially because Intellisense prompts you for each argument. If you need help understanding an argument, press F1 or look up the function in VBA Help.

Although this book was not meant to be a reference for VBA functions, this chapter explains many of the most used ones to give you an idea of VBA's power.

A point to remember when coding your functions: Be consistent in using data types. If you provide arguments of the wrong data type or assign a function to a different data type, you will cause an error.

TIP

I don't know of any developer who knows every available function off the top of his or her head, so don't expect or think you need to. The more you code, the more you will remember, so feel free to use the references Microsoft provides. Use the Help option from the VBE menu to open the Developer Reference. In the search box type `functions list`, and one of the options is Functions (Alphabetical List). This gets you to a listing of all functions. Most of the function names are meaningful, so it shouldn't be difficult to find a function for the task you have.

NOTE

In this chapter we frequently use the term *expression*. In my use an expression can be as simple as a value or text string or as complex as a formula using multiple operators and functions. Just remember that an expression expresses a value.

Converting Data Types

At times you might find the need to import or link to data from external sources, or you might have to use data differently than the planned purpose. In such cases, the need may arise for you to convert from one data type to another. VBA includes several functions for this purpose. When you use a conversion function, the function returns the converted value but doesn't change the stored value.

→ For more on data types see, "VBA DataTypes" **p. 28**.

This chapter goes over some of the more commonly used conversion functions. You can find a full list by opening the Developers Reference using the VBE Help menu and searching on *type conversion functions*.

- **CBool**—Converts a value to a `Boolean` data type.
- **CDate**—Converts a value to a `Date` data type.
- **CInt**—Converts a value to an `Integer` data type.
- **CStr**—Converts a value to a `String` data type.
- **CVar**—Converts a value to a `Variant` data type.

TIP

The most current conversion functions are prefixed with the letter *C*. It's better to use these functions in your conversions; however, you will also find included in VBA an older set of functions such as `Str` or `Val` for backward compatibility. The more current functions take your system's settings into account, whereas the older ones don't.

The `Val()` function has a use in addition to being a simple conversion function. It will return all numeric characters until it reaches a nonnumeric one. `CStr()` will return an error if you attempt to convert a string that contains nonnumeric data. For example, `Val("123abc")` will return the number 123 and `CInt("123abc")` will return a datatype mismatch error.

These functions have a simple syntax in common:

functionname(argument)

where *functionname* is the name of the function and *argument* is a value, variable, constant, or expression. The value of the argument is converted to a different data type depending on the function used, so it can be used elsewhere in your application. The value(s) used in the argument remain unchanged. It should be noted that not every data type can be converted to any other data type. The following sections explain the limitations.

Converting to a `Boolean` Data Type

A `Boolean` value is either `True` or `False`. The `False` value is either the number or character zero (0). Any other value is considered `True`. If the argument passed to the `CBool` function evaluates to a zero, `CBool` returns a `False`. If it evaluates to any other value, `CBool` returns a `True`. For example; all the following return a `True` because the arguments all evaluate to a nonzero value:

```
CBool("1")
CBool(1+0)
CBool(5)
CBool(-50)
```

Conversely, the following expressions return a `False` because each argument evaluates to zero:

```
CBool(0)
CBool("0")
CBool(15-15)
```

The argument passed to the `CBool` function must contain all numeric characters or operators. If you use alphabetic characters you get a type mismatch error. One place where using `CBool` becomes useful is in conditional statements. For example, you might need to determine whether two values match. In our Inventory application you might need to determine whether you are out of stock on an item. You could use the following expression, which would return a `False` if the incomings matched the outgoings:

```
CBool(Sum(Incoming)-Sum(Outgoing))
```

Converting to a `Date` **Data Type**

The `CDate` function converts any valid date/time value to a `Date/Time` data type. A valid date/time value can be either a number or a string that is formatted as a date or time. `CDate` determines valid date/time formats according to the regional settings you have chosen in Windows. You can use the following points to understand how dates are converted by `CDate`:

- If the argument is a numerical value, `CDate` converts the integer portion of the number according to the number of days since December 30, 1899. If the argument contains a decimal value, it's converted to a time by multiplying the decimal by 24 (for example, .25 would be 6:00 a.m.).

- If the argument is a string value, `CDate` converts the string if it represents a valid date. For example; `"1/16/51"`, `"March 16, 1952"`, and `"6 Jun 84"` would all be converted to a date. However, `"19740304"` would result in a type mismatch error.

- Access recognizes dates from January 1, 100, to December 31, 9999. Dates outside that range result in an error.

- I recommend that you use four-digit years for clarity. However, Access will work with two-digit years. If you enter a year less than 30, Access assumes you want a date in the twenty-first century. If you use a year of 30 or higher, it is assumed to be a twentieth century date.

- Remember that the / is also the division operator and the – is used for subtraction. So, if you enter dates such as 12/3/04 you will get unexpected results. Entering `CDATE(12/3/04)` returns December 31, 1899, because 12 divided by 3 divided by 4 = 1. So you need to put such dates within quotes.

Converting to an `Integer` **Data Type**

The `CInt` function takes a numeric or string value and converts it to an `Integer` data type. The *argument* is required and needs to represent a value within the range of –32,678 to 32,767. If the argument contains a decimal, Access rounds to the next whole number. A value of .5 or higher is rounded up; anything lower is rounded down. Some examples of `CInt` functions follow:

```
CInt(10.5)   = 11
CInt(25.333) = 25
CInt(10/3) = 3
CInt("1,000") = 1000
```

> **TIP**
>
> That last example illustrates one of the advantages of `CInt` over the older `Val` function. `CInt` uses the system's regional settings and, therefore, recognizes the thousands separator, whereas `Val` would convert "1,000" to 1.

The argument must evaluate to a numeric value; otherwise, it returns an error. If the argument evaluates to a value outside the range of the `Integer` data type, you get an overflow error.

Converting to a `String` Data Type

The `CStr` function converts just about every numeric value into a `String` data type. The required argument can be any variable, constant, expression, or literal value that evaluates to a string.

> **CAUTION**
>
> If you use a variable as the argument, make sure it's been initialized to a value. If you use `CStr` on an uninitialized variable, it returns a numeric value of 0.

Converting to a `Variant` Data Type

As I mentioned in the discussion of VBA data types in Chapter 3, "Using Variables, Constants, and Data Types," the `Variant` data type is the most flexible because it can accept almost any value. With `CVar`, you can convert just about any numeric or text string to the `Variant` data type. With numeric values there is a constraint to the same range for the `Double` data type.

> **CAUTION**
>
> `CVar` should be used only when there is a doubt of the data type you are converting or when the data type isn't important.

Converting Null Values

If you try to use a Null value in many expressions, you will probably encounter an error. For example, the following expression results in a runtime error if either of the values contains a Null:

```
varTotal = ValueA * ValueB
```

To avoid such errors you can utilize the `Nz` function to convert the value to a non-Null. The `Nz` function uses the following syntax:

```
Nz(value, [valueifnull])
```

The `Nz` function works similarly to an Immediate If (`IIF`) function. The following expressions are functionally equivalent:

```
varTotal = IIF(IsNull(ValueA),0,ValueA) * IIF(IsNull(ValueB),0,ValueB)
varTotal = Nz(ValueA,0) * Nz(ValueB,0)
```

The *valueifnull* is an optional argument; it defaults to 0 or a zero-length string based on the value's data type.

Working with Date Functions

VBA has many functions that help you deal with dates. As long as you understand how Access stores Date/Time values, you should have no problem in working with date functions and values.

→ For a description of the Date/Time datatype see "VBA DataTypes," **p. 28**.

In this section we go over most of the functions you use when dealing with dates.

Returning the Current Date

To return the current date (as stored on your system) use the following function, which gives you a number counting the days from 12/30/1899:

```
Date()
```

How this value is displayed depends on your regional settings. You can use the `Date$()` function to return a 10-character string representing the date. This string uses the format *mm-dd-yyyy*. The `Date()` function returns only the system date; if you need to include the time use the `Now()` function. As noted earlier, a date/time value is a number where the integer portion represents the date and the decimal portion represents the time. So the `Now()` function will return an integer and decimal that represents the current date and time. The `Now()` function defaults to displaying its value according to the regional settings on your PC. On my PC it displays 7/25/2007 5:06:34 PM.

Performing Date Arithmetic

Because dates are stored as numbers, you can do date arithmetic simply by adding or subtracting date values. However, VBA gives you a better way, the `DateAdd` function. Using this function, you can add 14 days, 14 weeks, 14 months, or 14 years to any date. Or you can find a time 60 hours earlier than the specified date and time.

The following is the syntax for `DateAdd`, where *interval* is a string that indicates the type of time period that you want to calculate:

```
DateAdd(interval, value, date)
```

Table 4.1 shows the various strings that can be entered as intervals. The *number* argument is a value or expression that specifies the number of intervals you want to calculate. The number used is an integer. If a decimal value is included, it's rounded to the nearest whole number, before performing the calculation. The *date* argument is a Date/Time value that is the base value to use in the calculation.

Table 4.1   Interval Settings

String Setting	Description
yyyy	Years
q	Quarters
m	Months
y	Day of year
d	Days
w	Weekdays
ww	Weeks
h	Hours
n	Minutes
s	Seconds

The y, d, and w intervals work interchangeably in the DateAdd function but have more meaning in other Date/Time functions. If the interval evaluates to a negative number, it returns an earlier date/time; a positive number returns a future date/time.

Determining the Difference Between Two Dates

The DateDiff function is used to determine the number of intervals between two date/time values. The following is the syntax for the DateDiff function, where *interval* is a string that indicates the type of time period used to calculate the difference between the first and second dates represented by *date1* and *date2* (refer to Table 4.1):

```
DateDiff(interval, date1, date2[,firstdayofweek[, firstweekofyear]])
```

Also included in the DateDiff function are two optional arguments: *firstdayofweek* and *firstdayofyear*. These are numerical constants that can be used to adjust the first day of a week or year when using the DateDiff function. Tables 4.2 and 4.3 show a list of the values for each constant. The default values are Sunday and January 1, respectively.

Table 4.2   First Day of Week Constants

Constant	Description	Integer Value
vbSunday	Sunday (the default)	1
vbMonday	Monday	2
vbTuesday	Tuesday	3
vbWednesday	Wednesday	4
vbThursday	Thursday	5
vbFriday	Friday	6
vbSaturday	Saturday	7

Table 4.3	First Week of Year Constants	
Constant	**Description**	**Integer Value**
vbFirstJan1	Use the week in which January 1 occurs (the default).	1
vbFirstFourDays	Use the first week that has at least four days in the new year.	2
vbFirstFullWeek	Use the first full week of the new year.	3

The results from this function might not always be as expected:

- If *date2* falls before *date1*, the function yields a negative value.

- The DateDiff function calculates a year has passed when a new year falls between the two dates, even if there are fewer than 365 days. So when using 12/31 and 1/1 as date1 and date2, respectively, the function returns a 1.

Figure 4.1 shows how these guidelines affect the function in the Immediate window.

Figure 4.1
The DateDiff function in action.

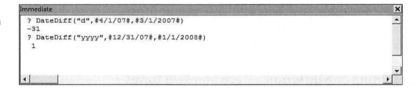

```
Immediate                                                              ×
? DateDiff("d",#4/1/07#,#3/1/2007#)
 -31
? DateDiff("yyyy",#12/31/07#,#1/1/2008#)
 1
```

> **NOTE**
> Notice that the dates in Figure 4.1 are enclosed by *octothorpes* (#—commonly known as a *pound sign*). This character is used to delimit date values, similarly to the way quotation marks are used with text strings. Access may recognize a date value and automatically insert the octothorpes, but it's a good practice to insert them yourself.

Extracting Parts of Dates

The DatePart function is used to extract a portion of a date from a date value. A Date/Time data type contains several components that correspond to the intervals listed in Table 4.1. For example, the following expressions return the values 4, 1, and 2007, respectively:

```
DatePart("m",#4/1/2007#)

DatePart("d",#4/1/2007#)

DatePart("yyyy",#4/1/2007#)
```

The DatePart function uses the following syntax, where *interval* is a String value that defines the part of the date you want to extract and *date* is a valid Date/Time value (refer to Table 4.1 for a list of interval values):

```
DatePart(interval, date[,firstdayofweek[, firstweekofyear]])
```

Also included in the `DatePart` function are two optional arguments: *firstdayofweek* and *firstdayofyear*. These are numerical constants that can be used to adjust the first day of a week or year when using the `DatePart` function. Tables 4.2 and 4.3 show a list of the values for each constant. The default values are Sunday and January 1, respectively.

> **TIP**
> Because you can extract any portion of a Date/Time value, it makes the most sense to store a date or time once as a valid Date/Time value. For example, even if you need to show only the month and year for a date, it would make sense to store a full date even if it's just the first or last day of the month.

Creating Dates from the Individual Parts

With `DatePart` you extract part of a date; conversely, with the `DateSerial` function you combine the parts of a date to return a date value. The `DateSerial` function uses the following syntax, where *Year*, *Month*, and *Day* can be any expression that evaluates to an integer value that represents the respective date part:

```
DateSerial(Year, Month, Day)
```

There are some rules for each of the arguments:

- *Year* is required and must be equal to an integer from 100 to 9999.
- *Month* is required, and integers from 1 to 12 (positive or negative) are considered.
- *Day* is required, and integers from 0 to 31 (positive or negative) are considered.

The `DateSerial` function can take integer values outside those ranges and calculate the difference to return a date value. This makes it very powerful if you use expressions for the arguments. For example, the following expression returns June 5, 2008 because the 18th month from the start of 2007 is June:

```
DateSerial(2007,18,5)
```

Similarly, the following returns May 15, 2007, by using the 30 days in April and adding the difference of 15 days to the next month:

```
DateSerial(2007,4,45)
```

Although this shouldn't be used as a substitute for `DateAdd` or `DateDiff`, it can make it easy to create dates from calculated values.

> **TIP**
> The expression `DateSerial(2007,5,0)` returns 4/30/07. Using 0 for the *Day* value can then be used to get the last day of a month. If you use `DateSerial(Year,Month+1,0)` you get the last day of the *Year* and *Month* used as arguments passed to the function.

Creating Dates from String Values

The DateValue function can be used to return a date value from a string value; it uses the following syntax, where *stringexpression* must conform to the formats used by the system's Regional settings:

DateValue(*stringexpression*)

The following three expressions return the date June 1, 2007:

DateValue("6/1/2007")

DateValue("June 1, 2007")

DateValue("1 Jun 07")

> **TIP**
>
> The functions TimeSerial and TimeValue perform similarly to the DateSerial and DateValue functions with time values.

Extracting a Specific Date or Time Portion

Table 4.4 lists several functions that return a specific portion of a date or time value. The syntax for these functions is simple:

Functionname(*date/time*)

Table 4.4   Date Component Functions

Function	Result
Day(*date*)	Returns the day of the month as an integer between 1 and 31
Hour(*time*)	Returns the hour as an integer between 0 and 23
Minute(*time*)	Returns the minute as an integer between 0 and 59
Second(*time*)	Returns the second as an integer between 0 and 59
Month(*date*)	Returns the month as an integer between 1 and 12
Year(*date*)	Returns the year as an integer between 100 and 9999

A Conversion and Date Example

Sometimes you might need to round a time value to the nearest quarter hour or hour. This example uses some of the conversion and date/time functions previously discussed to accomplish that task.

1. Create a blank form and put two text boxes on it. Label the boxes `txtTime` and `txtResult`.

2. Add an option group to the form with the options Hour and Quarter Hour. Name the group `optType`.

3. Add a button to the form (turn off the wizard first). Name the button `cmdRound`.

4. Set the Record Selectors and Navigation buttons to No. Set Scroll Bars to neither.

5. In the `On Click` event of the button use the following code:

```
Private Sub cmdRound_Click()
Dim intHrs As Integer, intMin As Integer
Dim dteTime As Date
' convert entered time to Time value

dteTime = CDate(Me.txtTime)
'extract parts of time

intHrs = DatePart("h", dteTime)
intMin = DatePart("n", dteTime)

If Me.optType = 1 Then 'test for nearest type
    'Round to nearest hour
    If intMin >= 30 Then
        dteTime = DateAdd("h", 1, dteTime)
        dteTime = DateAdd("n", -intMin, dteTime)
    Else
        dteTime = DateAdd("n", -intMin, dteTime)
    End If
Else
    'Round to quarter hour
    Select Case intMin
        Case Is < 8
            intMin = 0
        Case 8 To 23
            intMin = 15
        Case 24 To 38
            intMin = 30
        Case 39 To 53
            intMin = 45
        Case Else
            intHrs = intHrs + 1
            intMin = 0
    End Select
    dteTime = TimeSerial(intHrs, intMin, 0)
End If

'Populate Result control
Me.txtResult = dteTime

End Sub
```

6. Save form as `frmRound` (see Figure 4.2).

Figure 4.2
The completed
frmRound showing an
example of input and
result.

Using Mathematical Functions

VBA provides a rich, broad set of functions to perform mathematical and financial calculations. There are too many to cover in this section, so we provide an overview of the most commonly used functions.

The Abs Function

The Abs function returns the absolute value of a number, removing the sign. The following is the syntax for the Abs function, where *number* is any expression that evaluates to a numerical value:

Abs(*number*)

For example; this expression returns a 7:

Abs(-7)

The Int Function

The Int function removes any decimal value from a number, returning the integer portion. The function uses the following syntax, where *number* is any expression that evaluates to a numerical value:

Int(*number*)

For example; this expression returns 15 because it truncates the value, removing the decimal portion:

Int(15.9)

However, if the numerical value is negative, Int returns the nearest negative integer, so the following returns –16:

Int(-15.9)

Although seemingly the same, Int and CInt can't be used interchangeably. The Int function doesn't convert the data type of the argument. Using CInt is often the better option, but it doesn't always return the same result. So be careful in determining which one to use.

The Rnd **Function**

The Rnd function is used to generate a random number. It can be used with an optional argument represented as any valid numerical expression. The following is the syntax for the function:

```
Rnd(seed)
```

seed can be used to control the generated number as indicated in the following:

- If *seed* is a negative value, Rnd generates the same number.
- If *seed* is a positive number (other than 0) Rnd generates the next number in an internally determined sequence of numbers.
- If *seed* equals 0, Rnd generates the most recently generated number.
- If seed is omitted, Rnd generates the next number in an internally determined sequence of numbers.

The Rnd function generates a number in the range of 0 to 1, so if you need a whole number, you will have to multiply the generated value by a power of 10 and use the Int function to get your whole number.

> **TIP**
>
> Use the Randomize statement to reset the internal sequence so that Rnd generates apparently unique values that are repeated.

A Mathematical Functions Example

To illustrate mathematical functions, let's create a function to generate a number between 1 and 99.

1. Create a blank form and put two text boxes on it. Label the boxes txtSeed and txtPicks.
2. Add a button to the form (turn off the wizard first). Name the button cmdGenerate.
3. Set Record Selectors and Navigation buttons to No. Set Scroll Bars to neither.
4. In the On Click event of the button use the following code:

```
Private Sub cmdGenerate_Click()
'Generate number between 1 and 99
    Me.txtPicks = Int(Rnd(Me.txtSeed) * 100)
End Sub
```

5. Save form as frmGenerate (see Figure 4.3).

Figure 4.3
The completed
frmGenerate show-
ing an example of a gen-
erated number.

Using Financial Functions

Financial functions are used to perform many standard financial calculations such as interest rates, annuity or loan payments, and depreciation. Following are some financial functions you might find useful.

The Ddb Function

The Ddb function calculates the depreciation of an asset for a specified time using the predefined double-declining balance method. The following is the syntax for this function,
where *cost* is an expression representing the asset's opening cost and *salvage* is an expression that specifies the value of the asset at the end of *life*, an expression representing the
term of the asset's lifespan.

```
Ddb(cost, salvage, life, period[, factor])
```

The *period* argument represents the time span for which the depreciation is being calculated. All these arguments use Double data types. There is an optional *factor* argument that
specifies the rate of decline of the asset. If omitted, the double-declining method is used.

The FV Function

The FV function is used to calculate the future value of an annuity. The FV function returns
a double data type and uses the syntax

```
FV(rate, nper,pmt[,pv [, type]])
```

where *rate* is an expression resulting in a Double data type that represents the interest rate
per period, *nper* is an expression resulting in an Integer data type that represents the number of payment periods in the annuity, and *pmt* is an expression resulting in a Double value
that specifies the payment being made for each period. There are two optional arguments,
pv and *type*, which are Variant data types that specify the present value of the annuity and
whether payments are made at the start or end of each period.

The `Pmt` **Function**

The `Pmt` function is used to calculate the payment for an annuity or loan. This function uses the syntax

```
Pmt(rate, nper, pv[, fv[, type]])
```

where *rate* is an expression resulting in a `Double` data type that represents the interest rate per period, *nper* is an integer expression that defines the number of payments to be made, and *pv* identifies the present value and is also a `Double` data type. There are two optional arguments, *fv* and *type*, which are `Variant` data types that represent the future value of the payments and whether payments are made at the start or end of each period.

The `Rate` **Function**

The `Rate` function is used to calculate the periodic interest rate for an annuity or loan. The syntax for this function is

```
Rate(nper, pmt, pv[, fv[, type[, guess]]])
```

Where *nper* is an expression resulting in a `Double` data type that represents the number of period, *pmt* is an expression resulting in a `Double` data type that represents the payment per period, and *pv* is an expression resulting in a `Double` data type that defines the present value. There are also three optional arguments: *fv*, *type*, and *guess*, which identify the future value, determine whether payments are made at the start or end of each period, and allow you to give an estimate of the rate, respectively.

4

A Financial Functions Example

In keeping with the Inventory application theme of the sample file, this example looks at a scenario where you want to expand to cover a new product line. Because this new product line is from a new vendor, the vendor requires you to make a significant purchase the first time around. You don't have the $10,000 to make the initial purchase, so you need to figure out different loan scenarios to see whether you can afford a loan.

1. Open the basUDFs module or one of your own.

2. Enter the following procedure:
    ```
    Public function LoanPmt(dblRate As Double, intNper As Integer, _
    dblPv As Double) As Currency
        LoanPmt = Abs(Pmt(dblRate/12, intNper, dblPv))
    End Function
    ```

3. In the Immediate window enter the following statement and press Enter:
    ```
    ? LoanPmt(.05,36,10000)
    ```

Figure 4.4 shows the code and the result. This loan would cost you $300 per month for 36 months. You can now try out different scenarios with combinations of rate and term to see what your payments might be.

Figure 4.4
The LoanPmt function and its results.

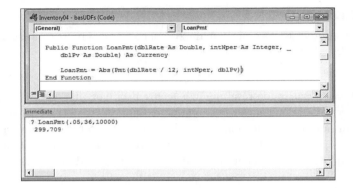

Manipulating Text Strings

You use string functions to manipulate groups of text data. The following are some examples of where you might use string functions:

- Checking to see whether a string contained another string
- Parsing out a portion of a string
- Replacing parts of a string with another value

The following string functions help you do all these tasks and more.

The Asc Function

Every individual character can be represented by a number value. These values are listed in the American Standard Code for Information Interchange (ASCII). To return the ASCII value of a character use the following syntax, where *string* is an expression that results in a Text data type. It returns an integer value between 0 and 255.

ASC(*string*)

> **CAUTION**
>
> The Asc function reads only the first character of the string if there are multiple characters.

With any text string you must use apostrophes or quotation marks to define and delineate the text string; otherwise, Asc returns an error. However, if the string is a numeric, the delimiters can be eliminated. For example, the following two functions both return the value 51:

Asc("3")

Asc(3)

The Chr **Function**

The Chr function is the reverse of the Asc function. Whereas Asc returns the numerical value from character, Chr returns the character from a number. The following is the syntax for this function. where *charactercode* is an integer value between 0 and 255:

```
Chr(charactercode)
```

As you saw previously, the character 3 is represented by the number 51. So the following functions returns a 3:

```
Chr(51)
```

> **NOTE**
> The numbers 0–255 represent the values of characters according to the ASCII table. An example of that table can be found at http://www.asciitable.com.

> **TIP**
> Many of the string functions return a value as a variant of the String subtype. An alternative set of string functions add a $ to the function name (for example, Chr$). These alternative functions return a literal string value. This provides a better performance because VBA doesn't have to evaluate the data type during processing.

The Case Functions

There is actually no case function. There are two functions, LCase and UCase, that can be used to change the case of a text string. They use the following syntax, where *string* is an expression that returns a string value. Both functions return the *string* in either lowercase or uppercase, respectively.

```
LCase(string)
```

```
UCase(string)
```

> **TIP**
> You can use the UCase function to convert entered data so that the data entry person doesn't have to concern himself with entering the proper case.

The Len **Function**

The Len function is used to determine the number of characters in a text string. This function uses the following syntax, where *string* is an expression that results in a Text data type. The function returns a long integer except where the string is Null, in which case it returns a Null value.

```
Len(string)
```

The Left, Right, and Mid **Functions**

Among the most used functions, these three return a portion of a string depending on the function and the arguments provided. All three result in a Variant Long subtype but support a $ version, which forces a String data type.

The Left and Right functions use a similar syntax:

```
Left(string, length)

Right(string, length)
```

Here, *string* is an expression that results in a Text data type to be parsed and *length* is an expression that results in an Integer data type that specifies the number of characters from either the left or right end of the string to return.

The Mid function can parse a text string from any part of the string. It uses the following syntax, where *string* is a required argument that represents an expression resulting in a Text data type and *start* is a required argument that specifies where to start parsing the string:

```
Mid(string, start[, length])
```

An optional argument, *length*, specifies how many characters from the *start* point to parse. If *length* is omitted or is greater than the number of characters to the end of the string, all characters from *start* are returned. Figure 4.5 shows the three functions parsing various parts of the same string.

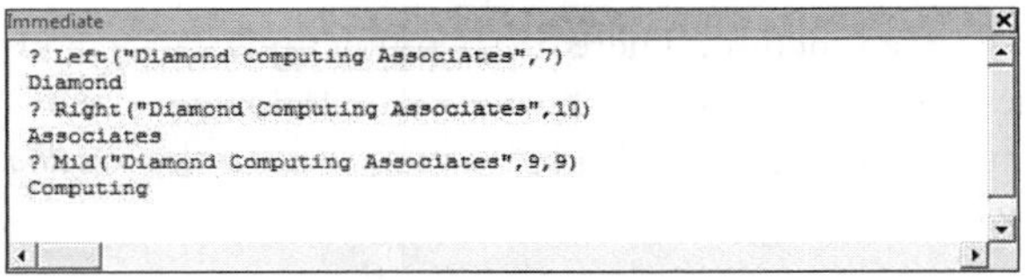

Figure 4.5
The Left, Right, and Mid functions parsing the same text.

```
Immediate                                                              ×
? Left("Diamond Computing Associates",7)
Diamond
? Right("Diamond Computing Associates",10)
Associates
? Mid("Diamond Computing Associates",9,9)
Computing
```

The Replace **Function**

The Replace function is used to replace one or more characters within a string with a different character or characters. This function takes the following syntax, where *string* is an expression representing the text string to be searched, *stringtoreplace* is an expression representing the string to be searched for, and *replacementstring* represents the string you want in place of *stringtoreplace*

```
Replace(string, stringtoreplace, replacementstring[, start[, count[, compare]]])
```

In addition, there are three optional arguments: *start*, which specifies where to start searching within the string; *count*, which specifies the number of replacements to process; and *compare*, which is a constant indicating the method used to compare *stringtoreplace* with *string*. Table 4.5 lists the constants that can be used.

Table 4.5 Comparison Constants

Constant	Value	Description
vbUseCompareOption	−1	Performs a comparison using the setting of the Option Compare statement.
vbBinaryCompare	0	Performs a binary comparison.
vbTextCompare	1	Performs a textual comparison.
vbDatabaseCompare	2	Microsoft Access only. Performs a comparison based on information in your database.

The Split Function

The Split function takes a delimited string and populates an array with the parts. The following is the syntax for the Split function, where *string* is a delimited string of values:

```
Split(string[, delimiter[, count[, compare]]])
```

This is the only required argument. The first optional argument is *delimiter*, which specifies the delimiting character separating the values. If you omit *delimiter* a space is assumed to be the *delimiter*. The second optional argument is *count*, which limits the number of values parsed. For example, there might be five values separated by commas in the string, but a *count* argument of 3 parses only the first three values. The final optional argument is *compare*. See Table 4.5 for the comparison constants.

The Trim Functions

Three functions can be used to trim leading or trailing spaces from a string. All three use the same syntax, where *string* is an expression that results in a Text data type:

```
Trim(string)
```

```
LTrim(string)
```

```
RTrim(string)
```

The Trim function removes both leading and trailing spaces, LTrim removes the leading spaces, and Rtrim removes the trailing spaces. All three functions return a Variant String subtype and support the $ format to force a Text data type.

Formatting Values

Often data is stored is differently from the way it's displayed on forms and in reports. The Format function is your tool to change how data is displayed. Access provides many predefined formats for you to use and allows you to customize your own formats. For example, a phone number might be stored as 10 digits but you can display it like (111) 222-3333 by applying a format. Another example are Date/Time values. As previously noted, they are stored as a Double number. However, the Format function can display the number in a variety of date or time formats.

CAUTION

Keep in mind that the `Format` function returns a `Variant` `String` subtype, which will probably be different from the original value's data type, and that the original data remains unchanged. This means that you should use `Format` only for display purposes; you don't want to use it in calculations.

The `Format` function uses the following syntax, where *expression* can be either a `String` or `Numeric` data type that results in the value you want to format:

`Format(expression[, format[,firstdayofweek[, firstweekofyear]]])`

There are three optional arguments, the first of which determines how the data is formatted. The other two optional arguments, *firstdayofweek* and *firstdayofyear*, are numerical constants that can be used to adjust the first day of a week or year when using the `DatePart` function. Tables 4.2 and 4.3 show a list of the values for each constant. The default values are Sunday and January 1, respectively.

Tables 4.6 and 4.7 show some of the predefined formats you can use.

Table 4.6 Numeric Named Formats

Format	Example	Result
General Number	`Format(12345.6789,"General Number")`	12345.6789
Currency	`Format(12345.6789, "Currency")`	$12,345.68
Fixed	`Format(0.1, "Fixed")`	0.10
Standard	`Format(12345.6789, "Standard")`	12,345.68
Percent	`Format(6789, "Percent")`	67.89%
Scientific	`Format(12345.6789, "Scientific")`	1.23E+03
Yes/No	`Format(0, "Yes/No")` `Format(3, "Yes/No")`	No Yes
True/False	`Format(0, "Yes/No")` `Format(3, "Yes/No")`	False True
On/Off	`Format(0, "Yes/No")` `Format(3, "Yes/No")`	Off On

The result for `Currency` is based on the United States regional settings; if you use a different regional setting, the `Currency` format uses those settings. For the `Boolean` types a zero results in a No, False, or Off result. Any other value gives the opposite result.

Table 4.7   Date/Time Named Formats

Format	Example	Result
General Date	Format("04/01/07", "General Date")	4/1/2007
Long Date	Format("04/01/07", "Long Date")	Sunday April 1, 2007
Medium Date	Format("04/01/07", "Medium Date")	01-Apr-07
Short Date	Format("04/01/07", "Short Date")	4/1/2007
Long Time	Format('13:13:13', "Long Time")	1:13:13 PM
Medium Time	Format('13:13:13', "Medium Time")	1:13 PM
Short Time	Format('13:13:13', "Short Time")	13:13

Applying User-Defined Formats

Although the predefined formats listed in Tables 4.6 and 4.7 cover many situations, at times you'll need to create your own formats. You can use a number of special characters and placeholders to define your own formats. Tables 4.8, 4.9, and 4.10 list these formats.

Table 4.8   Numeric User-Defined Formats

Format	Explanation	Example	Result
0	Display actual digit or 0 for each 0 used. Rounds if more digits than shown.	Format(12.3456, "000.00000")	012.34560
		Format(12.3456, "000.00")	012.35
#	Display actual digit or nothing. Rounds if more digits than shown.	Format(12.3456, "###.#####")	12.3456
		Format(12.3456, "###.##")	12.35
%	Multiples by 100 and adds percent sign	Format(.3456, "##%")	35%
E- E+ e- e+	Display scientific notation.	Format(1.234567, "###E-###)	123E-2
- + $ ()	Display a literal character.	Format(123.45, "$####.##")	$123.45
\	Display following character as a literal.	Format(.3456, "##.##\%"	.35%

4

Table 4.9   Date User-Defined Formats

Format	Explanation	Example	Result
d	Display day of month without leading zero	Format("04/04/07", "d")	1
dd	Display day of month with leading zero where needed	Format("04/04/07", "dd")	01
ddd	Display abbreviated day of week	Format("04/01/07", "ddd")	Sun
dddd	Display full day of week	Format("04/01/07", "dddd")	Sunday
ddddd	Display short date	Format("04/01/07", "ddddd")	4/1/2007
dddddd	Display long date	Format("04/01/07", "dddddd")	Sunday, April 1, 2007
m	Display month without leading zero	Format("04/01/07", "m")	4
mm	Display month with leading zero	Format("04/01/07", "mm")	04
mmm	Display abbreviated month name	Format("04/01/07", "mmm")	Apr
mmmm	Display full month name	Format("04/01/07", "mmmm")	April
q	Display quarter of year	Format("04/01/07", "q")	2
h	Display hours without leading zero	Format("13:13:13", "h")	1
hh	Display hours with leading zero	Format("13:13:13","hh")	01
n	Display minutes without leading zero	Format("13:07:13", "n")	7
nn	Display minutes with leading zero	Format("13:07:13", "nn")	07
s	Display seconds without leading zero	Format("13:13:07", "s")	7
ss	Display seconds with leading zero	Format("13:13:07", "ss")	07
ttttt	Display 12-hour clock	Format("13:13:13", "ttttt")	1:13:13 PM
AM/PM	With other time formats displays either upper- or lowercase AM/PM	Format("13:13:13", "hh:nn AM/PM")	1:13 PM
am/pm		Format("13:13:13", "hh:nn am/pm")	1:13 pm
A/P	With other time formats displays either upper- or lowercase A/P	Format("13:13:13", "hh:nn A/P")	1:13 P
a/p		Format("13:13:13", "hh:nn a/p")	1:13 p
ww	Display the number of the week (1–54)	Format("04/01/07", "ww")	14

Format	Explanation	Example	Result
w	Display the number of the day of the week	`Format("04/01/07", "w")`	1
y	Display the day of the year (1–366)	`Format("04/01/07", "y")`	91
yy	Display 2-digit year (00–99)	`Format("04/01/07", "yy")`	07
yyyy	Display 4-digit year (0100–9999)	`Format("04/01/07", "yyyy")`	2007

These formats can also be combined to display different date or time formats. The following are some examples:

```
Format("04/01/07", "yyyymmdd") = 20070401
```

> **TIP**
>
> This format is useful when exporting data to other formats and still maintaining chronological sort.

```
Format("4/01/07", "mmm dd") = Apr 01
Format("04/01/07", "mmm yyyy") = Apr 2007)
```

Table 4.10   String User-Defined Formats

Format	Explanation	Example	Result
@	Display actual character or space	`Format("VBA", "@@@@@")`	VBA
&	Display actual character or nothing	`Format("VBA", "&&&&&")`	VBA
<	Display character as lowercase	`Format("VBA", "<<<<")`	vba
>	Display character in uppercase	`Format("VBA", ">>>>")`	VBA

Domain Aggregate Functions

Domain Aggregate functions are specific to Microsoft Access because they are used to retrieve data from tables. Because you can't assign the results of a query directly to a variable, you must use Domain Aggregate functions to retrieve that data. There are other ways besides Domain Aggregate functions that will be covered later in this book. The advantages of the Domain Aggregate functions are that they can accept a set of criteria to retrieve just the data needed. All the Domain Aggregate functions use a similar syntax, where *expression* is the name of the field in a table or query, *domain* is the name of the table or query, and *criteria* is a comparison to define which record to extract the value from:

```
Function("[expression]", "domain", criteria)
```

Notice that the *expression* is usually surrounded by quotes and brackets and that the *domain* is also surrounded by quotes. I'll list some of the more commonly used Domain Aggregate functions.

The DLookup Function

The DLookup function is used to retrieve a value from a single field in a table or query. The following example returns the last name of the contact for Supplier G from tblSuppliers in the Inventory application:

```
DLookup("[LastName]", "tblSuppliers","[Company] = '" & "Supplier G" & "'")
```

The DLookup function retrieves that value from the first record matching the criteria. Because Company is a Text data type, you must concatenate the single quotes around the company name. If you are comparing a Numeric data type, no quotes are needed, and a Date/Time data type requires octothorpes (#) to delimit the value to be searched for.

The DCount Function

The DCount function is used to count the number of records in a table or query that match your criteria. An example of the DCount function follows:

```
DCount("*","tblEmployees","[Jobtitle] = 3")
```

This returns a result of 6 because there are six employees whose job title is Sales Representative.

The DMax/DMin Functions

The DMax and DMin functions return the highest or lowest values in the domain according to the criteria listed. An example of the DMin function follows:

```
DMin("[CreatedDate]","tblTransactions")
```

This returns 3/22/2006 4:02:28 PM, which is the earliest transaction in the Transactions table.

TIP

The DMax function is often used to produce a sequential numbering system that can be dependent on some other value. For example, say you wanted to number each transaction for each employee and start the numbering each time a new employee is added. In such a case you could use the following code snippet in the After Update event of the control where the employee is selected on your form:

```
Me.txtIncrement =
Nz(DMax("[Increment]","tblTransactions","[EmployeeID] = " &_
Me.cboEmployee),0)+1
```

This sets the control named txtIncrement to the highest value of the field Increment plus 1 for the selected employee. If no record for the employee is found, the Nz function causes the expression to return a 0, which is then incremented to 1.

Using the `Is` Functions

VBA provides a series of functions to help you trap errors that might arise from data type mismatches. These functions test a value to see whether it's a specified type.

- **`IsArray`**—Checks whether the value is an array
- **`IsDate`**—Checks whether the value is a Date/Time data type
- **`IsEmpty`**—Checks whether the value hasn't been initialized with a value
- **`IsError`**—Checks whether an expression results in an error
- **`IsMissing`**—Checks whether an optional argument has been passed to a procedure
- **`IsNull`**—Checks whether the value contains a Null
- **`IsNumeric`**—Checks whether the value is a number
- **`IsObject`**—Checks whether a variable contains a reference to an object

→ We cover arrays in more detail in Chapter 7, "Working with Arrays."

All these functions use the same syntax, where *value* is a value or expression being tested:

```
IsFunction(value)
```

The functions all return a `Boolean` data type, either `True` if the value meets the condition being checked or `False` if it doesn't.

Interaction

At times you need to provide information to the application's user or get information from them. This is interacting with the users. Two functions that can perform such an action are the `MsgBox` and `InputBox` functions.

The `MsgBox` Function

You use the `MsgBox` function to present information to users with an opportunity to respond to the information. You have control over how the message box appears and what response the user can make. The `MsgBox` function uses the following syntax, where *prompt* is the only required argument and represents a text string that constitutes the message presented by the message box:

```
MsgBox(prompt[, buttons][, title][, helpfile, context])
```

The users can respond through a choice of one or more buttons. Table 4.11 lists various button options you can use. You can supply a string value for *title* that displays in the title bar of the message box. The other two optional arguments—*helpfile* and *context*—are seldom used and go together. The *helpfile* argument is a string that points to a help file to be used if the user clicks the message box's Help button. The *context* argument is a numeric value that specifies a number to be used within the help file. (Note: Creating help files is outside the scope of this book.)

Table 4.11 `MsgBox` **Button Constants**

Constant	Description	Integer Value
`vbOkOnly`	OK button	0
`vbOKCancel`	OK and Cancel buttons	1
`vbAbortRetryIgnore`	Abort, Retry, and Ignore buttons	2
`vbYesNoCancel`	Yes, No, and Cancel buttons	3
`vbYesNo`	Yes and No buttons	4
`vbRetryCancel`	Retry and Cancel buttons	5

Table 4.12 lists constants for the icons that can be displayed in the message box. You can display both icons and buttons using the following syntax:

```
buttonconstant + iconconstant
```

As an example, the following function displays the message box shown in Figure 4.6. There are two buttons—OK and Cancel—and a question mark icon.

```
MsgBox("Do you want to save this record?", vbOKCancel + vbQuestion,"Warning")
```

Figure 4.6
A message box asking whether the user wants to save a record.

CAUTION

Besides the `MsgBox` function there is also a `MsgBox` action. The action displays the `Msgbox` without returning a value as a response.

Table 4.12 **Icon Constants**

Constant	Description	Integer Value
`vbCritical`	Critical message	16
`vbQuestion`	Warning message	32
`vbExclamation`	Warning message	48
`vbInformation`	Information message	64

When the user clicks one of the buttons, the function returns its value. Table 4.13 shows the values returned for each button.

Table 4.13   Button Values

Button	Returned Value	Integer Value
OK	vbOK	1
Cancel	vbCancel	2
Abort	vbAbort	3
Retry	vbRetry	4
Ignore	vbIgnore	5
Yes	vbYes	6
No	vbNo	7

The following code snippet is built around the message box function previously shown:

```
Private Function cmdSave_OnClick()
Dim strMsg As String
strMsg = "Do you want to save this record?"
If MsgBox("strMsg, vbOKCancel + vbQuestion,"Warning") = vbOK Then
     DoCmd.RunCommand acCmdSaveRecord
Else
     Me.Undo
End If
```

The InputBox Function

The Inputbox function displays a dialog box with a prompt that allows the user to enter a value that can then be assigned to a variable (see Figure 4.7). The following is the syntax for this function, where *prompt* is a String that displays a message for the user and is the only required argument:

```
InputBox(prompt[, title][, default][, xpos][, ypos][, helpfile, context])
```

The message is used to let the user know what data should be input. The *title* is a String that is displayed in the title bar of the window. The *default* is used to set a default value when the box opens. The *xpos* and *ypos* arguments allow you to precisely position the box in terms of the top and left of the screen. The *helpfile* and *context* arguments are the same as for the MsgBox.

Figure 4.7
An input box asking the user to enter a filename.

You usually use InputBox to retrieve a value from the user during processing of code. An example follows:

```
Dim strFilename As String
strFilename = InputBox("Enter file to be imported!", "Import file")
DoCmd.TransferText acExportDelim, , "Import", strFilename
```

> **TIP**
>
> I rarely use the InputBox function, preferring to use a form to allow the user to supply input. Using a form gives you much greater control over the input. With a form you can use interactive controls such as combo boxes or option groups to ensure that the correct data is entered. We'll deal with this more in later chapters.

CASE STUDY

Case Study: Add Work Days

Sometimes you might need to figure a delivery or follow-up date for a shipment. You want to calculate such dates based on business days, not calendar days. The following function allows you to enter a start date and the number of business days and returns the date equal to that number of business days:

1. Open the UDFs module or a new one.

2. Enter the following code into the module:

```
Public Function AddWorkdays(dteStart As Date, intnNumDays As Integer) As Date

Dim dteCurrDate As Date
Dim i As Integer

dteCurrDate = dteStart
AddWorkdays = dteStart
i = 1

Do While i < intNumDays
    If Weekday(dteCurrDate, vbMonday) <= 5 AND _
        IsNull(DLookup("[Holiday]","tblHolidays", "[HolDate] = #" & _
        dteCurrDate & "#")) Then
            i = i + 1
    End If

    dteCurrDate = dteCurrDate + 1

Loop
AddWorkdays = dteCurrDate

Exit_AddWorkDays:
End Function
```

3. Test the code by entering the following into the Immediate window. Figure 4.8 shows the results.

```
? AddWorkDays(#5/16/07#,15)
```

Figure 4.8
The results from using the
AddWorkDays function.

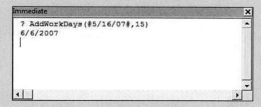

Building Procedures

Types of Procedures

The basic containers for your VBA code are *procedures*, which hold collections of VBA code statements that are executed line by line. Although individual statements can be executed from the Immediate window of the VBE, you must place your code into procedures to run the statements from your applications. Your procedures are placed into modules, which can be attached to a form or a report object, or they can stand alone. We've shown you some short procedures in previous chapters, but this chapter goes into creating and using procedures in more depth.

The first thing to understand is that there are two main kinds of procedures:

- Subroutines (Sub)
- Functions

A superset of procedures is referred to as *event procedures*. These are snippets of code executed when an event occurs. The only difference between a subroutine and an event procedure is how they are triggered.

→ We go more into event procedures in Chapter 8, "Object and Event-Driven Coding."

Subroutines

A subroutine differs from a function in that it doesn't return any value; it simply executes the code within the subroutine. Basic subroutines start with the word Sub, a name for the subroutine, and an empty set of parentheses. Subroutines end with the command End Sub. Within those two lines can be any number of code statements, including calls to other subroutines.

You use subroutines when you need to process some data; for example, looping through a recordset, adjusting a value, or adding records to a table when a condition is met. In such cases you don't need to return a single value. You use functions when you need to return a value that requires some complex calculations. Generally, a function is the right side of an assignment expression (x = y()) so that the value returned by the function is assigned to a variable.

You can enter a subroutine into a module manually by typing the Sub and End Sub lines and the code in between. But the easier way is to use the Insert Procedure icon from the VBE toolbar. Figure 5.1 shows the icon and the selection.

Figure 5.1
The Insert Procedure icon and submenu.

This opens the Add procedure dialog (shown in Figure 5.2). You can enter the name of the procedure and select its Type and Scope (more on scope in Chapter 9, "Understanding Scope").

Figure 5.2
The Add Procedure dialog filled in for Sample1.

Let's look at a simple procedure that prints out the name of the computer:

```
Sub Sample1()
Dim strCompName As String

strCompName = Environ("computername")
Debug.Print strCompName
End Sub
```

This little routine defines a String variable and assigns the computer name to it using the Environ() function; then it uses Debug.Print to print the contents of the variable to the Immediate window. Figure 5.3 shows the procedure being run.

Figure 5.3

The Sample1 proce-
dure being run from the
Immediate window.

We have been running these procedures through the Immediate window, but that's only for testing and demonstration purposes. Normally, you run your procedures through the Access user interface, or you can call the subroutine from within another routine using the following syntax:

```
Call procedurename
```

→ You learn more running procedures from the Access interface in Chapter 10, "Working with Forms."

Functions

The other type of procedure is the *user-defined function (UDF)*. The two differences between functions and subroutines are that functions are identified by a Function...End Function keyword pair and functions return a value. Therefore, a function is used to assign a value to a variable. For example, using the Case Study from Chapter 4, "Using Built-In Functions," we would have the statement

```
dteDueDate = AddWorkDays(#4/1/07#,20)
```

Let's look at a simple procedure:

```
Function Sample2()
    Sample2 = "Diamond Computing Associates"
End Function
```

The function procedure begins with the Function keyword and the name of the procedure and ends with the command End Function. In between, you can have as many lines of VBA code as needed. There is one required statement for a function, and that's the return value. You need to assign a value to the procedure name so that the computed value is returned. In the preceding example, the procedure name Sample2 is assigned a value of a company name. If you forget to include the return value assignment statement, the function returns a Null value. Figure 5.4 shows this procedure run from the Immediate window.

Figure 5.4

The Sample2 proce-
dure being run from the
Immediate window.

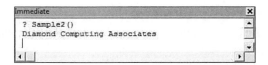

Notice the question mark preceding the function name. This is used to tell VBA to execute the function and display the return value. It is shorthand for the Visual Basic Print command.

> **TIP**
>
> The ? can be used to display the results of any expression that returns a value in the Immediate window. For example, typing **? 5*6** returns 30.

Functions are often called from within other procedures to calculate a value and return it to the calling procedure. A user-defined function is used just like one of the built-in Access functions described in Chapter 4.

Assigning a Data Type to a Function

Functions have data types, just as variables do. This enables you to control the result of the function. You assign a data type by adding an `As` keyword after the parentheses, just as you would identify any variable. For example:

```
Function Sample7() As String
```

If you don't specify the data type, it will default to `Variant`. Get in the habit of explicitly identifying data types.

Public Versus Private

We have been showing you sample code with just the `Sub` or `Function` keywords to open the procedure. In actual coding, you almost always identify a procedure with the additional `Public` or `Private` keyword. A procedure identified with the `Public` keyword can be called from anywhere in your application, whereas `Private` procedures can be called only from within the module where it's declared. Following are examples of the use:

```
Public Sub procedurename()
    'Can be called from anywhere
End Sub
Private Sub procedurename()
    'Called from this module
End Sub
Public Function procedurename()
    'Can be called from anywhere
End Function
Private Function procedurename()
    'Called from this module
End Function
```

You will find that most functions are public and are placed in global modules so that they can be reused in various places within your application—although many of your procedures will be private within an object's module.

> **CAUTION**
>
> A private procedure cannot be run from the Immediate window.

Passing Arguments

A lot of the sample code shown so far has been simple and not very useful in real-world applications. One of the keys to making code useful is to make it flexible so that it can work in different situations. One way this is done is by passing arguments to the procedure. Notice that each procedure has a pair of parentheses in the opening line. These parentheses provide a place to include arguments for the procedure, including multiple arguments separated by commas. The syntax for an argument is

variable AS *datatype*

Here's a small function that returns a discount on a price:

```
Public Function Discountprice(curPrice As Currency)
    Discountprice = curprice *.9
End function
```

The declaration statement for Discountprice includes a required argument of a price. This argument's value is assigned to the variable curPrice, which can then be used within this procedure as necessary. Figure 5.5 shows the function being run from the Immediate window with various values.

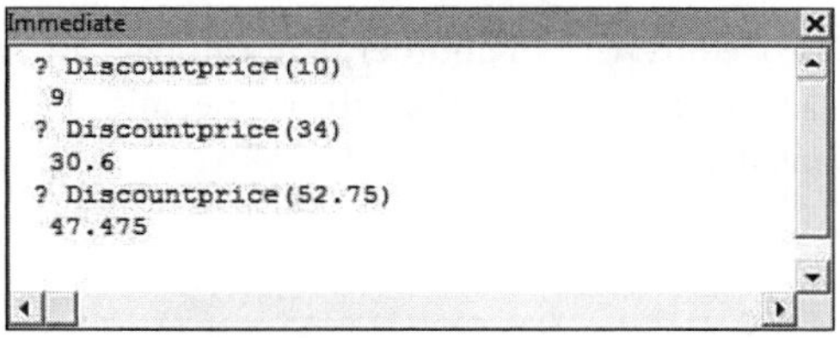

Figure 5.5
The Discountprice function being run from the Immediate window.

```
Immediate
? Discountprice(10)
 9
? Discountprice(34)
 30.6
? Discountprice(52.75)
 47.475
```

Using Optional Arguments and Default Values

You can also specify that arguments be optional, so that you don't have to include them in your procedure call. For example:

```
Public Function Fullname(strFirst As String, strLast As String, & _
    Optional strMI As String)
    Fullname = strFirst
    If isNull(strMI) Then
        Fullname = Fullname & " " & strMI & " "
    Else
        Fullname = Fullname & " "
    End If
    Fullname = Fullname & strLast
End Function
```

If you run the full name function from the Immediate window like this, you get *Scott B Diamond* in return:

```
? Fullname("Scott", "Diamond", "B.")
```

If you run it without the optional argument you get *Scott Diamond* in return:

```
? Fullname("Scott", "Diamond")
```

Optional arguments can also be given default values. Let's rework the `Discountprice` function:

```
Public Function DiscPrice(curPrice as Currency,  _
    Optional dblDisc As Double = .9) As Currency
    DiscountPrice = curPrice * dbDisc
End Function
```

If you run the function like this you get 80:

```
? DiscountPrice(100,.8)
```

If you run it like this you get 90:

```
? DiscountPrice(100)
```

> **NOTE** Values passed as arguments to a procedure must be entered properly for the data type. This means that `String` types must be delimited with quotes (""), Date/Time types with the octothorpe (#), and numerical types without any delimiter.

Passing Arguments By Reference

When you are calling one procedure within another, you can pass an argument by reference. When doing so the variable is passed to the subroutine, and the called procedure uses the exact same variable. Consider this example:

```
Sub Sample3()
    'demo pass by reference
    Dim strMessage As String
    strMessage = "Hello"
    Sample4 strMessage
    Debug.Print strmessage
End Sub

Sub Sample4(strMsg As String)
    strMsg = "Goodbye"
End Sub
```

When you run `Sample3` from the Immediate window, it prints the message *Goodbye*. Because `Sample4` changes the value, it's changed back in the calling procedure as well. The advantage to passing values by reference is the speed of response, but there could be unanticipated results if you weren't expecting the variable to change. To account for this, there is an alternative of passing arguments *by value*.

Passing Arguments By Value

The difference between passing a value by reference and by value is that the latter creates a copy of the value and passes that copy to the successor procedure. The `ByVal` keyword is used to declare the argument as being passed by value. I've rewritten the previous sample to use the `ByVal` keyword:

```
Sub Sample5()
    'demo pass by reference
    Dim strMessage As String
    strMessage = "Hello"
    Sample6 strMessage
    Debug.Print strmessage
End Sub

Sub Sample6(ByVal strMsg As String)
    strMsg = "Goodbye"
End Sub
```

Now run `Sample5` from the Immediate window, and you see it returns "Hello." Because a copy of the value is passed to the called procedure, only the copy is changed in the successor procedure.

Error Handling

One thing I've learned about writing code for others is that users always do the unexpected. When you write code for yourself, you have an idea of what that code will do and how to use it. So when you execute your code you are unlikely to make the mistakes that your users might. Therefore, you won't encounter errors that they might find.

So you need to provide for handling potential errors so that they don't cause your applications to crash and become unusable. This makes error handling of primary importance. VBA gives you different methods to deal with errors encountered during processing.

Using `On Error Resume Next`

One way to deal with errors is to simply ignore them; that's what the `On Error Resume Next` statement does for you. When an error is encountered, it just ignores the error and continues to the next statement and executes it. After you set error handling, it remains in effect until you remove or change it.

In the following example, a value is being distributed over a group of people. The user enters the value and the number of people.

```
Function Sample8(intValue As Integer, intPeople As Integer)
On Error Resume Next
Sample8 = intValue/intPeople
End Function
```

If the user makes an error and enters a 0 as the second argument, you get a Division-by-Zero error. Figure 5.6 shows the code with the `On Error` statement commented out and the resulting error.

In Figure 5.7, the `On Error` statement is restored and the function runs, leaving a blank line.

As you can see, using `On Error Resume Next` can give unexpected results, so it's better to deal with errors more explicitly.

5

Figure 5.6
A Division-by-Zero error occurs.

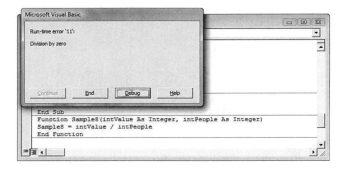

Figure 5.7
No error occurs, but no result is returned.

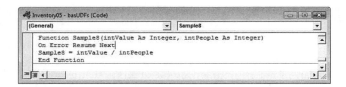

Using On Error Goto

The format for the On Error Goto statement is in three parts. The first part is the statement itself, which goes at the top of your procedure. The second part is a segment of code to handle the error. The final part is a redirection statement that allows you to skip the error-handler portion. The following example takes the code from Sample8 and adds the error-handling segments:

```
Function Sample9(intValue As Integer, intPeople As Integer)
On Error Goto Err_Sample9
Sample9 = intValue/intPeople

Exit_Sample9:
    Exit Function

Err_Sample9:
    MsgBox Err.Number & " " & Err.Description, vbOkOnly
    Resume ExitSample9
End Function
```

The preceding procedure introduces several new concepts:

■ The On Error Goto statement includes a label name that tells VBA where within the procedure to go when an error is encountered. In this example, it's the label titled Err_Sample9.

In previous versions of Access, when you used the Command Button Wizard, Access automatically generated minimum error handling code. This code took the following form:

```
On Error Goto Err_procedurename

Exit_procedurename:
Exit Function
...
Err_procedurename:
    MsgBox Err.Description
    Resume Exit_procedurename
```

I use the same format in my sample codes. However, with Access 2007, Microsoft introduces embedded macros, so the wizards now generate an embedded macro, without any error handling. Although macros now offer an On Error statement, it's not as flexible as VBA's. That's another reason to use VBA rather than macros.

- The code includes the labels `Exit_Sample9` and `Err_Sample9`. A label is code that ends with a colon (:). The VBA `Goto` and `On Error Goto` statements can be used to redirect processing to a label.

- After the `Exit_Sample9` label is an `Exit Function` statement, which skips any subsequent code and exits from the function.

- `Err.Number` and `Err.Description` are variables that return the number and description of the currently incurred error.

- The `Resume` statement can redirect code execution to a named label. This can help if you can identify and fix or ignore the error in your code, and then resume processing.

This chapter gave you a foundation for building your procedures. In Chapter 6, "Conditional and Looping Statements," we start to get into the main tools for programming—your flow of control statements.

5

Conditional and Looping Statements

Introducing Flow of Control Statements

A large portion of programming can be summed up by two concepts: `If...Then...Else` and `Do...While`. These concepts, known as *conditional branching* and *looping*, make up approximately 75% of your code. Branching allows you to perform different tasks based on the value of a condition. Looping allows you to repeat a task while a condition exists. Each of these types of statements has different variations. Collectively they are referred to as *flow of control* statements because they allow you change the order in which statements are processed. Once you understand how these statements are used, you will be able to write code that can accomplish almost any task.

Using `If...Then...Else`

The main branching statement is `If...Then...Else`. In its simplest form it uses syntax like the following:

```
IF condition is true THEN
    statements
END IF
```

This statement tests a condition to see whether it's true. If true it performs the set of instructions; otherwise, it skips to the next statement after the `END IF`.

A Simple If Statement

If you require code to manage inventory, odds are you frequently need to check whether an item is in stock. The following simple function does that:

```
Public Function IsInstock(lngItemID As Long) As Boolean
IsInstock = False
If DLookup("[ActualQuantity]", "qryInventoryTransactionsExtended", _
"[InventoryID] = " & lngItemID) > 0 Then
    IsInstock = True
End If
End Function
```

The function sets the default value IsInstock to False and then tests to see whether the value of the Dlookup function is greater than 0. If it is, it sets the IsInstock variable to True. It uses a passed-in value of the ItemID to determine what Item to count for. The function refers to the qryInventoryTransactionsExtended query, which was set up to count current stock for all items.

More Complex Conditions

Conditions can be used to test for multiple logical results using the AND and OR operators along with parentheses to group items. The next function can be used to determine whether an item needs to be reordered and whether the item is from the supplier from whom you are preparing to order.

```
Public Function ReorderItem(lngItemID As Long, lngSupplier As Long) As Boolean
Dim varInStock As Variant
Dim varReorder As Variant
'Retrieve quantity on hand and Reorder level
varInStock = DLookup("[ActualQuantity]", "qryInventoryTransactionsExtended", _
"[InventoryID] = " & lngItemID)
varReorder=DLookup("[Reorderlevel]","tblinventory", "[InventoryID] = " _
& lngItemID)
ReorderItem = False
'Test if stock is less than reorder level
If varInStock < varReorder AND DLookup("[SupplierID]","tblinventory", _
"[InventoryID] = " & lngItemID) = lngSupplier THEN
    ReorderItem = True
End If
End Function
```

The function tests both for whether the amount in stock is greater than the reorder level and whether the supplier is a selected supplier. As noted, it's possible to use multiple conditions in your If statements when necessary. Three operators can be used to express conditions:

- The AND operator requires that all conditions be met to return a True result.
- The OR operator requires that at least one of the conditions be met to return a True result.
- The NOT operator takes the inverse of the result and returns False if the conditions evaluate to True and vice versa.

Table 6.1 illustrates how these operators might work.

Table 6.1 Logical Operator Examples	
Condition	**Results**
`Weekday(date)=7 AND Hour(date) <12`	Returns a `True` only if it's Sunday morning
`Weekday(date)=1 OR Weekday(date)=7`	Returns a `True` if the date is either Saturday or Sunday
`NOT Weekday(date)=1`	Returns a `True` if the date is not a Sunday

Including an `Else` Clause

The `If...End If` grouping has some additional clauses that expand its capabilities. First, let's look at the `Else` clause. In the first example of the `ReorderItem` function we set the value for the function to `False` and then changed it to `True` if the condition was met. The other way to handle that is with the `Else` clause. Look at the revised code:

```
Public Function IsInstock2(lngItemID As Long) As Boolean
If DLookup("[ActualQuantity]", "qryInventoryTransactionsExtended", _
"[InventoryID] = " & lngItemID) > 0 Then
     IsInstock2 = True
Else
     IsInStock2 = False
End If
End Function
```

Using the `Else` clause we can define a set of instructions to execute depending on the result of the condition.

Including an `ElseIf` Clause

Another clause to look at is the `ElseIf` clause that allows you to deal with multiple conditions in sequence. Following is an example of how to use the `ElseIf` clause:

```
Public Function SupplierDiscount(lngSupplier As Long) As Currency
'Apply discount specific to Supplier
If lngSupplier = 1 Then
     SupplierDiscount = .12
ElseIf lngSupplier = 2 Then
     SupplierDiscount = .08
ElseIf lngSupplier = 3 Then
     SupplierDiscount = .15
ElseIf lngSupplier = 4 Then
     SupplierDiscount = .06
ElseIf lngSupplier = 5 Then
     SupplierDiscount = .2
ElseIf lngSupplier = 6 Then
     SupplierDiscount = .11
ElseIf lngSupplier = 7 Then
     SupplierDiscount = .16
ElseIf lngSupplier = 8 Then
     SupplierDiscount = .1
ElseIf lngSupplier = 9 Then
     SupplierDiscount = .18
```

6

```
ElseIf lngSupplier = 10 Then
    SupplierDiscount = .25
End If
End Function
```

This function looks at each supplier and returns a discount percentage depending on the supplier. Each condition is tested in turn. After a condition returns a True, that code is executed and the rest of the conditions are skipped.

Using Select Case

Similar to the ElseIf clause is the Select Case statement, which takes a value and performs some code based on its value. We'll look at the same function using the Select Case instead of ElseIf:

```
Public Function SupplierDiscount2(lngSupplier As Long) As Currency
'Apply discount to Supplier
Select Case lngSupplier
    Case 1
        SupplierDiscount2 = .12
    Case 2
        SupplierDiscount2 = .08
    Case 3
        SupplierDiscount2 = .15
    Case 4
        SupplierDiscount2 = .06
    Case 5
        SupplierDiscount2 = .2
    Case 6
        SupplierDiscount2 = .11
    Case 7
        SupplierDiscount2 = .16
    Case 8
        SupplierDiscount2 = .1
    Case 9
        SupplierDiscount2 = .18
    Case 10
        SupplierDiscount2 = .25
    Case Else
        SupplierDiscount2 = 1
End Select
End Function
```

The Select Case evaluates a value and then uses that value in each Case to determine what code to run. Each Case clause is checked sequentially and when the value is matched, the code within that Case is executed. The Select Case statement allows a Case Else clause to provide a default if none of the cases match.

The Select Case statement is easier to read and cleaner than using ElseIf. However, ElseIf allows you to test different variables, whereas Select Case is restricted to one variable.

Although these examples do a good job of illustrating how `ElseIf` and `Select Case` work, they are not the best way to handle this situation. Normally, you would store the discount in a field in the Suppliers table and retrieve it using a `DLookup()`. This makes it much easier to maintain the discount.

Using For...Next

The next set of flow of control statements are looping statements. These allow you to execute a code snippet multiple times under certain conditions. Let's look at the `For...Next` loop first. This loop can be used to repeat an action a specified number of times. The `For` portion of the statement defines how many times to repeat the loop. That number can be a hard-coded number or an expression that evaluates to an integer value.

Before we do, I'll show you why loops are valuable. Consider a situation where you want to print a reorder report separately for each supplier. Without a loop you might use code like this:

```
Public Sub PrintReorder()
DoCmd.OpenReport "rptInvToReorder", , , "[SupplierID] = 1"
DoCmd.OpenReport "rptInvToReorder", , , "[SupplierID] = 2"
DoCmd.OpenReport "rptInvToReorder", , , "[SupplierID] = 3"
DoCmd.OpenReport "rptInvToReorder", , , "[SupplierID] = 4"
DoCmd.OpenReport "rptInvToReorder", , , "[SupplierID] = 5"
DoCmd.OpenReport "rptInvToReorder", , , "[SupplierID] = 6"
DoCmd.OpenReport "rptInvToReorder", , , "[SupplierID] = 7"
DoCmd.OpenReport "rptInvToReorder", , , "[SupplierID] = 8"
DoCmd.OpenReport "rptInvToReorder", , , "[SupplierID] = 9"
DoCmd.OpenReport "rptInvToReorder", , , "[SupplierID] = 10"
End Sub
```

Without a loop, you would have to run the same line of code for each supplier. Now let's look at the same situation but using a `For...Next` loop:

```
Public Sub PrintReorder()
    Dim intI As Integer
    'Loop through each supplier
    For intI = 1 To 10
        DoCmd.OpenReport "rptInvToReorder", , , "[SupplierID] = " & intI
    Next intI
End Sub
```

As you can see this is much more efficient, running the same line of code for each instance of `intI`, which is referred to as the counter.

> **NOTE**
>
> In many coding examples, the counter is represented by a single letter such as i, j, or k. I prefer to stay within my naming convention and use the `int` prefix. Sometimes I will use a more meaningful name, especially if I'm writing code for someone else. In this example, I might use `intSupplier`.
>
> Also, it's unnecessary to specify the counter in the `Next` statement. Here, too, my personal preference is to include it for readability.

Using the `Step` Clause

The default for a `For...Next` loop is to increment the counter by 1 for each pass through the loop. VBA provides more flexibility using a `Step` clause. The `Step` clause allows you to change both the amount and direction of the change in the counter. The following examples show how to use the `Step` clause:

- `For intI = 2 To 12 Step 2`—Performs the loop six times using counter values of 2, 4, 6, 8, 10, and 12. The counter is incremented by 2 for each pass through the loop.
- `For intI = 10 To 1 Step -1`—Performs the loop 10 times, decrementing the counter by 1 with each pass.

> **CAUTION**
>
> Be careful when using a `Step` clause. If you use a clause that would not result in any loops (for example, `For I = 1 To 10 Step -1`) Access does not produce an error; it just ignores the loop.

Other Ways to Set the Counter

You can make your code even more flexible by adjusting the counter on-the-fly. You can do this either by passing values to your function to use as the counter ranges or by using an expression to calculate the ranges. The following functions print a daily transactions report for a specified range of dates:

```
Sub PrintDaily(dteStart As Date, dteEnd As Date)
Dim dteCurrent As Date
'Loop for each date in the range
For dteCurrent = dteStart To dteEnd
    DoCmd.OpenReport "rptDailyInvTrans", , , "[TransDate] = #" & dteCurrent & "#"
Next dteCurrent
End Sub
```

This function prints a daily report for each date between the supplied start and end dates:

```
Public Sub PrintWeek()
Dim dteCurrent As Date
'Loop through each date in the range
For dteCurrent = Date - 7 To Date
```

```
    DoCmd.OpenReport "rptDailyInvTrans", , , "[TransDate] = #" & dteCurrent & "#"
Next dteCurrent
End Sub
```

This function prints a daily report for the previous seven days (`Date - 7`) from the current date (`Date`). As you can see you have a great deal of flexibility in setting the range that the `For...Next` loops through.

Table 6.2 Examples of `For...Next` **Counters**

Counter	Explanation
`Date() To DateAdd("m",1,Date())`	Loops through all dates from today to a month from today.
`1 To Dcount("[keyfield]","queryname")`	Loops for the number of records in the specified queryname.
`DMin("[datefield]","queryname") To DMax("[datefield]","queryname")`	Loops for each date from the earliest to the latest date in queryname.
`1 To Len(string)`	Loops thru each character in string.

Nesting `For...Next` **Loops**

You can place a loop within another loop; this is called *nesting*. Using nested loops you can compact your code to an even greater extent. Each nested loop is run the number of times called for by its counter for each time the loop in which it is contained runs. For example, if the outer loop is set to run 6 times and the inner loop 4 times, the inner loop will run 24 times. This example gets away from the sample database and provides a tool for picking lottery numbers:

```
Public Function Lottery(intNumbers As Integer, intUpper As Integer) As String
Dim intI As Integer, intJ As Integer
Dim arrPicks(20) As Integer
'Start first loop to generate each number
For intI = 1 To intNumbers
    'Genrate random number
    arrPicks(intI) = Int((intUpper - 1 + 1) * Rnd(intI) + 1)
    'Start second loop to make sure number has not been picked
    For intJ = 1 To intI
        If intJ <> intI Then
            If arrPicks(intI) = arrPicks(intJ) Then
                intI = intI - 1
                Exit For
            End If
        End If
    Next intJ
Next intI

'concatenate numbers into a single string
For intI = 1 To intNumbers
    Lottery = Lottery & arrPicks(intI) & ", "
```

6

```
Next intI
Lottery = Left(Lottery, Len(Lottery) - 2) 'remove extra characters
End Function
```

The outer loop generates random numbers, as many as indicated by the `intNumbers` argument. The number generated is in a range limited by the `intUpper` argument. The purpose of the inner loop is to make sure there are no duplicate numbers, so it checks each previously generated number against the current number. If a match is found, it regenerates the current number. You can see the results this function generates in Figure 6.1.

➜ This function introduces arrays. For more on arrays, **see** Chapter 7, "Working with Arrays."

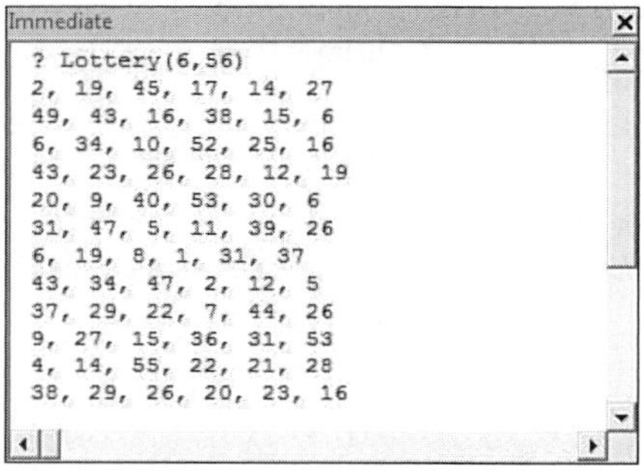

Figure 6.1
The `Lottery` function generates different sets of numbers each time it is run.

```
Immediate                                        ×
? Lottery(6,56)
2, 19, 45, 17, 14, 27
49, 43, 16, 38, 15, 6
6, 34, 10, 52, 25, 16
43, 23, 26, 28, 12, 19
20, 9, 40, 53, 30, 6
31, 47, 5, 11, 39, 26
6, 19, 8, 1, 31, 37
43, 34, 47, 2, 12, 5
37, 29, 22, 7, 44, 26
9, 27, 15, 36, 31, 53
4, 14, 55, 22, 21, 28
38, 29, 26, 20, 23, 16
```

Aborting a For...Next **Loop**

In some instances you might need to exit a `For...Next` loop before it goes through all the iterations called for. In such instances, you can use the `Exit For` statement. In this example we have several orders that were placed by customers but put on hold until new stock was received. You need to fill these orders until the new stock is used up. If that happens, you must prematurely exit the loop. To illustrate this you first create a form to select the product to process:

1. Open a blank form (select Create, Blank Form).
2. Add a combo box to select the item. (Figure 6.2 shows the query behind the combo.)
3. Name the combo box cboItems.
4. Save the form as frmProcOnHold.
5. Add a button to the form with the following code in the On Click event:
```
Private Sub cmdProcess_Click()
Dim intCurr As Integer
Dim intTransCount As Integer, intI As Integer
Dim db As Database
Dim rs As Recordset
Dim strSQL As String

'Generate  SQL to return On Hold items
strSQL = "SELECT TransactionID, TransactionItem, Employee, " _
& "TransactionType, Quantity, CreatedDate "
strSQL = strSQL & "FROM tblTransactions "
```

```
strSQL = strSQL & "WHERE [TransactionItem] = " & Me.cboitems & " _
& " And [TransactionType] = 3 "
strSQL = strSQL & "ORDER BY CreatedDate;"

'Open a recordset with On Hold items
Set db = CurrentDb()
Set rs = db.OpenRecordset(strSQL)

'Get number of on hold items
intTransCount = rs.RecordCount
'Retrieve quantity on hand
intCurr = DLookup("[CurrentStock]", "qryInventoryStockLevels", _
"[TransactionItem] = " & Me.cboitems)

'Loop through recordset and test if enough stock is on hand
For intI = 1 To intTransCount
    intCurr = intCurr - rs.Fields("Quantity")
    If intCurr < 0 Then
        Exit For
    Else
        rs.MoveNext
    End If
Next intI

End Sub
```

Figure 6.2
frmProcOnHold in Design view with Query Design mode for the combo's Rowsource.

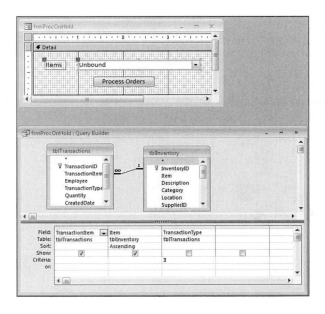

When you click the button the procedure goes through the On Hold transactions for the selected item and exits the loop before the current stock is used up.

> **NOTE**
> This code is purposely incomplete. Although it illustrates the technique for exiting a For...Next loop, it really doesn't do anything to process the transactions while there is enough stock.

> **NOTE**
> This code snippet introduces two new concepts: embedded SQL and recordsets. These concepts are discussed in much greater detail later in this book. Because loops frequently are employed to cycle through a set of records I will use them in code examples and explain them later.

→ Another form of the For...Next loop, called For...Each, is designed for use with object variables. **See** "Using Collections," **p. 105**.

Using Do **Loops**

Another type of loop is referred to as a Do loop. Unlike For...Next loops where you execute the loop a specified number of times, Do loops repeat the code within the loops until a condition is met. Use a Do loop when you don't know how many times you will need to execute the loop.

A Simple Do **Loop**

Let's revisit the first example used for the For...Next loop. In that example, we printed a reorder report for each supplier. Because the sample database has only 10 suppliers with IDs of 1–10, it was possible to do this in a For...Next loop. In most cases, though, the number of suppliers may vary, and their IDs may not be sequential. So this function would be better off with a Do loop:

```
Public Sub DoPrintReorder()
Dim db As Database
Dim rs As Recordset

'Open the Suppliers table as a Recordset
Set db = CurrentDb()
Set rs = db.OpenRecordset("tblSuppliers")
rs.MoveFirst 'go to the 1st record
    Do
        DoCmd.OpenReport "rptInvToReorder", , , "[SupplierID] = " _
        & rs.Fields("SupplierID")
        Rs.Movenext 'go to the next record
    Loop Until rs.EOF
End Sub
```

You will frequently use a loop like this where you cycle through all the records in a table or query until you reach the end of the file (EOF). This loop captures the current value of each record's SupplierID and uses that to filter the OpenReport method. Therefore, it doesn't matter how many suppliers there are or whether the IDs are sequential.

> **CAUTION**
>
> Be careful when setting your condition to make sure you will eventually meet the condition. For example, in the previous code example, if you forget to include the `Movenext` statement, the loop will never reach the end of the file and will just keep running. If that happens, you can press Ctrl+Break to suspend the loop and enter Debug mode.

Do **Loop Flavors**

Do loops come in four different flavors. In two of the flavors, the loop is performed `While` a condition is `True`; in the other two it's performed `Until` a condition is `True`. In two of the flavors, the check is performed at the start of the loop; in the other two, it's performed at the end of the loop. The example in the previous section executes the loop until a condition is met and checks at the end of the loop:

```
Do
     Statements
Loop Until condition
```

In the previous example the Do loop ends as follows:

```
Do
     Statements
Loop Until rs.EOF
```

The next flavor uses the `While` keyword again, checked at the end of the loop:

```
Do
     Statements
Loop While condition
```

For example:

```
Do
     Statements
Loop While NOT rs.EOF
```

The next flavor goes back to the `Until` keyword but places it at the beginning of the loop:

```
Do Until condition
     Statements
Loop
```

For example:

```
Do Until rs.EOF
     Statements
Loop
```

The final flavor uses the `While` keyword at the beginning of the loop:

```
Do While condition
     Statements
Loop
```

6

For example:

```
Do While NOT rs.EOF
     Statements
Loop
```

When to use each loop is not always clear. You might have to use Debug mode to check that the loop is executed the right number of times. If you put the check at the end, the loop will be run at least once, which isn't the case if the Do Until or Do While syntax appears at the start of the loop. In those cases it's theoretically possible that the exit condition will already be met when the loop starts, so the code in the statements would be skipped. Otherwise, the four flavors are roughly equivalent.

Aborting a Do Loop

Just like in the For...Next loop you might also need to exit a Do loop before you reach the condition terminating the loop. The Exit Do statement performs the same function as the Exit For statement did with For...Next loops. Let's take the same example used in the section "Aborting a For...Next Loop" earlier in the chapter and modify it for a Do loop:

```
Private Sub cmdProcessDo_Click()
Dim intCurrStock As Integer
Dim db As Database
Dim rs As Recordset
Dim strSQL As String

'Generate SQL statement
strSQL = "SELECT TransactionID, TransactionItem, Employee, _
TransactionType, Quantity, CreatedDate "
strSQL = strSQL & "FROM tblTransactions "
strSQL = strSQL & "WHERE [TransactionItem] = " & Me.cboitems & " _
And [TransactionType] = 3 "
strSQL = strSQL & "ORDER BY CreatedDate;"

Set db = CurrentDb()
Set rs = db.OpenRecordset(strSQL)

intCurrStock = DLookup("[CurrentStock]", "qryInventoryStockLevels", _
"[TransactionItem] = " & Me.cboitems)

Do Until rs.EOF
    intCurrStock = intCurrStock - rs.Fields("Quantity")
    If intCurrStock < 0 Then
        Exit Do
    Else
        rs.MoveNext
    End If
Loop

End Sub
```

This procedure works just the same by testing whether the order exceeds the current stock level and exiting the loop when it does.

Using GoTo

The last type of flow of control statement is branching. The GoTo statement is used to alter the next statement executed by transferring execution to the statements following a named label within your code. The syntax is simple:

GoTo *label*

where *label* is the name of a label in your code. A label takes the form of

labelname:

The GoTo statement is not highly regarded by most experienced programmers. It can lead to so-called spaghetti code that is often difficult to read and follow as program execution jumps around. In most cases, you can use If...Then...Else or other flow of control statements to avoid using GoTo.

I go along with the many who avoid using the GoTo statement. In some rare instances it makes sense to use it—mostly to transfer control to some cleanup code placed at the end of your procedure.

GoTo is required in one place: as part of the On Error statement.

→ For more about the On Error statement, **see** "Error Handling," **p. 73**.

Case Study: Calculating Bonuses

Your company is doing well, and you want to pay bonuses to employees based on different factors. You want to pay higher bonuses to lower level employees and pay more to those who had a higher quantity of items sold. The procedure that follows calculates those bonuses for you.

First we need to do some setup. Open the tluJobtitles table add a field named BonusPct as a Number type with a Double subtype. Next, use the Form Wizard to create a form based on tluJobtitles that has controls for the Job title and Bonus %. You then need to add percentages for each Job title. I used the percentages listed in Table 6.3.

Table 6.3   Job Titles

JobTitle	BonusPct
Sales Coordinator	0.3
Sales Manager	0.25
Sales Representative	0.35
Vice President, Sales	0.15
Marketing Manager	0
Marketing Assistant	0

6

Really, you can use any percentages you want. Finally, you need to add a new table named tblBonus with the following four fields:

- BonusID—Autonumber
- EmployeeID—Number (Long Integer)
- BonusYear—Number (Integer)
- Bonus—Currency

Figure 6.3 shows the table in Design mode.

Figure 6.3
The new tblBonus in Design mode.

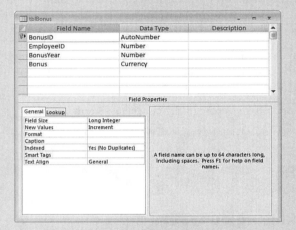

> **NOTE** The changes to the table listed earlier are already made in the sample file for Chapter 6 if you prefer not to create them yourself.

After you have set up the database you can enter the code in your global module. The following is the code listing:

```
Public Sub Bonus()

Dim db As Database
Dim rs1 As Recordset, rs2 As Recordset
Dim strSQL As String
Dim lngJob As Long
Dim dblBonusPct As Double
Dim curBonus As Currency, curTotBonus As Currency

On Error GoTo Bonus_Error

'Open Employees table
Set db = CurrentDb()
Set rs1 = db.OpenRecordset("tblemployees")
```

```
rs1.MoveFirst
'Loop thru Employees table capturing Title and Bonus %
Do
    lngJob = rs1.Fields("JobTitleID")
    dblBonusPct = DLookup("[BonusPct]", "tluJobTitles", _
    "[JobtitleID] = " & lngJob)
    'Open qryTransbyEmp if there is a %
    If dblBonusPct > 0 Then
        Set rs2 = db.OpenRecordset("qryTransbyEmp")
        'Find current employee
        rs2.FindFirst "Employee = " & rs1.Fields("EmployeeID")
        If rs2.NoMatch Then
            GoTo Exit_Bonus
        End If
        'Initialize Bonus sum and loop thru Transactions
        curTotBonus = 0
        Do While rs2.Fields("Employee") = rs1.Fields("EmployeeID")
            ' Calculate Bonus base on quantity & %
            Select Case rs2.Fields("Quantity")
                Case Is < 100
                    curBonus = 100 * dblBonusPct
                Case 100 To 200
                    curBonus = 200 * dblBonusPct
                Case 200 To 300
                    curBonus = 300 * dblBonusPct
                Case 300 To 400
                    curBonus = 400 * dblBonusPct
                Case Is > 400
                    curBonus = 500 * dblBonusPct
            End Select
            curTotBonus = curTotBonus + curBonus
        rs2.MoveNext
        Loop
    End If
'Add record to bonus table
Append:
    strSQL = "INSERT INTO tblBonus (EmployeeID, BonusYear, Bonus) "
    strSQL = strSQL & "VALUES(" & rs1.Fields("EmployeeID") & ", " _
    & Year(Date) - 1
    strSQL = strSQL & ", " & curTotBonus & ");"
    CurrentDb.Execute strSQL
    rs1.MoveNext
Loop Until rs1.EOF

GoTo Exit_Bonus:
'Error trapping
Bonus_Error:
    If Err.Number = 3021 Then
        Resume Append
    Else
        MsgBox Err.Number & vbCrLf & Err.Description, vbOKOnly, "Error"
    End If
'Cleanup
Exit_Bonus:
    Set rs1 = Nothing
```

6

```
        Set rs2 = Nothing
        MsgBox "Bonus Allocation complete!", vbOKOnly, "Complete"

End Sub
```

So let's see how this module works.

After declaring the variables I set up error trapping. Next the employees table is opened as a recordset, and the record pointer is positioned at the beginning of the recordset.

> **NOTE** As noted earlier we discuss recordsets in much greater detail later in this book. For now it's only necessary to understand they are used to define a set of records for processing.

The outer loop is then started. This loop cycles through each employee, grabbing the employee's job title ID and using it to determine the employee's bonus percentage. The next portion tests to see whether the employee is eligible for a bonus (percentage not zero). If they aren't eligible, the next record is pulled in, and the loop increments. If they are eligible, the transactions table is opened using a query, sorted by employee, as a recordset. The first record for the current employee is found, and the inner loop is started. The inner loop takes the quantity of items sold and uses a `Select Case` statement to determine a factor by which to multiply the percentage. This amount is then added to the employee's total, and the next record is processed. When the employee changes, an `Append` SQL query is generated and executed that adds a record for the employee storing the bonus year and bonus amount. The loop starts over again.

The error-trapping routine tests for an error 3021, which is a "no Active record" error. This occurs when the transactions table reaches its end. Although I could have changed the looping to prevent this from happening I wanted to also illustrate using error trapping. Because this error simply signals the end of the transactions table, I decided to catch the error and redirect processing to the `Append` section to add the final record. The final piece is some cleanup code. Before ending the procedure you should set any opened recordsets to Nothing.

Working with Arrays

7

Introducing Arrays

With one exception all the variables we have used in previous chapters have been specific as to data type and held a single value. That one exception was the lottery number generator introduced in Chapter 6, "Conditional and Looping Statements." That code used a different type of variable called an *array*. An array has the capability to hold a set of values of the same data type. Arrays are often visualized as rows and columns of data, much like a spreadsheet appears to the user. In VBA an array is a set of values, called *elements*, that can be defined by name and dimensions where each element is treated as an individual variable.

Arrays are used to store a set of values temporarily. Instead of using a temporary table, which requires more overhead in terms of code and memory usage, arrays are often a better alternative.

A classic example of a two-dimensional array is a multiplication table. Each element in the array is represented by a row number and a column number. The intersection of row and column is a value defined by the row and column numbers. That value is derived by multiplying those two numbers. Table 7.1 shows a portion of such an array visually.

Table 7.1 Example of a Two-Dimensional Array

Indexes	1	2	3	4	5
1	1	2	3	4	5
2	2	4	6	8	10
3	3	6	9	12	15
4	4	8	12	16	20
5	5	10	15	20	25

Declaring a Fixed-Size Array

Because arrays are variables, they need to be declared like any other variable. They have to be assigned a name and data type. Remember the data type selected is applied to each element within the array. In addition, fixed-size arrays are declared with boundaries that determine the number of elements that will be held. The boundary values are used to refer to an individual element within an array. The syntax for declaring a fixed-size array is

```
Dim arrayname([lower to] upper) As datatype
```

where *arrayname* is the name you assign to the array variable; *lower* is an optional argument defining the lower boundary of the array; *upper* is a required argument for a fixed-size array, defining the upper boundary of the array; and *datatype* is a valid VBA data type. You can omit the data type, and VBA will declare the array and its elements as a `Variant` data type. You can omit the lower range because it's optional, and VBA will default to 0 as the lower range. The default lower boundary can be changed and will be discussed later in this chapter.

In the lottery number generator we used the statement:

```
Dim arrPicks(20) As Integer
```

This statement defined an `Integer` array of 21 elements (0–20). Although this was more than we needed, it provided a cushion of flexibility for different types of lotteries. It's better to declare a larger array than you might need and not use elements.

Understanding an Array's Index

Of course you need a way to differentiate between the various elements of an array. This is done using the array's index, which is the set of values between, and including, the boundary values. Each element in an array is assigned an index that defines its position within the array. The index is expressed with a subscript within parentheses after the array name. So the statement:

```
Dim arrPicks(1 To 6) as Integer
```

defines a six-element array with index values of 1, 2, 3, 4, 5, 6. In the declaration from the lottery number generator, the index would be the numbers 0 through 20. You can specify the index to be any sequential set of numbers. Table 7.2 illustrates some different examples of this.

Table 7.2 Array Indexes

Declared Array	Index Values
`Dim arrMyArray(0 to 5) As Integer`	0, 1, 2, 3, 4, 5
`Dim arrMyArray(2 to 8) As Integer`	2, 3, 4, 5, 6, 7, 8
`Dim arrMyArray(-5 to 1) As Integer`	−5, −4, −3, −2, −1
`Dim arrMyArray(-4 to 0) As Integer`	−4, −3, −2, −1, 0
`Dim arrMyArray(5) As Integer`	0, 1, 2, 3, 4, 5

7

Using `Option Base`

As mentioned, if you don't specify a lower limit, it defaults to 0. However, the default lower limit can be changed for the module. This is done by including an `Option Base` statement in the General Declarations section of the module. The syntax for the `Option Base` statement is

```
Option Base 0 ¦ 1
```

With this statement you can set the default to either 0 or 1. If you want to set the lower limit to any other value, you have to explicitly declare it.

➔ The General Declarations section is detailed in "Explaining VBA Modules," **p. 15**.

> **TIP**
>
> Using `Option Base 1` you can change the default lower limit. However, you should consider explicitly declaring the lower limit to create more readable code. This can help avoid errors if you forget what the lower limit is set for.

Working with Array Elements

Array elements are referenced using a subscript enclosed within parentheses. The subscript refers to the index number of that element. So referencing an element would look like this:

```
arrMyArray(2) = 20
arrMyArray(15) = 150
```

Assuming both these arrays start with an index of 1, the first assigns a value of 20 to the second element of the array, and the second assigns a value of 150 to the 15th element of the array.

Assigning Array Elements

After you have declared your array, now comes the harder part: populating the elements. As the two examples in the previous section show, values are assigned to array elements like any variable, with an assignment statement. The syntax for such an assignment is

```
arrayvariable(index) = variable
```

However, because an array has multiple values you generally don't want to enter an assignment statement for each element.

Most of the time, you use a loop to populate the elements. The following is the lottery number generator from Chapter 6:

```
Public Function Lottery(intNumbers As Integer, intUpper As Integer) As String
Dim intI As Integer, intJ As Integer
Dim arrPicks(20) As Integer
'Start first loop to generate each number
For intI = 1 To intNumbers
    'Genrate random number
```

7

```
    arrPicks(intI) = Int((intUpper - 1 + 1) * Rnd(intI) + 1)
    'Start second loop to make sure number has not been picked
    For intJ = 1 To intI
        If intJ <> intI Then
            If arrPicks(intI) = arrPicks(intJ) Then
                intI = intI - 1
                Exit For
            End If
        End If
    Next intJ
Next intI

'concatenate numbers into a single string
For intI = 1 To intNumbers
    Lottery = Lottery & arrPicks(intI) & ", "
Next intI
Lottery = Left(Lottery, Len(Lottery) - 2) 'remove extra characters
End Function
```

In this procedure each lottery number is assigned to an element of the array (arrPicks). The For...Next counter in each of the loops is used to supply the Index value for each element of the referenced array, so that with each pass through the loop another element of the array is populated.

➔ To review For...Next loops **see** "Using For...Next", **p. 81**.

Using Array Element Values

Using the values of array elements is the same process as using any other type of variable; just make sure you indicate the element you want to use! For example:

variable = arrayvariable(index)

If you look at the last loop of the lottery number generator each pass of the loop adds one of the generated picks to a string variable so the picks can be printed.

Arrays with Multiple Dimensions

An array can be thought of as being composed of rows and columns, like a spreadsheet as previously mentioned. In the previous discussions we have dealt with arrays of one column and many rows, a *one-dimensional array*. Arrays can have multiple columns as well, thus making them *multidimensional*. To declare such an array you specify the ranges of each dimension separated by commas. For example, the following statement defines a two-dimensional array of 10 elements in the first dimension (rows) and 6 elements in the second dimension (columns):

```
Dim arrFactor(1 to 10, 1 to 6) as Double
```

To reference an element in a multidimensional array, you have to specify the index value of each dimension separated by commas. For example, the following assigns the value *x* to the third row and fifth column of the array:

```
arrfactor(3,5)=x
```

7

To illustrate a multidimensional array let's go back to the Case Study in Chapter 6 where we calculated bonuses. Instead of using nested loops, we can use a multidimensional array to calculate the bonus and in doing so alter the way the bonus is calculated:

```
Public Function Bonus(intQty As Integer, intJob As Integer) As Currency

Dim dblBonusPct As Double
Dim arrBonus(0 To 5, 1 To 4) As Double
Dim i As Integer, j As Integer

On Error GoTo Bonus_Error

'populate array with bonus amounts.
For i = 0 To 5
    For j = 1 To 4
        dblBonusPct = DLookup("[BonusPct]", "tluJobTitles", _
        "[JobtitleID] = " & j)
        arrBonus(i, j) = i * 100 * dblBonusPct
    Next j
Next i

intQty = Int(intQty / 100)
If intQty > 5 Then
    intQty = 5
End If
Bonus = arrBonus(intQty, intJob)

GoTo Exit_Bonus:
'Error trapping
Bonus_Error:
        MsgBox Err.Number & vbCrLf & Err.Description, vbOKOnly, "Error"
'Cleanup
Exit_Bonus:
    Set rs = Nothing

End Function
```

As you can see the code has been shortened and simplified. In the previous version we cycled through all the employee and transaction records and created a table of bonuses. In this version we create an array of bonuses, where each row represents the quantity range and each column the job title. So we can reference each bonus amount by using the quantity calculation and the job Title ID. This version is a function that returns the bonus for a single employee based on her total sales and job title. This is designed to work within a query to produce a listing of bonuses. In the sample file for this chapter you will find *qryAnn1Bonus*, which produces such a list.

Access VBA allows you to create arrays with up to 60 dimensions. I can't imagine a situation where you might use that many. In fact, I would venture to say you would rarely use more than two or possibly three dimensions. Two-dimensional areas are quite common as they represent a matrix of values. Think back to the multiplication tables you memorized in elementary school. Those were classic two-dimensional arrays, where the intersection of the two numbers was the result. You can envision a three-dimensional array as a cube, where you have height, width, and depth. An example would be sales figures for a marketing

7

staff, over an array of products, over a time period. The rows would be each salesperson, the columns would represent each product, and the depth would be shown as the reporting time periods.

Expanding to Dynamic Arrays

In all the previous examples, we declared the size of the array when it was dimensioned using a `Dim` statement. As you recall, this is referred to as a fixed-size array. However, you can omit the boundaries to create a dynamic array. When doing so, you need to use a `ReDim` statement in your code to specify the boundaries before you can assign values to the elements. The syntax for this is as follows:

```
Dim arrMyArray() AS datatype
...
ReDim [Preserve] arrMyArray([lower to] upper) AS datatype
```

By using a dynamic array with a `ReDim` statement you can then use variables to define the range of the array.

About `ReDim`

The `ReDim` statement is used to alter the size and memory allocation for a dynamic array. This statement is used after the array is declared but before it's used. `ReDim` can be used multiple times within a code snippet to adjust a dynamic array to the specific usage. The syntax for the `ReDim` statement as mentioned previously is

```
ReDim [Preserve] arrayvariable([lower To] upper) As datatype
```

The keyword `Preserve` is used to save the data stored in an existing array when the upper boundary of the last dimension is increased. Without the `Preserve` keyword the contents of the entire array are deleted. When using the `Preserve` keyword, you can change only the upper boundary of the last dimension; otherwise, an error is raised during program execution.

Let's go back to the lottery number generator and edit it to allow for a dynamic array. Instead of just the `Dim` line, we edit that line and add a `ReDim`:

```
Dim arrPicks() As Integer
ReDim arrPicks(1 To intNumbers) As Integer
```

The edited code removes the size (20) that was in the original statement making it a dynamic array. The `ReDim` is added using the value passed to indicate the number of numbers to pick as the upper bound. So instead of wasting storage by setting the array large enough to accommodate different lottery games, we just use what's needed for the game you are playing. If you `ReDim` an array, the elements of the array are lost.

`Erase` Statement

You use the `Erase` statement to reinitialize arrays. With a fixed-size array, the elements are cleared out; with a dynamic array the storage space assigned to the array is released.

7

Depending on the nature of the array, the `Erase` statement will act slightly differently. Table 7.3 shows how the `Erase` statement will react to various types of arrays.

Table 7.3 Erase **Statement Actions**

Type of Array	Effect of Erase on Fixed-Array Elements
Fixed numeric array	Each element in the array is set to zero.
Fixed string array (variable length)	Each element in the array is set to a zero-length string ("").
Fixed string array (fixed length)	Each element in the array is set to zero.
Fixed variant array	Each element in the array is set to `Empty`.
Array of user-defined types	Each element in the array is set as if it were a separate variable.
Array of objects	Each element in the array is set to the special value `Nothing`.

Object and Event-Driven Coding

Understanding Objects

An *object* within Access is anything that has properties that can be manipulated. Because Access is, at least partially, an object-oriented development platform, almost everything you use within Access is an object. From a field in a table, to a form, to a control on a report, to a query and everything in between. These are all objects, and much of Access design is manipulating the properties of those objects. You can set the properties directly through the Property dialog box. (Figure 8.1 shows the property sheet for a control object on a form.) But a good part of the power of Access comes from being able to set and manipulate properties through VBA.

Let's try to use a real-world example to explain objects. Consider the Barbie doll. The dolls are mass produced and so are very similar, but each doll has its own properties of size, skin color, hair color, and so on. The dolls have legs and arms that can be manipulated so that, at any one time, an arm could be up or down or pointing forward. The dolls can be clothed, and those clothes can have their own properties of style, color, size, and so on. You also have accessories—such as houses and cars—that can change the doll's environment.

So you can see that a Barbie doll has many properties that influence how it can appear and be used. Access objects are similar. A combo box, for example, can be added as a control on a form or report and behave differently on each. The list that appears in the combo can be changed as can the data that is stored with it. The font, background color, and size, are all properties that can be changed for the control.

Figure 8.1
The Data tab of the Property sheet for a combo box control object.

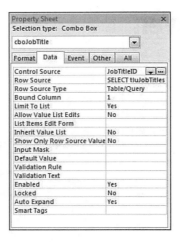

Objects play an important part in the design of your database as this chapter shows. So it's important to understand how to use them. It may help if you think of Access objects as real-world, three-dimensional objects that you can hold and manipulate.

Creating Objects in Code

Many objects—such as forms reports, tables, and so on—can be created through the menus. But because this is a book about VBA, this chapter deals mostly with VBA objects, most of which can only be created through VBA code. So the first order of business in dealing with such objects has to be creating them. The following code opens an instance of the form frmCoInfo. This form is used to store the basic information about the company that is using this application.

```
Sub CreateObject1()
'Create and display a form Object
    Dim frm As Form_frmCoInfo
    Set frm = New Form_frmCoInfo
    frm.Visible = True
    MsgBox "press OK to continue", vbOKOnly

End Sub
```

Running this code snippet opens an instance of the form with a message box that asks whether you want to continue, as shown in Figure 8.2. When you click OK, the form instance disappears.

To explain this code further, we start by declaring an object variable named frm of the Form_frmCoInfo type. Access creates a matching class for each form that has a code module created.

Figure 8.2
The Company Information
form opened with a
message box.

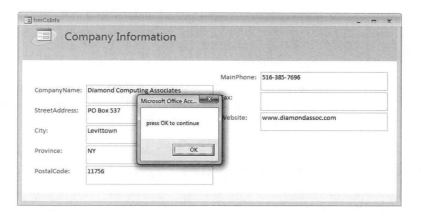

8

> **NOTE**
> Only forms that have some VBA code in the class module appear on the list of form objects.

Because the class is not an object itself, you have to instantiate the class to use the object within your VBA code. The SET statement is used to instantiate a class. It says to Access it should create a new instance of the Form_frmCoInfo class and assign it to the frm variable.

The next line makes the form visible because, by default, a new instance is created as a hidden object. The last line is used to display a message box that pauses the code until a button on the box is clicked. After the button is clicked, the code snippet is ended. With its end, the form disappears because the frm variable is removed from memory.

> **NOTE**
> In its current state, this code is essentially useless. However, we will build on this snippet over the course of this chapter to make it a useful piece of code.

➔ You can create variables so that they can be used beyond one procedure. This is discussed in Chapter 9, "Understanding Scope and Lifetime."

You can, however, eliminate the SET statement to simplify your code as shown in the following example. However, using the SET statement makes the code more readable.

```
Sub CreateObject2()
'Create and display a form Object
    Dim frm As New Form_frmCoInfo
    frm.Visible = True
    MsgBox "press OK to continue", vbOKOnly

End Sub
```

This code snippet uses the `Dim` statement to both declare and instantiate in one line of code.

> **CAUTION**
>
> Although using the `Dim` statement to both declare and instantiate saves code, it doesn't indicate when the object is actually created. That doesn't happen until the first time the object is used within your code. Using the `SET` statement makes it easier to mark where the variable is used.

Reading and Setting Object Properties

As I said at the beginning of this chapter an object is defined by manipulating its properties. The values assigned to each property describe the current state of an object. When an object from a class is instantiated, the properties of that object are assigned a value. The value can be null, it can be constrained to a specific set of values (for example, yes/no), or it can be some value that would be meaningful for that property (for example, a font size or color number). Each property value can be read from or written to in your VBA code. The following example illustrates both:

```
Sub ReadWriteproperties()
'Create and display a form Object
    Dim frm As New Form_frmCoInfo
    frm.Visible = True
    If frm.AllowEdits Then
        frm.RecordSelectors = True
    Else
        Frm.Recordselectors = False
    End IF
    MsgBox "press OK to continue", vbOKOnly

End Sub
```

This code snippet reads the `AllowEdits` property and checks whether it's True or False. It then sets the `Recordselectors` property accordingly.

> **TIP**
>
> You can shorten and simplify this code with the statement:
>
>   `frm.RecordSelectors = frm.AllowEdits`
>
> Because the value of `AllowEdits` is either True or False and you want the `Recordselectors` value to be the same, just do a straight assignment. This trick can be used often to assign a Boolean conditionally.

The syntax for referencing a property is

object.property

You can use the value of the property any way you need to depending on the requirements of your application.

Properties fall into three categories:

- **Read/Write**—The property can be read and written to.
- **Read-only**—The property can only be read.
- **Write-only**—The property can only be written to.

Most properties fall into the read/write category. You generally run into read-only properties as a property that can't be changed after the object is created. An example of this is the form's Name property. Write-only properties are a rarity; one of the few examples would be a password property that you can allow to be changed but not read for security reasons.

Invoking Methods

An object can be told to do certain things. What an object knows how to do are called *methods*. Methods perform an action within your code. Some examples of methods would be OpenForm, RunCommand, Execute, and many others. Methods are referenced using the same syntax as properties:

```
object.method
```

Here's an example that invokes the SetFocus method of the Forms class:

```
Sub TestMethod()
'Invoke one of an object's methods
    Dim frm As New Form_frmCoInfo
    frm.Visible = True
    frm.SetFocus
    MsgBox "Press OK to continue", vbOKOnly
End Sub
```

Some methods can have arguments; for example, the Move method has arguments for left, top, width, and height that allow you to specify the position and dimensions of a form.

Using Collections

A *collection* is a special object that contains a group of objects. Access maintains some collections so they can be used in VBA and don't need to be instantiated. The Forms collection, which lists open forms, is an example of that. Other collections include Reports, Macros, and Modules. You will generally use collections to find or list instances of the objects they contain. The following code example lists all the tables in your application:

```
Sub ListTables1()
    Dim obj As AccessObject, dbs As Object
    Set dbs = Application.CurrentData
    ' List AccessObject objects in AllTables collection.
    For Each obj In dbs.AllTables
            ' Print name of obj.
            Debug.Print obj.Name
    Next obj
End Sub
```

This code snippet introduces a variation of the `For...Next` loop, the `For...Each` loop, which loops through a collection. In this case it prints name of each member to the Immediate window.

To make this code snippet more useful, we can add a test to limit the listing to open tables:

```
Sub ListTables2()
    Dim obj As AccessObject, dbs As Object
    Set dbs = Application.CurrentData
    ' Search for open AccessObject objects in AllTables collection.
    For Each obj In dbs.AllTables
        If obj.IsLoaded = True Then
            ' Print name of obj.
            Debug.Print obj.Name
        End If
    Next obj
    This variation used the IsLoaded property of each member to only print the
loaded tables.
```

Every collection includes a `Count` property and an `Items` method. Additional methods may also allow for further manipulation of the collection.

Working with an Object Model

Collections of objects are usually depicted in a hierarchical, graphical model such as the one shown in Figure 8.3.

Figure 8.3
A portion of the Forms object model.

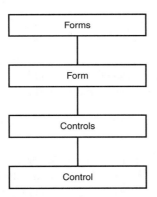

In this diagram the top box represents the Forms collection, which is made up of Form objects, represented by the second box. The Form object has a Controls collection represented by the third box, made up of individual controls placed within the Form object. The fourth box is the individual control placed on the form. The importance of this diagram is that, to get to the individual control, you must identify the collections or objects of which the control is a part. So, when referencing that control on a form, you must identify that it is part of the Forms collection, belonging to a specifically named Form object. From there you name the control itself.

Using the Object Model

This next snippet of code can be useful in working with forms, especially unbound forms. It opens a form and populates the controls of that form from a record in a table:

```
Public Sub Fetch()
Dim db As Database, rs As Recordset
Dim frmCoInfo As New Form_frmCoInfoUnbound
Dim cnt As Control
Dim strField As String

'Setup Recordset
Set db = CurrentDb()
Set rs = db.OpenRecordset("tblCoInfo")

'Loop through each control
For Each cnt In frmCoInfo.Controls
    'Test each control to make sure it's a textbox,
    'then populate with the corresponding field value
    If cnt.ControlType = "TextBox" Then
        strField = Right(cnt.Name, Len(cnt.Name) - 3)
        cnt = rs.Fields(strField)
    End If
Next cnt

frmCoInfo.Visible = True
MsgBox "Press OK to continue", vbOKOnly
End Sub
```

After opening the form and recordset, this code loops through each control on the form. It tests to make sure it's a text box, and if it is it pulls the corresponding field name from the table and populates the control. To set up for this code, I create an unbound copy of the frmCoInfo. The text controls were named with txt plus the field name. So the code strips off the txt. Figure 8.4 shows the form with the controls populated.

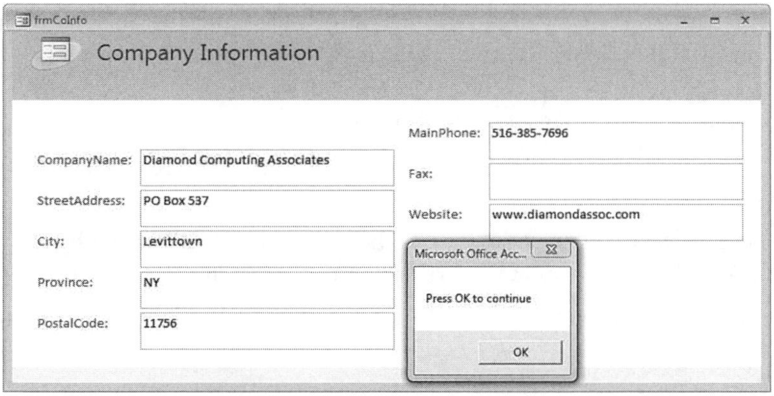

Figure 8.4
The unbound version of the form with controls populated.

Of course, to be really useful, this code would work with all types of data controls and any form. An example of that will be shown later.

Using References

Objects are provided by many programs that VBA can utilize. For instance, each application that is part of the Microsoft Office suite includes its own object model. If you want to access the object model from some application other than the one where VBA is currently running, you need to set a *reference* to that object model. Such a reference informs VBA that you plan to use objects from another object model.

You set a reference from the Tools, References menu in the VBA editor. When you do, it opens the dialog box displayed in Figure 8.5. References that have already been set are listed at the top and checked off. Then comes a list of all references available on that computer, sorted alphabetically.

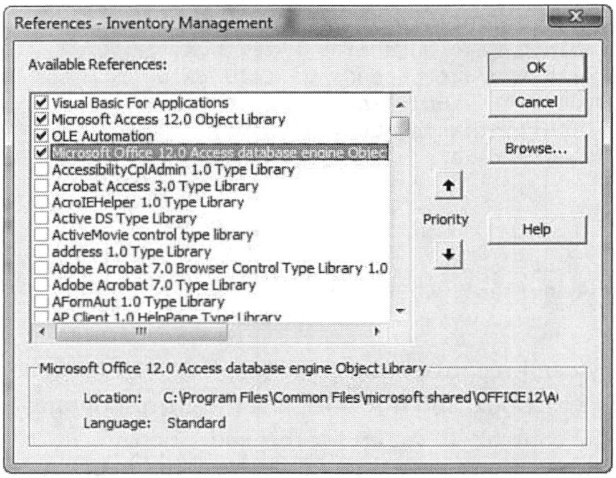

Figure 8.5
The References
dialog box.

To set the reference, scroll to the reference you want to use and just check the box. After you have done this, you can use any of the objects for that model. As an example, the following code snippet opens an instance of PowerPoint:

```
Sub TestPP()
Dim objPP As New PowerPoint.Application
    objPP.Visible = True
    MsgBox "Powerpoint should now be visible", vbOKOnly
End Sub
```

Because the Office applications each have their own Application object, you need to be specific about which application you are calling the object model from. The syntax for this is

```
Application.object
```

For example:

```
Access.Report
Powerpoint.Application
```

The Object Browser

After you start using objects, you may feel overwhelmed at the hundreds of methods, objects, and properties available to you. This is where the Object Browser tool comes to your aid in navigating through the sea of choices.

You open the Object Browser from within the VBA Editor by selecting View, Object Browser from the menu or pressing the F2 key. The Object Browser, shown in Figure 8.6, opens as a window within the VBE.

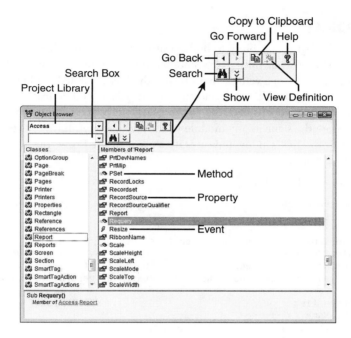

Figure 8.6
The Object Browser.

Following are a few of the tasks you can perform using the Object Browser:

- Choose one of the libraries or models by selecting from the drop-down list of objects loaded in your project. You can also select the All Libraries option to see everything.

- Scroll down the list on the left side of the window to select a class. You can also use the Search box to search for matching text.

- After you select a class the right side of the browser displays all the events, methods, and properties attributable to that class. The collection of these is referred to as *members* of the class.

- Selecting a member displays a definition of that member in the Definition window at the bottom of the Browser.

- The Help button is context sensitive and shows help for the selected member.

■ The Forward and Back navigation buttons allow you to shift among the members of the class.

■ The Copy to Clipboard button moves the selected member into the clipboard.

> **TIP**
>
> I find the Object Browser speeds coding by providing a faster way to find and get help with objects.

Creating Objects

VBA also includes the capability to build your own classes and objects in addition to those provided by Microsoft or third-party vendors. In this section we build a class that allows you take a text file from a vendor that updates the Discontinued field in tblinventory. You start off by opening the VBE and selecting Insert, Class Module from the menu. An empty class module window opens with the *Option Compare Database* stub. Although the editing window appears the same as any module window, the icon in the Projects window is different and the Properties window indicates it's a class. In the Properties window, set the name property to clsCorpUpdateCSV.

The code for the class follows:

```
Option Compare Database
Option Explicit

'Private variables for standard properties
Private strCSVFile As String      'Name of the CSV file with updates
Private intChannel As Integer     'The "Channel" of communcation to the file
Private lngRecordsUpdated As Long  'The number of records that were updated

'Simple properties
Public TableName As String
'Initialize the class
Private Sub Class_Initialize()
    intChannel = FreeFile
End Sub

'Define the standard properties
Property Let FileName(strFileName As String)

    If Len(Dir(strFileName)) > 0 Then
        strCSVFile = strFileName
    Else
        strCSVFile = ""
        MsgBox "Corp Update File name is invalid", vbInformation
    End If

End Property

Property Get FileName() As String
    FileName = strCSVFile
End Property
```

```
Property Get RecordsUpdated() As Long
    RecordsUpdated = lngRecordsUpdated
End Property

'Define the Methods
''''''''''''''''''
Public Sub OpenUpdateCSV()
'Opens the update CSV

    'Set up error handler
    On Error Resume Next

    'Open the file
    If Len(strCSVFile) = 0 Then
        MsgBox "No file has been specified.", vbInformation
    Else
        Open strCSVFile For Input Access Read As #intChannel
        If Err.Number <> 0 Then
            MsgBox Err.Description & "(" & Err.Description & ")"
            Close #intChannel
            strCSVFile = ""
            Err.Clear
        End If
    End If

End Sub

Public Sub ApplyUpdates()
'Applies the updates to the specified table

    Dim strSQL As String            'A place to store a SQL statement
    Dim strCSVLine As String        'The record in CSV format
'An array of field values from a record in the CSV
    Dim aStrCSVRecord() As String

    'Exit the procedure if no file name is present
    If Len(strCSVFile) = 0 Then
        MsgBox "CorpUpdate csv file is not specified.", vbInformation
        Exit Sub
    End If

    'Open the inventory table and loop the CSV to update the records
    strSQL = "SELECT * FROM [" & TableName & "] ORDER BY [SupplierID], [Item]"
    With CurrentDb.OpenRecordset(strSQL)

        'Make sure all the records have been read
        .MoveLast

        'Loop the CSV
        Do Until EOF(intChannel)

            'Read the line in the CSV,
            'note that lines that begin with a # are comments
            Line Input #intChannel, strCSVLine

            'Read the CSV Line, and apply to a record
            If Left(strCSVLine, 1) <> "#" Then
```

8

```
                'Parse the CSV line
                aStrCSVRecord = Split(strCSVLine, ",")

                'Find and update the record
                .FindFirst "[SupplierID] = " & Trim(aStrCSVRecord(0)) & _
                        " And [Item] = '" & Trim(aStrCSVRecord(1)) & "'"
            If Not .NoMatch Then
                    .Edit
                    .Fields("Discontinued") = CBool(aStrCSVRecord(2) & "0")
                    .Update

                    lngRecordsUpdated = lngRecordsUpdated + 1

            End If

        End If

    Loop

    'Close the table
    .Close

    End With

End Sub

'Terminate the class
Private Sub Class_Terminate()
    Close intChannel
End Sub
```

There are two ways to implement properties within a class. The simple way is just declaring a variable. The Tablename property is implemented as a simple property. A more complex way is using a *property procedure*. You need to use a Property Let and Property Get procedure for such properties. The Filename property illustrates this. The Property Let procedure is used to set the value for a variable; the Property Get procedure is used when reading the value of the variable.

If you just use Property Let procedures to implement a property, the property will be read-only. The RecordsUpdated property is a read-only property.

There are two methods within the class. Using a Public Function or Public Sub creates a method within the class. The examples are the OpenUdateCSV and ApplyUpdates methods.

To use this class, you call it like you would any class. The following code uses the new clsCorpUpdateCSV:

```
Public Sub GetCorpUpdate(Optional strFilename As String)

    Dim csvFile As clsCorpUpdateCSV

    'Create the object
    Set csvFile = New clsCorpUpdateCSV
```

```
        'Set up the object
        With csvFile

            'Get the file name to import and table to update
            .TableName = "tblInventory"
            If Len(strFilename) = 0 Then
                .FileName = InputBox("Type the full path and name of the file", _
                        "File Name", CurrentProject.Path & "\CorpUpdate.csv")
            Else
                .FileName = strFilename
            End If

            .OpenUpdateCSV
            .ApplyUpdates

            MsgBox "The Corporate updates were applied. " _
                    & .RecordsUpdated & " records were updated."

        End With

    End Sub
```

This code gives you the opportunity to input the full path and filename as a prompt or a passed value to give you some flexibility. We have included a sample CSV file in the folder for this chapter. Running this code results in the message box shown in Figure 8.7.

Figure 8.7
This message appears after importing the supplied CSV file.

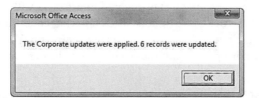

> Microsoft Office Access
>
> The Corporate updates were applied. 6 records were updated.
>
> OK

Working with Events

Events are a set of properties available to many objects. Event properties are tied to some action that occurs within your application. Some common events are the `After Update` event of a data control, the `On Click` event of a button, and the `On Current` event of a form. Event properties allow you to attach some code to be executed when the event occurs called an *event procedure*. When you click the ellipses next to an `Event` property, you get three choices: Macro Builder, Expression Builder, or Code Builder, as shown in Figure 8.8. Generally, you use the Macro Builder and Code Builder only for events.

As mentioned earlier, macros were originally included in Access to provide a level of automation consistent with macro languages in other applications within the Office suite. As VBA developed, use of macros has been discouraged because VBA provides a much richer and more powerful automation tool. With Access 2007, Microsoft adds error trapping to the macro language. In addition, embedded macros have been added.

➔ For more on macros, **see** "Macros," **p. 8**.

Figure 8.8
The Choose Builder dialog.

Most developers avoid using macros because of their more limited flexibility. Because this is a book on using VBA, we concentrate on showing you how to use VBA within event procedures. This means that we use the Code Builder when entering code within event procedures. When you select the Code Builder for an Event property, the VBE is opened, the Class module for the object is opened, and the opening and closing statements for the event are inserted.

You don't have to use the Code Builder to enter event code modules. You can do it directly from within the VBE. As shown in Figure 8.9 there are two pull-down lists at the top of the form's Class module. The left-hand pull-down allows you to select from all objects on the form. The right-hand pull-down allows you to select from the events available for the selected control. Doing so also inserts a code stub into the class module.

Figure 8.9
The VBE with the stub for an AfterUpdate event for the txtPostalCode control in the frmCoinfo Class module inserted. Also shown is the event list pulled down.

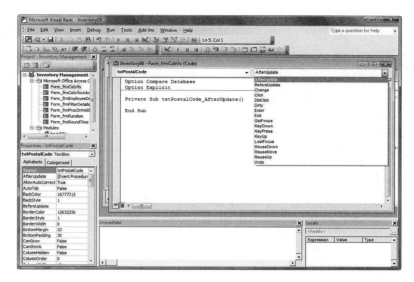

Understanding Scope and Lifetime

9

Scope Explained

The dictionary defines *scope* as extent of treatment, activity, or influence; range of operation. In VBA terms, scope covers where, within your VBA, a variable can operate or have influence. In Chapter 5, "Building Procedures," in the section "Public Versus Private," we discussed the scope of procedures. Variables function similarly using the concepts of *scope* and *lifetime*. A variable's *scope* defines how other code within your application can see it. The *lifetime* of a variable dictates when it contains valid data.

A variable's scope falls into one of three categories:

- **Local**—The variable is confined to the procedure where it was declared.
- **Module**—A variable is available for all procedures within the module where it was declared.
- **Public**—A variable is available within your entire application.

Most variables are local. They are declared and used only within the procedure where they were declared. Less often you may need to make a variable visible to other procedures within the module. This would be especially true of class modules such as form or report modules. In rare cases, you need to make a variable available throughout the entire application.

Procedure-Level Variables

Almost all the variables we have used so far have been procedure-level variables. Such variables can be used only by the procedure where they are declared. Only that procedure can reference the variable to assign or read the value stored in it.

Because procedure-level variables can be used only by the one procedure, you can reuse the variable name in other procedures within the module. However, you can't declare a variable (using a `Dim` or other variable declaration statement) with the same name in the same procedure. This results in an error.

To demonstrate procedure-level scope we'll create two procedures that use a variable of the same name. Open the VBE (press Ctrl+G or Alt+F11), and then open a blank standard module making sure the `Option Explicit` declaration is at the top.

→ For more on `Option Explicit`, **see** "Declaring Variables and Constants", **p. 25**.

Then type in the following procedures:

```
Function ProcLevel1()
Dim strMessage As String
strMessage = "Message from ProcLevel1"
MsgBox strMessage, vbOKOnly
End Function

Function Proclevel2()
strMessage = "Message from ProcLevel2"
MsgBox strMessage, vbOKOnly
End Function
```

> **NOTE** The previous procedures are already in the sample file for this chapter if you don't want to type them in. They are in the module `basProcLevelScope`.

Place the cursor within the first procedure and press F5. The variable `strMessage` is assigned a value of the string `"Message from ProcLevel1"`, and a message box with that message is displayed as shown in Figure 9.1.

Figure 9.1
The message box generated by `ProcLevel1`.

This is simple code not dissimilar to other examples we've used. The second procedure uses a variable with the same name, but there is no declaration of the variable. With the cursor within the second procedure, again press F5. This results in the error message shown in Figure 9.2. Because there is no `Dim` statement declaring the variable it is unknown to this procedure.

Figure 9.2
An error message is generated by ProcLevel2 because the variable has not been defined.

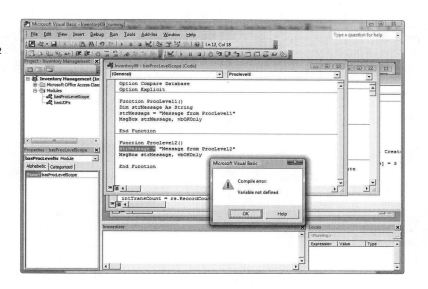

Click OK; then click the Reset icon on the toolbar to clear the error message. You can fix this problem in one of two ways:

- Add a Dim statement in ProcLevel2 for the variable and remove the one for ProcLevel1.
- Add a module-level variable for strMessage.

Module-Level Variables and Constants

Every procedure in a module can see and reference a module-level variable or constant. Such variables (and constants) are declared within the module's Declarations section, not within individual procedures.

This is demonstrated by moving the Dim statement from the ProcLevel1 to the Declarations section. You can do this either by using Cut and Paste or by highlighting the line and dragging it above the Function line. Figure 9.3 shows a new module that we added to the sample file with the declaration of strMessage in the Declarations section.

To test this, position the cursor within the first procedure and press F5; then click OK on the message box. Then position the cursor within the second procedure and again press F5. With each execution you see one of the two message boxes shown in Figure 9.4.

Because the scope of the variable has been changed to a module level, the variable is available to both procedures.

Figure 9.3
The new module
`basModLevelScope`.

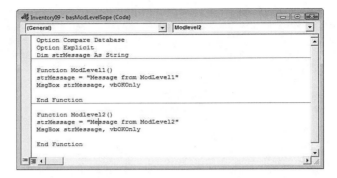

Figure 9.4
The message boxes
generated by the
adjusted code.

Public Variables and Constants

The remaining level of scope is public. Public variables are available externally to the module that created them. To demonstrate this, you will need to create the test yourself; we have not included this in the sample because once declared, the test will find the variable. Follow these steps:

1. Create a new standard module by selecting Insert, Module from the VBE menu.
2. Enter the following code snippet into the module:

```
Function PublicLevelTest()
    strMessage = "Message with Public variable"
    MsgBox strMessage, vbOKOnly
End Function
```

3. Position the curser within this code snippet and press F5. The result will be the same error as shown in Figure 9.2. The variable has not been made public, so it's not defined for this module.
4. Click OK, and then click Reset to clear the error.

Now we'll make the variable public and test this code again:

1. Open the modular-level test module you created (or `basModLevelScope` from the Inventory09 sample file).
2. Replace the keyword `Dim` with the keyword `Public` in the Declarations section. Figure 9.5 shows the module with the changed scope. You can declare a variable as `Public` only in the General Declarations area.

Figure 9.5
The
`basModLevelScope`
module with
`strMessage` set as a
public variable.

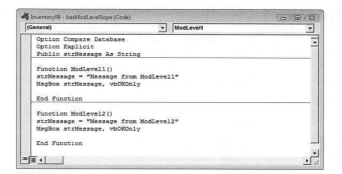

3. Now position the cursor within the `PublicLevelTest` procedure and press F5 again. The correct message box should now appear.

> **TIP**
> Constants are declared as public using the following syntax:
>   `Public constant AS datatype = value`

> **NOTE**
> Another level can be used only in object (form/report) or class modules. This level uses the `Friend` keyword instead of `Public` or `Private`. The difference is that the `Friend` scope is available only within the Access project. `Public` variables can be referenced from external projects.

Measuring the Lifetime of a Variable or Constant

Although the scope dictates what procedures can use a variable or another procedure, a variable's *lifetime* refers to when and how long the variable holds a value in memory. Following are some guidelines to help you understand lifetime better:

- A variable's lifetime is the period in which it retains its value.
- Although a variable may change value during its lifetime, it will always have some value.
- A variable will lose its value (and its lifetime will end) when it loses scope; for example, when the code that declares it ends processing. This means that, although there is a relation between scope and lifetime, they aren't the same.

At the time a procedure begins execution (the procedure is called) all variables declared within the procedure's scope are initialized. Each variable is assigned an initial value according to the list in Table 9.1. The variables retain the initialized values until another value is explicitly assigned within your VBA code.

Table 9.1   Value of Initialized Variables

Data Type	Initialized Value
Numeric	0
Variable-length string	"" (zero-length string)
Fixed-length string	The result of Chr(0), a nonprintable character
Variant	Empty
Object	Nothing

Next, we will examine the connection between the scope of a variable and its lifetime.

- If a variable is declared within a procedure using the Dim statement that variable's lifetime is equal to the procedure's lifetime. The variable retains a value only while the procedure is running.

- If a variable is declared in the General Declarations area of a standard module, it retains a value until the database file is closed and all code ceases executing. This is referred to as *application lifetime*.

- If a variable is declared in the General Declarations area of a class module, it retains a value only within an instance of that class and as long as the instance remains open. This is referred to as *object lifetime*.

- If a variable is declared as a Public variable (instead of using a Dim statement) the variable retains its value until the code stops executing. Public variables always are considered to have *application lifetime*.

The Lifetime of a Procedure-Level Variable

A procedure-level variable's lifetime is equal to the procedure's scope. The variable is declared within the procedure, and when the procedure finishes executing the variable's lifetime ends.

The variable's value can be reassigned several times during the processing of the procedure, but it needs to be declared only once.

The Lifetime of a Module-Level Variable

Now we turn to the lifetime of a module-level variable. We're going to use the basModLevelScope module in the sample file for Chapter 9 to demonstrate.

1. Create a variable by declaring it in the General Declarations section with the following code:

```
Dim intModLevelTest As Integer
```

2. Add the following functions to the module:

```
Function ModLevel3()
    Debug.Print intModlevelTest
End Function

Function ModLevel4()
    intModlevelTest = 100
    Debug.Print intModlevelTest
End Function
```

3. Place the cursor within ModLevel3 and press F5. The procedure sends the value 0 to the Immediate window. Because intModlevelTest hasn't been assigned a value as yet, it still has the initialized value.

4. Now run ModLevel4 in the same way. You now see 100 in the Immediate window.

5. Return the cursor to ModLevel3 and press F5 again. Now you see 100 written to the Immediate window, as shown in Figure 9.6. As you can see, the variable can be referenced from both procedures, and it retains its value from procedure to procedure.

Figure 9.6
The two functions demonstrate the lifetime of the variable intModLevelTest.

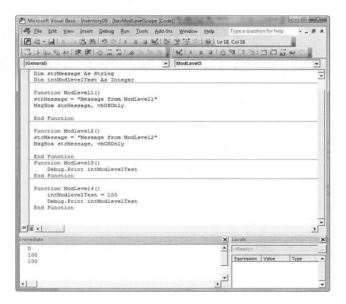

You still would not be able to reference intModLevelTest from a different module. VBA doesn't see it and returns a runtime error. The variable is still alive; however, it remains usable within the scope of the module where it was declared. This behavior is an issue of scope, not lifetime.

The Lifetime of a Public Variable

You can access a public variable anywhere within your application. When initialized, they are alive until specifically destroyed. You can change the value of a variable, but it still returns a value.

To demonstrate the immortality of a public variable, let's go back to the basModLevelScope and change the Declaration of intModLevelTest from Dim to Public. Next, create a new module and enter the following function:

```
Function PublicLevelTtest()
    Debug.Print intModlevelTest
End Function
```

See Figure 9.7 for the results of executing PublicLevelTest(). Because the variable is public, PublicLevelTest can reference it from another module. As you can also see, the value of the variable is also carried over. Module-level variables and public variables may have the same lifetime, but they won't share the same scope. So a variable might not be available to every procedure, even while it's residing in memory.

Figure 9.7
A public variable lives as long as code is running within the application.

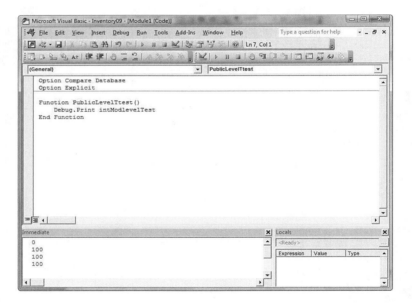

Using Static Variables

Static variables allow you to extend the life of a procedure-level variable beyond the procedure where it's declared. To do so you need to use the Static keyword in your declaration statement. The syntax for this is

```
Static variablename [As datatype]
```

The advantage of a static variable is that it retains its value between calls to its procedure. However, like a procedure-level variable, its scope remains only with the procedure.

We use the following simple example, to demonstrate the use of a static variable:

```
Function StaticVariableTest1()
    Dim intStaticTest As Integer
    intStaticTest = intStaticTest + 1
    Debug.Print intStaticTest
End Function
```

As probably seems obvious at this point, each time you execute this module, it displays a 1 in the Immediate window. Figure 9.8 illustrates this.

Figure 9.8
Each time you execute
StaticVariable-
Test it displays a 1 in
the Immediate window.

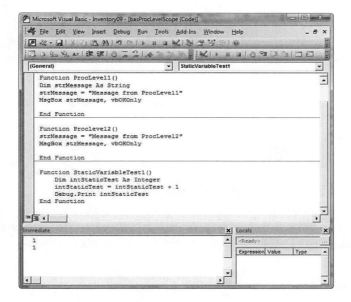

Now change the Declaration statement replacing Dim with Static. Run the procedure again. Again it displays a 1. But run it again, and it displays a 2. Because the variable retained its value it is now incremented by 1. Run it one more time, and this time it displays a 3, because it is again incremented by 1.

> **NOTE**
>
> Object variables need to be reset after you are finished using them. This is accomplished by setting the variable to Nothing. The syntax for this is
>
> ```
> Set objectvariable = Nothing
> ```
>
> You should include the set-to-nothing statement at the end of each procedure and in the cleanup part of your error handlers. This way you ensure the object variable is reset to nothing.

Figure 9.9
Each time you execute the edited `StaticVariable-Test` it increments its value by 1.

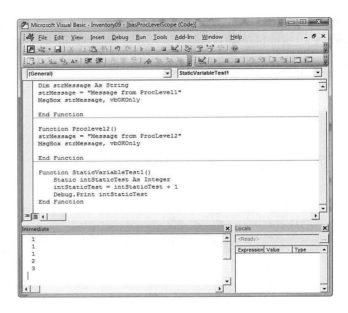

CASE STUDY

Case Study: Tracking the Current User

Sometimes you might need to track the current users of your application. There are several ways to do this; one possibility is the use of a global variable. You can use a login form that requires the user to select his name and enter a password. After confirming the password, you can store the employee ID in a global variable so it can be used throughout the application.

The first thing you need to do is create a login form:

1. From the Create ribbon, select Form Design to open a new blank form in Design view. Name it `frmLogin`. Set the Modal and Popup properties to Yes. Set the Navigation buttons and RecordSelectors to No and Scroll Bars to Neither.

2. Using the wizard, add a combo box to list the employees. Name it `cboEmployee`.

3. Add a text box to enter the password. Set the `Input` mask of the text box to password. Name the textbox `txtPassword`.

4. Open the basUDFs Module in Design mode and add the following line to the `Declarations` section of the module:

   `Public lngUser As long`

5. Using the Code Builder open the `AfterUpdate` event of the password text box. Add the following code snippet:

   ```
   Private Sub txtPassword_AfterUpdate()

   'test password
   If Me.txtPassword = "LetMeIn" Then
   ```

```
          'assign password to public variable
          lngUser = Me.cboEmployee
          DoCmd.Close acForm, "frmLogin", acSaveNo
     Else
          'warn user of invalid password
          MsgBox "Invalid Password", vbOKOnly
     End If
     End Sub
```

6. Save the form and return to Form view.

7. Select an employee, type in the password **LetMeIn**, and press Enter.

The form should close. Now, you can test that the user ID for the logged user has been saved and can be accessed from anywhere, by opening the VBE and typing the following in the Immediate window:

```
? lnguser
```

The result should be the employee ID of the user you selected on the form.

9

Working Within the User Interface

II

Working with Forms

10

Opening and Closing Forms

The first part of this book was devoted to building a foundation in the VBA language. This part shows you how to apply the foundation building blocks to create practical applications. This chapter deals with using VBA with your forms. If you've been developing Access applications, you are familiar with creating forms. Now we show you how to use VBA to automate them.

First, let's take a look at opening and closing forms using VBA.

Opening a Form

We introduced you to the `OpenForm` method back in Chapter 2, "Using the Visual Basic Editor." The `DoCmd` object is your main means for using VBA as a way to use many of the capabilities to automate Access. You can't create or destroy a `DoCmd` object; all you can do is use the methods of that object. You use these methods within VBA to work directly with other Access-specific objects.

Opening a form from VBA means using the `DoCmd.OpenForm` method. This method has a number of optional arguments in addition to the one required argument. The syntax for the method is

```
DoCmd.OpenForm formname, [view], [filtername],
➥[wherecondition], [datamode],
➥[windowmode], [openargs]
```

The *formname*, as might be obvious, is a required argument. It's necessary for specifying what form to open. The other arguments, all optional, give you greater control over the behavior of the form, when it's opened:

- The *view* argument allows you to choose what type of view with which the form opens. The Intellisense feature allows you to choose from these seven intrinsic constants as options: acDesign, acFormDS, acFormPivotChart, acFormPivotTable, acLayout, acNormal, and acPreview. The constants acDesign and acLayout open the form in one of Access's two views for creating forms. The constants acFormDS and acFormPivotTable open the form in a tablelike view. The constant acFormPivotchart uses a PivotChart, acNormal opens the form in its Normal view/Edit view, and acPreview shows you what the form will look like when printed. For more specifics on these views and how to use them see *Microsoft Access 2007 Forms, Reports, and Queries* (ISBN: 0-7897-3669-1) by Paul McFedries, another volume of the Business Solutions series.

- The *filtername* argument allows you to use a saved query to filter the records shown in the opened form.

- The *wherecondition* argument allows you to filter the records shown in the opened form by setting specific criteria in an expression (for example, "[Country] = 'USA'").

- The *datamode* argument allows you to restrict the user's ability to enter new records in the form or edit existing ones. The intrinsic constants that can be used here are acFormAdd, for adding new records; acFormEdit, for editing existing records; acFormPropertySettings, to edit only the form's properties; and acFormReadOnly, for only viewing records.

- The *windowmode* argument controls whether a form is opened as a dialog box (acDialog), hidden (acHidden), opened as an icon (acIcon), or opened normally (acWindowNormal).

- The final argument is *openargs*, which allows you to pass a value to the new form.

In its simplest form, the OpenForm method can open a form with all optional arguments as defaults. The following procedure opens the Employee Details form (frmEmployeeDetails):

```
Sub OpenEmpform()
'Open form using default arguments
    DoCmd.OpenForm "frmEmployeeDetails"
End Sub
```

This opens frmEmployeeList in the last view that was saved, giving access to all the data in its Recordsource, using the last saved data and window mode. However, you will generally want to use the power of VBA to modify the way the form opens. The following code opens the same form but only showing sales representatives:

```
Sub OpenEmpformFiltered()
'Open form showing only Sales Reps
    DoCmd.OpenForm "frmEmployeeDetails", , , "[JobTitleID] = 3"
End Sub
```

But let's take this a little further. Say you are using a form as a menu. From the Create ribbon, open a blank form using the Form Design icon. On the form use the Combobox wizard to place a combo box that selects a job title from `tluJobTitles`. Name the combo `cboTitle`. You now use the Code Builder to enter the following code in the `AfterUpdate` event:

```
Private Sub cboTitle_AfterUpdate()
'Open form showing selected title
    DoCmd.OpenForm "frmEmployeeDetails", , , "[JobTitleID] = " & Me.cboTitle
End Sub
```

Save the form as `frmMenu`. Now you can use the same form and code to open the form filtered for any job title. As you can see this opens many possibilities by allowing the user to supply the arguments to control how the form is opened.

Passing Arguments Using OpenArgs

The `OpenArgs` argument is useful and deserves some special mention here. `OpenArgs` is both an argument of the `OpenForm` method and a property of a form. The value entered for the `OpenArgs` argument can be used by the called form.

> **TIP**
>
> Reports also have an `OpenArgs` property, which works similarly to the `Form` property.

One common usage for this functionality is to open a form to a specific record. The following example illustrates that:

1. Open the `frmEmployeeList` form in Design view.
2. Unselect the Use Control Wizard icon on the Design ribbon.
3. Select the Command button icon and draw a button in the header of `frmEmployeeList`.
4. Set the caption for the button to View Employee and name the button `cmdViewEmp`.
5. In the `On Click` event enter the following line of code:
   ```
   DoCmd.OpenForm "frmEmployeeDetails",,,,,,Me.txtEmployeeID
   ```
6. Save the form.
7. Open the `frmEmployeeDetails` form in Design view.
8. Select the `On Load` event and enter the following code:
   ```
   Private Sub Form_Load()
   Dim rs As Object
   If Not IsNull(Me.OpenArgs) Then

       Set rs = Me.Recordset.Clone
       rs.FindFirst "[EmployeeID] = " & Me.OpenArgs
       If Not rs.EOF Then Me.Bookmark = rs.Bookmark

   End If
   End Sub
   ```
9. Save the form.

To test this code, reopen `frmEmployeeList` and select a record (see Figure 10.1).

Figure 10.1
The Employee List form.

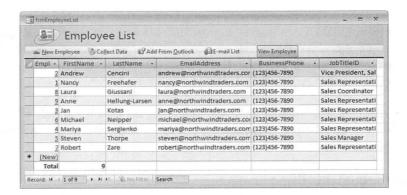

Click on the View Employee button, and the Employee Details form opens with the selected employee's record.

Closing a Form

Now that you have opened a form, you will probably want to close it. The `DoCmd.Close` method is used for that. This method is applicable to a variety of Access objects, not only forms. It has three optional arguments and uses the following syntax:

```
DoCmd.Close [objecttype], [objectname], [save]
```

- The *objecttype* argument indicates which type of object you are closing.
- The *objectname* argument indicates the name of the object you want to close.
- The *save* argument indicates whether to save any design changes made since the object was last saved.

> **NOTE**
> Because all the arguments for the `Close` method are optional, you don't have to provide any. By default the object that currently has focus will be closed.

To close the Employee Details form, you can use the following code snippet:

```
Sub CloseEmpDetails()
'Close the frmEmployeeDetails form
    DoCmd.Close acForm, "frmEmployeeDetails"
End Sub
```

TIP There are two ways to specify arguments for a method. The first way is to enter the arguments separated by a comma. If you use this method, you have to include a comma for each argument regardless of whether you specify a value for it. The other option is to explicitly list the argument name and its value. For example; `ObjectName:="frmEmployeeDetails"`. The argument name is followed by a colon and the equal sign. Both methods allow you to use Intellisense to select a value for the argument, but using the first method lists the arguments for you. I'm going to use the first method in all the illustrations in this book.

While a form is open and you make changes to the design or properties of the object, when you go to close the object, Access asks whether you want to save the changes. This can confuse users who might not realize it refers to design changes and not data. Changes such as setting a new filter trigger the save prompt. So the `DoCmd.Close` method provides a way to override this, because you generally don't want users to save changes. The following code snippet closes the Employee Details form without saving any changes:

```
Sub CloseEmpDetailsNoSave()
'Close the frmEmployeeDetails form
    DoCmd.Close acForm, "frmEmployeeDetails", acSaveNo
End Sub
```

The Form Module

All the sample procedures we've used in this chapter up to now have been part of a standard module. VBA code snippets can also be linked directly with a form (or report). Every form object in your Access application can be associated with its own *form module*. This form module becomes part of the form object so that if you copy the form, either within the Access file or to another one, the form module is copied with it. The form module can store regular procedures and functions but is used most often for event procedures.

→ See "Form Events," **p. 137**.

Form and Control Properties

Like every object, a form has properties. These properties can be manipulated from VBA to make adjustments to the form. The properties can be seen by opening the property from the Design ribbon. Figure 10.2 shows the Format tab of the property sheet with some of the properties listed.

As you can see from Figure 10.2, a form's property sheet displays numerous properties you can deal with—properties too numerous to list and describe here. To find out more about each property, position your cursor in the property and press F1 to load the built-in VBA Help for that property. Later in this section I list a few of the properties users generally find themselves using most often.

10

Figure 10.2
The Format tab of a
form's properties sheet.

First, to set a property for a form object or a control on a form, you use the following syntax:

`Forms.formname[.controlname].propertyname [= expression]`

In this instance `Forms` indicates the Forms collection. `Formname` is the name of the form. If the form is currently active, you can use the abbreviation `Me.` instead of `Forms.formname`. The `controlname` is optional and is used if you are referring to a control within a form. The `propertyname` is the name of the property you are changing. In some cases assigning a value to the property using an expression is necessary. But a few properties require no value. Following are some examples:

- `Forms.frmEmployeeDetails.Requery`—Requeries the `Recordsource` of the form.

- `Forms.frmEmployeeDetails.AllowDatasheetView = No`—Prevents the user from switching the form to Datasheet view.

- `Forms.frmEmployeeDetails.NavigationButtons = Yes`—Displays the built-in navigation buttons at the bottom of the form.

- `Forms.frmEmployeeDetails.AllowAdditions = No`—Prevents new records from being added to the form.

- `Forms.frmEmployeeDetails.Cycle = Current Record`—When the cursor gets to the last control on the form, pressing Tab returns to the first control in the tab order.

- `Forms.frmEmployeeDetails.txtEmail.Width = 2"`—Sets width of the `txtEmail` control to 2 inches.

- `Forms.frmEmployeeDetails.txtEmail.FontSize = 12`—Sets font size of the `txtEmail` control to 12 points.

- `Forms.frmEmployeeDetails.txtEmail.Visible = Me.chkEmail`—Hides or displays the `txtEmail` control depending on whether a check box control is checked.

- `Forms.frmEmployeeDetails.cboJobTitleID.RowSource = strSQL`—Sets the `Rowsource` of a combo to a SQL `Select` statement stored in a variable named `strSQL`.

As noted, you can manipulate many other properties through VBA. Go over the property sheets to get an idea of what's available, but don't expect to memorize them.

Form Events

The form module can contain custom functions and procedures. Event procedures are another type of procedure. The execution of such procedures is triggered by something happening to the form or a control on the form. For example, many controls have an `On Click` event that occurs when you use the mouse to click on the control. In this section we're going to add functionality to `frmEmployeeDetails` so that you can double-click on the employee's email address and have your default email client open to compose email with the address already filled in.

> **NOTE** The code is already in the Inventory10.accdb sample file provided. You can either make a copy of the form and delete the double-click event procedure or work from the Inventory9.accdb sample.

1. Open `frmEmployeeDetails` in Design view.
2. Select the EMailAddress control, open the property sheet, and click the ellipsis next to the double-click event.
3. Select the Code Builder, as shown in Figure 10.3.

Figure 10.3
Choose the Code Builder to enter code for the double-click event.

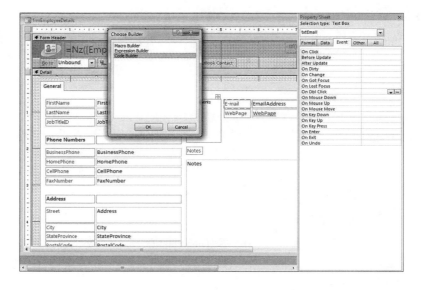

4. Enter the following code snippet:

```
Private Sub txtEmail_DblClick(Cancel As Integer)
If IsNull(Me.txtEmail) Then
    MsgBox "There is no E-mail for this employee", vbOKOnly
Else
    Application.FollowHyperlink "mailto:" & Me.txtEmail
End If
End Sub
```

5. Save the form and double-click the control to test it.

A large part of your VBA code will be entered into form events. Your code snippets are triggered by events that occur on forms. You should familiarize yourself with the various events that can occur with forms and controls so you know what event to choose for your workflow needs. Some events most often used include form events and control events. Form events include

- `On Open/On Load`—Occur when you open a form. `On Open` occurs before a record is displayed; `On Load` occurs after.
- `After Update`—Occurs after a record has been changed.
- `On Current`—Occurs whenever the current record changes.

Examples of control events include

- `On Click/On Dbl Click`—Occur when you single- or double-click on a control.
- `After Update`—Occurs when a change is made to the value of the control.

CASE STUDY

Case Study: Adding to a Combo Box

Combo boxes are used to select from a list of items. Often these lists are static, but many times they get updated. In this case study, we show two situations: adding a new category and adding a new supplier. This will all be done from `frmInvDetails`.

> **NOTE**
> The code is already in the Inventory10.accdb sample file provided. You can either make a copy of the form and delete the double-click event procedure or work from the Inventory9.accdb sample.

1. Open `frmInvDetails` in Design view.

2. Select the Category combo box.

3. Open the property sheet from the Design ribbon.

4. Select the `NotInList` event, click the ellipsis, and select the Code Builder (see Figure 10.4).

Figure 10.4
Choose the Code Builder to enter code for the NotInList event.

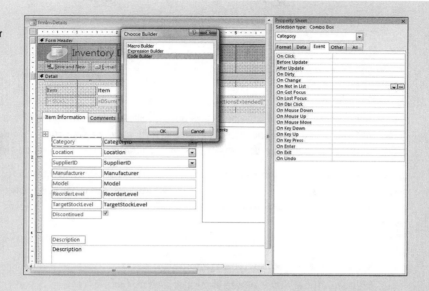

10

The VBE is opened, and the stub of the NotInList event is inserted. Notice that two arguments—NewData and Response—are inserted (see Figure 10.5).

Figure 10.5
The NotInList event stub.

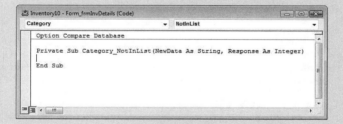

The NewData argument is the value entered into the combo box that is not in the list produced from the RowSource. The Response argument tells the combo box whether a value has been added.

5. Enter the following code snippet:

```vb
Private Sub Category_NotInList(NewData As String, Response As Integer)
Dim strSQL As String
Dim strMsg As String
Dim ctl As Control
Set ctl = Screen.ActiveControl

strMsg = "The Category, " & NewData & ", you entered is not listed!" & _
        vbCrLf & "Do you want to add it?"
    If MsgBox(strMsg, vbYesNo, "Not listed") = vbYes Then
        strSQL = "INSERT INTO tluCategory (Category) "
        strSQL = strSQL & "VALUES('" & NewData & "');"
```

```
            CurrentDb.Execute strSQL
            Response = acDataErrAdded
        Else
            ctl.Undo
            Response = acDataErrContinue
        End If
    End Sub
```

The user is first asked to confirm whether he wants to add the unmatched value. If he does, this snippet uses an Append query to add a record to the table referenced in the combo box's Rowsource. The acDateErrAdded constant then tells the combo that the value was added, and it's selected for you. Now test the code by adding a new category (Snacks).

Because tluCategory is a lookup table containing only the Category ID and its name, nothing more needs to be done here. The next example looks at adding a supplier where there would be more information to enter besides just the supplier name. So the code is modified to capture the ID of the added record and open frmSuppliers to the newly added record.

1. Reopen frmInvDetails if it's not already open.
2. Select the Suppliers combo and open the property sheet.
3. Select the NotInList event, click the ellipsis, and select the Code Builder.
4. Enter the following code snippet:

```
Private Sub Supplier_NotInList(NewData As String, Response As Integer)
Dim strSQL As String
Dim strMsg As String
Dim lngSupplierID As Long
Dim ctl As Control
Set ctl = Screen.ActiveControl

strMsg = "The supplier, " & NewData & ", you entered is not listed!" & _
        vbCrLf & "Do you want to add it?"
    If MsgBox(strMsg, vbYesNo, "Not listed") = vbYes Then
        strSQL = "INSERT INTO tblSuppliers (Company) "
        strSQL = strSQL & "VALUES('" & NewData & "');"
        CurrentDb.Execute strSQL
        Response = acDataErrAdded
        lngSupplierID = DMax("[SupplierID]", "tblSuppliers")
        DoCmd.OpenForm "frmAddSupplier", , , "[SupplierID] = " & lngSupplierID
    Else
        ctl.Undo
        Response = acDataErrContinue
    End If
End Sub
```

5. Test the code by entering a new supplier into the Supplier combo box on frmInvDetails.

The NotInList event code is modified to capture the newly added record's primary key. That value is then used in a WHERE clause in the OpenForm method to filter the newly opened form for the newly added Supplier. When you close the Add Supplier form, you are returned to frmInvDetails, with the newly added supplier selected in the combo.

More on Event-Driven Coding

Responding to Events

Much of Access programming is event-driven; your VBA code doesn't just execute at will. The code you write is not constantly running as in a more traditional program. Access itself manages a lot of the interaction between the user and the data. So the code snippets you construct will be triggered by events that occur as the user interfaces with your application design. Events such as entering data into controls, clicking buttons, changing records, and more are used to execute code snippets.

Using events is so vital a concept in automating Access applications that we will spend a significant amount of time going over the process. You will learn that events occur in a particular order, and each has a particular purpose.

Let's first review how this all works together, by looking at the button on the frmDateRange. Right-click on frmDateRange in the Navigation pane and select Design View as shown in Figure 11.1.

After the form is opened, select the button, and open the Properties sheet to the Event tab as shown in Figure 11.2.

Notice that the button has been assigned the name cmdPreview. The On Click event property for the button has been set to [Event Procedure]. This lets Access know that a VBA code snippet is attached to this event of that button. Access then knows that when the On Click event occurs (the user clicks on the button with her mouse) that it should execute the code in that procedure.

Figure 11.1
Select Design View for
`frmDateRange`.

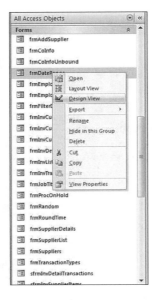

Figure 11.2
The Event tab of the
Properties sheet for the
`cmdPreview` button.

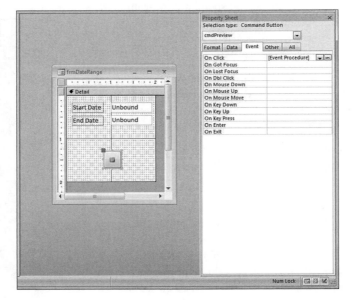

> **TIP**
>
> `[Event Procedure]` is not the only thing that might appear in the event property. It's also possible to see `[Embedded Macro]` or the name of a separate macro. In those cases the event executes the macro to which it refers. It's also possible but rare for an expression to appear in the property.

To see the code snippet that is executed when the event occurs you need to use the VBE. You can quickly view the event code by clicking on the ellipsis button to the right of the [Event Procedure] entry. This opens the VBE, makes the form module the active window, and scrolls to the selected event procedure. You then see the following code snippet:

```
Private Sub cmdPreview_Click()
    On Error GoTo cmdPreview_Click_Err
    DoCmd.OpenReport "rptInvTransByDate", acViewPreview
Exit_cmdPreview_Click:
    Exit Sub
cmdPreview_Click_Err:
    MsgBox "Error " & Err.Number & ":" & Err.Description
    Resume Exit_cmdPreview_Click
End Sub
```

For an event procedure to work properly the following conditions must be met:

- The event property must have [Event Procedure] as its setting.

> **NOTE**
> When you enter a procedure with the correct module name for the event, VBA automatically enters [Event Procedure] in the property box.

- The code has to be entered in the form (or report) module of the object from where it is triggered.
- The procedure must be named using the syntax *objectname_eventname*.

You must also declare any arguments that the event procedure will use. We discuss that in more detail later in this chapter.

The Event Sequence for Controls

Let's start off by looking at events that are linked to the controls (buttons, combo boxes, labels, and so on) on your form (or report).

> **TIP**
> Those new to Access often have a tendency to refer to data controls (text boxes, combo boxes, check boxes, and so on) on a form as fields. But a control is not a field. A *field* is a piece of data within a record. A *control* is an object on a form (or report) that can be used to display data or perform some other function. The data it can display may or may not be bound to a field in a table. This is a subtle but important distinction. Understanding this helps you understand how controls are used to automate your applications.

We begin by discussing events involved with switching focus and modifying data, and then cover a selected group of events for individual controls.

> **NOTE**
>
> The scope of this book doesn't permit us to cover every event available. Many events are of little practical use, and you will never use them. Because this book is designed to teach you practical skills for automating Access, we limit what we discuss here.

Focus Events

Using Access forms means moving around from control to control using the Tab and/or Enter keys or using the mouse cursor. As the user does this, a number of events are triggered. You can place code in the event procedures for these events to perform a variety of tasks to automate your application.

Four events to consider are

- Enter—Gets triggered just prior to a control receiving the focus from another control on the same form.
- Exit—Gets triggered just prior to a control losing the focus to another control on the same form.
- GotFocus—Gets triggered when a control gains focus.
- LostFocus—Gets triggered when a control loses focus.

> **TIP**
>
> *Focus* refers to when an object can interact with either mouse or keyboard input. Only one control on a form can have focus. This control is referred to as the *active control* and is generally indicated by a blinking cursor or dotted outline.

Some simple code snippets illustrate the order these events are triggered. We use frmCoInfo for these examples. Open that form in Design mode. You can either open the form's module and type in the following code or use the Code Builder option from the property dialog for each event. (Or you can simply use the form from the sample file for this chapter.) We start with Company Name text box.

```
Private Sub txtCompanyName_Enter()
    MsgBox "Company Name Enter", vbOKOnly
End Sub

Private Sub txtCompanyName_Exit(Cancel As Integer)
    MsgBox "Company Name Exit", vbOKOnly
End Sub

Private Sub txtCompanyName_GotFocus()
    MsgBox "Company Name Got Focus", vbOKOnly
End Sub

Private Sub txtCompanyName_LostFocus()
    MsgBox "Company Name Lost Focus", vbOKOnly
End Sub
```

```
Private Sub txtStreetAddress_Enter()
    MsgBox "Street Address Enter", vbOKOnly
End Sub

Private Sub txtStreetAddress_Exit(Cancel As Integer)
    MsgBox "Street Address Exit", vbOKOnly
End Sub

Private Sub txtStreetAddress_GotFocus()
    MsgBox "Street Address Got Focus", vbOKOnly
End Sub

Private Sub txtStreetAddress_LostFocus()
    MsgBox "Street Address Lost Focus", vbOKOnly
End Sub
```

The purpose here is to display a message box as each event is triggered. To test the code, save and close the form. Now double-click the form to activate it, and you see the first message box displayed as in Figure 11.3.

Click OK on the message box, and the Got Focus message is displayed as in Figure 11.4.

Figure 11.3
The Company Name Enter message is displayed when the form is activated.

Figure 11.4
The Company Name Got Focus message is displayed when the form is activated.

Note that these messages boxes are displayed even before the form because the Company Name control is set as the first control in the Tab sequence. Now Tab out of the Company Name text box. When you do, the next series of message boxes, shown in Figures 11.5 through 11.8, appear.

Figure 11.5
The Company Name Exit message is displayed when you Tab out of the control.

Figure 11.6
The Company Name Lost Focus message is displayed when you Tab out of the control.

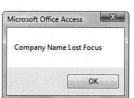

Figure 11.7
The Street Address Enter message is displayed when you Tab into the control.

Figure 11.8
The Street Address Got Focus message is displayed when you Tab into the control.

Now try clicking into a different form, and you see the Street Address Lost Focus message as shown in Figure 11.9.

Figure 11.9
The Street Address Lost Focus message is displayed when you switch to another form.

The `Exit` and `Enter` events don't get triggered in this instance because these events are concerned only with movements within the same form. Next, switch back to `frmCoInfo`, and the Street Address Got Focus message is shown (refer to Figure 11.8).

Finally, try changing to a different application (Word, Internet Explorer, or anything else) and then going back into Access. You do not see the focus events being triggered here. Access registers only those actions that occur within Access.

Data Events

The next set of events we cover are data events. These events pertain to data that the user is entering or involve data being interchanged between tables and the controls. Because a control can be bound to a field in a table or can be unbound, some data controls apply only to bound controls:

- `BeforeUpdate`—Triggered after data in the control is modified but before it's committed to the form
- `AfterUpdate`—Triggered after data in the control is modified and committed to the form

Another grouping of events is applicable only for controls that allow data to be entered in them (text boxes or combo boxes):

- `KeyDown`—Triggered each time the user presses a key
- `KeyPress`—Triggered when a key's value is sent to Access
- `Dirty`—Triggered when a change is made to the bound record of the form
- `Change`—Triggered as soon as a change is made to the control's value
- `KeyUp`—Triggered when the user releases a key

Following are some code snippets you can put behind events for the `MainPhone` control on the `frmCoInfo` form to illustrate when these events are triggered:

```
Private Sub txtMainPhone_AfterUpdate()
    MsgBox "Main Phone AfterUpdate", vbOKOnly
End Sub
```

```
Private Sub txtMainPhone_BeforeUpdate(Cancel As Integer)
    MsgBox "Main Phone BeforeUpdate", vbOKOnly
End Sub

Private Sub txtMainPhone_Change()
    MsgBox "Main Phone Change", vbOKOnly
End Sub

Private Sub txtMainPhone_Dirty(Cancel As Integer)
    MsgBox "Main Phone Dirty", vbOKOnly
End Sub
Private Sub txtMainPhone_KeyDown(KeyCode As Integer, Shift As Integer)
Dim strMsg As String
    strMsg = "Main Phone KeyDown, KeyCode = " & CStr(KeyCode)
    strMsg = strMsg & " Shift = " & CStr(Shift)
    MsgBox strMsg, vbOKOnly
End Sub

Private Sub txtMainPhone_KeyPress(KeyAscii As Integer)
    MsgBox "Main Phone KeyPress, KeyAscii = " & CStr(KeyAscii)
End Sub

Private Sub txtMainPhone_KeyUp(KeyCode As Integer, Shift As Integer)
Dim strMsg As String
    strMsg = "Main Phone KeyUp, KeyCode = " & CStr(KeyCode)
    strMsg = strMsg & " Shift = " & CStr(Shift)
    MsgBox strMsg, vbOKOnly
End Sub
```

Now save the form; then place the cursor in the Phone control at the end and type a backspace. You should see the message boxes shown in Figures 11.10 through 11.13.

Figure 11.10
Message box showing the results of typing.

Figure 11.11
Message box showing the results of typing.

Figure 11.12
Message box showing the results of typing.

Figure 11.13
The Main Phone messages are displayed when you make a change in the value.

Now press 5 to complete the phone number, and the message boxes shown in Figures 11.14 and 11.15 are displayed.

Figure 11.14
Message box showing the results of typing.

Figure 11.15
Message box showing the results of typing.

You can see that the procedures for the Keypress, KeyDown, and KeyUp events have arguments. The values of these arguments are automatically populated by Access. They contain the value of the key being used. The KeyCode and KeyAscii arguments contain the ASCII code of the key. The Shift argument indicates whether the Shift, Alt, or Ctrl keys were also pressed. Table 11.1 shows the values returned for those keys.

Table 11.1   Shift Argument Values

Key	Value	Constant
None	0	
Shift	1	acShiftmask
Ctrl	2	acCtrlMask
Alt	4	acAltmask

Control-Specific Events

Certain controls have events closely aligned with the purpose of the control. The button control is a prime example of that. The Click and Dbl Click events are intrinsically linked to buttons because buttons are used mostly by clicking on them with the mouse.

Buttons, toggle buttons, check boxes, and radio buttons all usually trigger the Click event when the user clicks on the control. However, when these controls are used within an option group (as toggles, check boxes, and radio buttons are most often used), one of the data events of the group is triggered.

Combo box controls have an event peculiar to them—the NotInList event. This event is triggered when the LimitToList property is set to Yes and the user enters a value not in the list returned by the control. This event is then used to allow for adding a new value to the list (either a Value List or a table).

→ This event is illustrated in "Case Study: Adding to a Combo Box," **p. 138**, and "Adding to the List—Or Not," **p. 159**.

The Event Sequence for Forms

So far we've shown you control events, but forms also have their own events. Sometimes they work in concert with control events.

> **NOTE**
> At this point you should have seen how to use message boxes to determine the order of events. So we won't go over this code anymore; we'll just discuss the events.

Navigation Events

Whenever a form is opened, five events are triggered in the following order:

1. Open
2. Load
3. Resize
4. Activate
5. Current

Because the Open event is triggered first, it's the earliest point in the life cycle of the form where you can execute VBA code. Next comes the Load event, which is triggered just after data is called into the form from the data store. The Resize event is triggered each time the size of a form is changed. Changing the size from nothing to its initial size is considered a size change. The Activate event is triggered when the form or a control on it gains focus. The Current event gets triggered whenever a different record is displayed on the form. As you might be able to tell, only the first two events are exclusive to the opening of a form. The other three events can be triggered by other actions after the form is open.

> **TIP**
> If there is a need to execute some procedure each time the user navigates to a different (or new) record, the Current event is where you need to put your code.

On closing a form, you trigger a different set of events:

1. Unload
2. Deactivate
3. Close

These three events unload the data from the form, remove the focus to another object, and close the form.

When moving the focus from one form to another the Deactivate event for the current form is followed by the Activate event of the subsequent form.

11

Data Events

Forms have a broad set of events that deal with data. This makes sense because forms are designed to be the interface between the user and data tables.

> **TIP** The data events for a form make it much easier to use bound forms (forms where the Recordsource is a table or query). These events are triggered when data is called from or sent to the Recordsource. With unbound forms, these events are not triggered, and the developer needs to write code to handle the I/O.

If you are in a new, blank record on a form, as soon as you press the first keystroke, the following five events are triggered:

1. Current

2. Enter (for the control that gains focus)

3. GotFocus (for that control)

4. BeforeInsert

5. AfterInsert

The first three events were covered earlier in this chapter. The last two are part of a before-and-after pair. The BeforeInsert event is triggered when a new record is being created. It lets Access know that the record is getting ready to be stored and that the form contains the data to be stored. You can use this event to modify the data in the bound controls so that the modifications will be saved in the table. Conversely the AfterInsert event is triggered when the record is successfully added to the bound table.

We previously covered the BeforeUpdate and AfterUpdate events as they relate to controls. They are triggered as you move among the controls, editing their values. When you are ready to save the data, either by moving focus to another record or form, or by committing the record via VBA, the BeforeUpdate and AfterUpdate events of the form are triggered. As in the Insert pair, the BeforeUpdate event allows you to modify data before it's saved, whereas the AfterUpdate event is triggered when the record is saved.

The deletion of a record triggers three events:

1. Delete

2. BeforeDelConfirm

3. AfterDelConfirm

The Delete event is triggered when the Delete command is issued but before the record is actually deleted. The BeforeDelConfirm event occurs just before Access displays the dialog box that prompts you to confirm deletion. You can then cancel the deletion. The AfterDelConfirm event occurs after the deletion is completed.

Behind the Scenes: Data Buffers

Working with data through a form involves using different areas of memory to store the data at various points during the processing. These areas are referred to as *buffers*. Figure 11.16 illustrates the flow of data through the buffers. Each area represents one of the buffers where data can be stored with the arrows showing the flow of the data.

Figure 11.16
How data is buffered during processing.

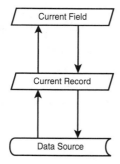

When a record is first called into a bound form, that record's data is retrieved from the table where it's stored. The data is then held in a buffer containing the single record. Each control pulls the data from that buffer for display. When the user starts typing in a control, the data for that control is then placed in a second buffer.

When the user moves to a different control, the data from the control buffer is written back to the record buffer for the form. This triggers the BeforeUpdate and AfterUpdate events for the control. However, pressing Esc discards the changes and wipes out what's in the control buffer. If that happens the events are not triggered.

As the user edits data in the controls, the edited record is still held within the form buffer. This means that it can still be cleared by pressing the Esc key twice. You have to actually commit the record before it's moved from the form buffer back to the underlying table. The BeforeUpdate and AfterUpdate form events are then triggered, and the table is updated.

The Event Sequence for Reports

You will find events in reports as well, though they are less extensive than those provided for forms. Part of the reason for this is that reports are not interactive. Users can't make changes to the data in controls through a report. When a report opens, only two events are triggered:

1. `Open`

2. `Activate`

These two events are the first time you can run code within the report and when it gains focus of the application. When the report closes, two similar events are triggered:

1. `Deactivate`

2. `Close`

Some other events also are associated with reports. The most important to consider is the `NoData` event. This event is triggered if there is no data to be displayed within a bound report band. Because most reports are bound to queries, this event becomes useful in providing a message rather than just a blank report.

Reports are divided into bands, with each band having a specific purpose. It's outside the scope of this book to go into detail about the report writer within Access. But we need to mention them to refer to the events that occur within each band. Those events are

1. `Format`

2. `Retreat`

3. `Print`

The `Format` event is triggered after Access has determined there is data to be displayed within the band but prior to when it applies the formatting for the band. The `Retreat` event gets triggered if Access decides it has to reformat a band because of some other action within the form. For example, if you have properties set to keep blocks of data together, it might require reformatting. And the `Print` event is triggered after the band has been formatted but before it's actually sent to the printer.

A `Page` event also needs to be mentioned. This event is triggered for each page in the report, just prior to it being printed.

Cancelling Events

Some events can be cancelled from within the code for the event. If this is done, the action that triggered the event is also stopped. Events that can be cancelled have a `Cancel` argument generated as part of the stub when you use the Code Builder. Cancelling the event is accomplished by setting the `Cancel` argument to `True` within the code snippet. For example, the following code seeks to confirm whether the user wants to leave the end date on `frmDateRange` without entering a date:

```
Private Sub txtEnd_Exit(Cancel As Integer)
If IsNull(txtEnd) Then
    If MsgBox("No value entered, Continue exiting?", vbYesNo) = vbYes Then
```

```
        Cancel = True
        Me.cmdpreview.SetFocus
    End If
End If
End Sub
```

As stated, when you Cancel the event, the action that triggered it is also cancelled. If the user answers Yes, the event and the Tab out of the control are cancelled, so you need the SetFocus to move the cursor. Otherwise, the user will be stuck in that control.

The Before events—BeforeUpdate, BeforeInsert, and BeforeDelConfirm—are all events that can be cancelled. The ability to cancel allows the user to back up from making changes she didn't want to make or if invalid data was entered.

CASE STUDY

Case Study: Validating Data

One use of some events is doing more complex validation of data than the Validation property permits. This case study illustrates using some events to make sure the entered data is valid.

We are going to use frmDateRange for these examples. This form supplies a range of dates for the Transactions by Date report. The form consists of two text boxes and a button to run the report. The first thing we are going to do is make sure that the user enters a valid date value in the controls. Follow these steps:

1. Open the form in Design mode.

2. Select the txtStart control and open the Code Builder for the On Exit event.

3. Add the following code:

```
Private Sub txtStart_Exit(Cancel As Integer)

If Not IsNull(Me.txtStart) Then
    If Not IsDate(Me.txtStart) Then
        MsgBox "the value entered is not a valid date!", vbOKOnly
        Cancel = True
    End If
Else
    MsgBox "No Value entered!", vbOKOnly
    Cancel = True
End If
End Sub
```

This code ensures that a valid date is entered into the control.

When entering a date range, the end date is usually after the start date. So you want to make sure the user enters a date value that is chronologically after the start date. This time we again add the following code to the On Exit event:

```
Private Sub txtEnd_Exit(Cancel As Integer)
If IsNull(txtEnd) Then
    If MsgBox("You didn't enter a value do you want to exit?", _
      vbYesNo) = vbYes Then
        Cancel = True
        Me.cmdpreview.SetFocus
    End If
Else
    If Me.txtStart > Me.txtEnd Then
        MsgBox "Start date is after End date!", vbOKOnly
        Cancel = True
    End If
End If
End Sub
```

The other part of the code was entered in a previous example. The new code is in the highlighted section. This new code tests to see whether the end date is earlier than the start date. If it is, it produces an error.

Working with Selection Controls

Selection Controls

Controls are objects the developer uses to allow the user to interface with the application. One category of controls allows you to select from several options in a list. The three types of controls in this category are combo boxes, list boxes, and option groups. Although all three of these controls enable you select from a list, each has its own special properties and its own advantages and disadvantages. There will be specific instances where you will want to use one type of control over another. This chapter discusses list controls and option groups.

Populating a List Control

Combo and list boxes fall into the category of list controls because they present a list of items to the user. They differ from option groups in that the lists they present can be variable. This provides the developer with a great deal of flexibility by permitting the list presented to the user to be configured as needed by the workflow of the application.

Combo and list boxes have two properties in common that allow the developer to programmatically change the contents of the lists presented to the user:

- RowSourceType—Tells Access that the list is taken from a table or query, a hard-coded list of values, or the field names from a table or query.

- RowSource—Dependent on the row source type, this property tells Access where to get the list the control displays.

Table 12.1 shows the three row source types and what they use for the list they display.

Table 12.1 Row Source Types

RowSourceType	Property Value	Row Source Explanation
Table/Query	"Table/Query"	The name of a table or query or a SQL statement
Value List	"Value List"	A typed-in list of items separated by semicolons
Field List	"Field List"	The name of a table or query or a SQL statement

> **NOTE**
>
> The Field List RowSourceType is one you will probably rarely use. Access uses it for some of its wizards, which are sometimes written in VBA, so the property is left open for use.

If you've worked at designing forms, you are probably already familiar with these properties. You've seen them when adding these types of controls to your forms. Like most properties, however, they can be manipulated through VBA.

Although you can change both the RowSourceType and Rowsource properties, generally, you will change only the Rowsource. A list control is set up either as a Value List or as a Table/Query when you design the form, so it's unlikely you would want to change that programmatically.

There are many instances, however, when you would want to change the Rowsource. Some examples follow:

- To filter the list based on another value selected by the user.

> **TIP**
>
> This is an often-used, standard technique referred to as *synchronized* or *cascading* combo boxes. An example would be filtering a list of cities for a specified country.

- To add values to a list when applicable.
- To use a different table or query as the source of the list; for example, you might be looking up values from different lookup tables, based on another value in the record.

To set the Rowsource property you use the following syntax:

```
control.Rowsource = datasource
```

where *datasource* is a table, query, or SQL statement or a value list as applicable to the application.

A Filtering List Control

The example in this section uses two combo boxes to allow the user to filter the records displayed in the form. We are going to use frmEmployeeList and add two combo boxes to the form's header. The first combo box chooses the field to filter by; the second chooses the values to filter by.

Let's start by opening `frmEmployeeList` in Design view. Drag the form header down a couple of ticks to allow room to insert the two combo boxes. Next, turn off the Control Wizard; we will be setting the properties manually and in code. Then insert a combo box control in the header beneath the row of buttons (see Figure 12.1).

Figure 12.1
`frmEmployeeList` in Design view, showing the expanded header with one combo box inserted.

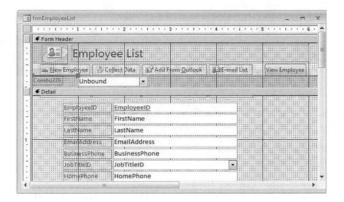

From here, you must manually set certain properties as follows:

1. Enter the word **Fields** in the Caption property of the label.
2. Set the Name property to cboFields.
3. Set the Row Source Type property to Value List.

> **NOTE**
> You could use a Field List in this instance, especially if you wanted to allow the user to select any field to filter by. But because we limit the user to four fields, we will use a Value List.

4. Type **FirstName; LastName; JobTitleID; City** in the RowSource property.

Next we add the second combo box and set some of its properties:

1. Insert a second combo box to the right of cboFields.
2. Enter the phrase **Filter By** as the Caption property of the label.
3. Set the Name property to cboValues.
4. Make sure the Row Source Type property is set as Table/Query.

Your form should now look like the one shown in Figure 12.2.

Figure 12.2
frmEmployeeList in Design view, showing the expanded header with the two combo boxes inserted.

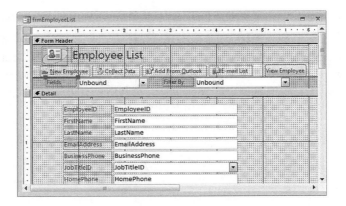

Now we go back to cboFields, and open the Code Builder for the After Update event. Then enter the following code:

```
Private Sub cboFields_AfterUpdate()
Dim strSQL As String

If Me.cboFields = "JobTitleID" Then
    strSQL = "SELECT JobTitleID, JobTitle FROM tluJobtitles ORDER BY JobTitle;"
    Me.cboValues.ColumnCount = 2
    Me.cboValues.ColumnWidths = "0" & Chr(34) & ";2" & Chr(34)
Else
    strSQL = "SELECT DISTINCT " & Me.cboFields & " FROM tblEmployees;"
    Me.cboValues.ColumnCount = 1
End If

Me.cboValues.RowSource = strSQL
End Sub
```

Because JobTitleID is a numeric data type, you need to treat it differently from the other fields, which are text data types—hence, the If statement. You need to query a different table and set the combo box to deal with two columns instead of one.

Next, enter the following code in the After Update event of cboValues:

```
Private Sub cboValues_AfterUpdate()
If Me.cboFields = "JobTitleID" Then
    Me.Filter = "[" & Me.cboFields & "] = " & Me.cboValues
Else
    Me.Filter = "[" & Me.cboFields & "] = '" & Me.cboValues & "'"
End If
Me.FilterOn = True
End Sub
```

Again, you need to deal with the Job Title somewhat differently. This code sets up and applies the filter. To test the code, open frmEmployeeList and select a field in cbofields. Then pull down the Values list and you will see only values that pertain to the selected field. When you select a value from that combo box, the form shows only matching values. Figure 12.3 shows the completed form with the Sales Representative job title selected and filtered.

Figure 12.3
frmEmployeeList
in View mode, showing
the completed form
in use.

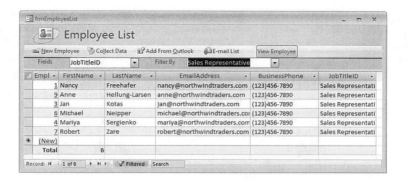

Adding to the List—Or Not

A combo box control has a property that is not available in list box controls. Combo boxes allow you to enter a value that is not in the list, just by typing that value in. Two properties are involved in this capability: the LimitToList property and the NotInList event.

→ **See** the Case Study in Chapter 10 that used the NotInList event, **p. 138**.

The LimitToList property is a Boolean value. When set to Yes, the combo box cannot accept any value that is not in the Rowsource of the combo box. If the user attempts to enter a nonlisted value, the error message shown in Figure 12.4 appears (unless you use the NotInList event).

Figure 12.4
Entering an unlisted
value produces an error
message.

12

When the combo box is set to No, you can type in any value (unless there is a validation rule), and it will be accepted. If the combo box is bound to a field in a table, the value entered is stored in that field. However, if the combo box uses a Value List, the entered value is not added to the list.

That's where the NotInList event comes into play. As we saw in Chapter 10, "Working with Forms," when the Rowsource is a query of another table, the NotInList event can be used to add a record to that table. It also can be used to add a value to a Value List.

Let's go back to frmEmployeeList. Earlier in this chapter we added a combo box to select a field on which to filter the form. That control uses a Value List. Figure 12.5 shows the form in Design view with the list.

Figure 12.5
frmEmployeeList
in Design view with the
property sheet showing
the Value List.

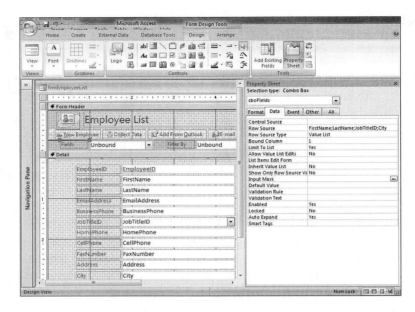

When you pull down the list, the four fields currently entered are shown, as illustrated in Figure 12.6.

Figure 12.6
frmEmployeeList
with the Fields combo
box pulled down.

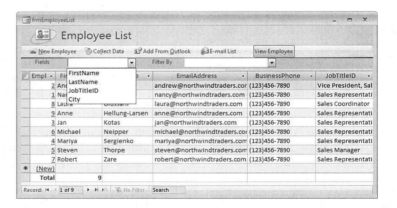

If you type in another value (for example, State) the value would be accepted, but nothing happens with it. If you pull down the list again, State is not on the list (see Figure 12.7).

Figure 12.7
frmEmployeeList
with the newly entered
value and the Fields
combo pulled down.

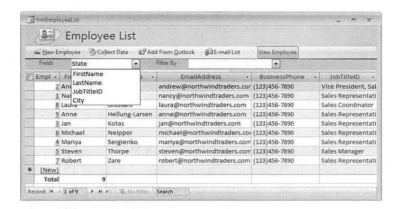

Access 2007 has a new feature that recognizes that an entry is not in the Value List and asks whether you want to add the entry to the list. If you answer Yes, a dialog box opens where you can enter new items, as shown in Figure 12.8. This feature works only with bound combo boxes.

Figure 12.8
A new feature allows you
to add items to the list
using a dialog box.

12

However, our purpose here is to show you how to use VBA to automate Access. You need to set this up so that you can add a value to the list using VBA and the NotInList event. The following steps will get you there:

1. Enter Design view and set the LimitToList property for cboFields to Yes.

2. Enter the Code Builder for the NotInList event of cboFields.

3. Enter the following code:

```
Private Sub cboFields_NotInList(NewData As String, Response As Integer)
Dim strMsg As String

'Populate message text
strMsg = "The value " & NewData & " Is not in the Value List."
strMsg = strMsg & vbCrLf & "Do you want to add it?"

'add value to list if user confirms
```

```
If MsgBox(strMsg, vbYesNo) = vbYes Then
    Response = acDataErrAdded
    Me.cboFields.RowSource = Me.cboFields.RowSource _
        & ";" & NewData
Else
    Response = acDataErrContinue
    Me.cboFields.Undo
End If

End Sub
```

4. Close the VBE and return the form to View mode.

5. Retype **State** in the `cboFields` combo box.

6. Access displays the message box shown in Figure 12.9. Click Yes, and the new entry is accepted and added to the Value List. Figure 12.10 shows the pull-down with the new entry added. Figure 12.11 shows the Property Sheet for the control with the new `RowSource`.

Figure 12.9
A message box prompts the user to indicate whether she wants to add the unlisted value.

Figure 12.10
The pull-down shows the added value.

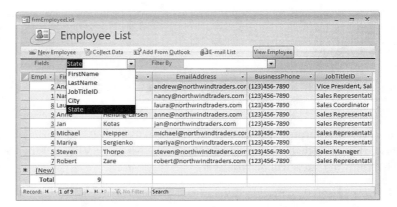

Figure 12.11
The Property Sheet shows the modified RowSource.

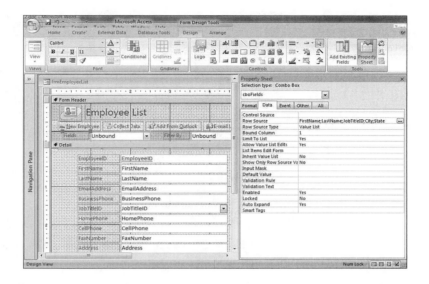

When the user types in a value that is not in the list, the `NotInList` event is triggered. This causes the message box shown in Figure 12.9 to be displayed. The `If` statement checks the response given and either adds the value to the list or not depending on the choice. If the user chooses to add, the `Response` argument is reset to `acDataErrAdded`, and the value is concatenated onto the list. Otherwise, the `Response` argument is reset to `acDataErrContinue`, and the typing is erased with the `Undo` command.

Updating a Table/Query List

You will use a Table/Query `RowSourceType` most often in programming. It gives you maximum flexibility by allowing you to simply add a value to a table when needed. This way, values can be added directly by entering them into the table through a form, or on-the-fly by using the `NotInList` event. Using a query or SQL statement as the `Rowsource` allows you greater control over what's displayed in the pull-down list.

How you add an item to the `Rowsource` depends on how you have set up your database. One of the main reasons for using lists is to standardize data entry. For example, you have a City field in the Employee table. If you want to query the table for all employees who live in a certain city, you want to make sure that the data is entered the same way. You don't want employees living in New York City to have New York City, New York, and NYC as their city. One way of dealing with this is to use a lookup table that lists the possible values. The sample database has a few lookup tables (with a `tlu` prefix). However, with a city, there may be too many items to create a lookup table. In such a case, you want the combo box to query the actual field.

Open `frmEmployeeDetails` in Design view and right-click on the City control. Select Change To, Combo Box as shown in Figure 12.12.

12

Figure 12.12
Change the City text box
to a combo box.

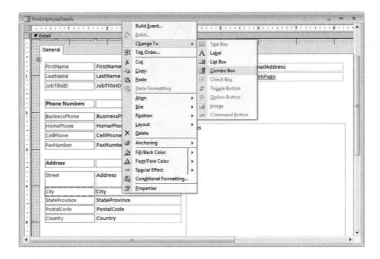

Open the Property dialog and change the name to cboCity. Set the RowSourceType to
Table/Query, set the LimitToList property to No, and enter the following SQL statement as
the Rowsource (see Figure 12.13):

SELECT DISTINCT City FROM tblEmployees ORDER BY City;

You need to use the DISTINCT keyword here because you want to show each city only once.
Because multiple employees may live in the same city, you don't want show multiple values
for the same city.

→ For a brief overview of SQL, **see** the appendix, "A Review of Access SQL."

Figure 12.13
The Rowsource has
been entered for the
changed City control.

The control now displays a sorted list of cities that it pulls from the table, as shown in Figure 12.14.

Figure 12.14
The City list displayed in the `cboCity` control.

The user can now just type in a value, and it will be accepted and stored. However, the pull-down is not updated until you close the form and reopen it. You want the list to be updated immediately. The easiest way to do this is to requery the control using VBA. To do so, open `frmEmployeeDetails` in Design view, select `cboCity`, and open the Property Sheet. Select the `After Update` event and use the Code Builder to enter the following code:

```
Private Sub cboCity_AfterUpdate()
    Me.Dirty = False
    Me.cboCity.Requery
End Sub
```

By resetting the `Dirty` property to `False`, you force the record to be saved. The `Requery` method then causes the control to redo the query that is its `Rowsource`. Put the form back into Form view and change the city by typing in a new value (the example uses Wantagh). Then pull down the list again and you see the newly added city as part of the list (see Figure 12.15).

12

Figure 12.15
The newly added city is
shown in the pull-down
list.

Next we look at a situation where the Rowsource of the control uses a table other than the
one to which the form is bound. Such instances occur when you are using a lookup table or
when you are populating a foreign key field. An example of this is the JobTitleID control
on frmEmployeeDetails.

Open the form in Design view and select the JobTitleID control (named cboJobTitle).
Then use the Code Builder to enter the following code:

```
Private Sub cboJobTitle_NotInList(NewData As String, Response As Integer)
Dim strSQL As String
Dim strMsg As String

'populate message text
strMsg = "The value " & NewData & " is not a listed JobTitle!"
strMsg = strMsg & vbCrLf & "Do you wish to add it?"

'Add data to table if user confirms
If MsgBox(strMsg, vbYesNo) = vbYes Then
    strSQL = "INSERT INTO tluJobTitles (JobTitle) Values('"
    strSQL = strSQL & NewData & "');"
    CurrentDb.Execute strSQL
    Response = acDataErrAdded
Else
    Response = acDataErrContinue
    Me.cboJobTitle.Undo
End If

End Sub
```

Return the form and type **HR Manager** as the Job Title. You get a message box, as shown in
Figure 12.16, asking whether you want to add the value.

Figure 12.16
A message box prompts
the user whether he
wants to add the
unlisted value.

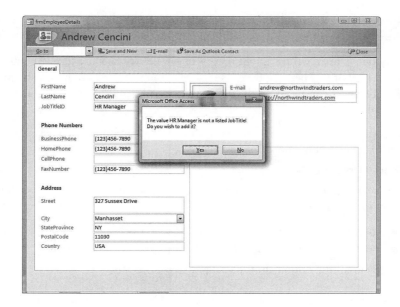

If you select Yes, the value is added, and you are returned to the form. Figure 12.17 shows
the value added to the Job Titles lookup table.

Figure 12.17
The value HR Manager is
added to the Job Titles
lookup table.

If the user makes a mistake, she can back out of adding the new value by selecting No
when prompted to add the value. The `If` statement sets the `Response` to `acDataErrContinue`
and uses the `Undo` method to clear the entry.

Working with Option Groups

An *option group* is a control that contains a collection of other Boolean controls, such as

- Check box
- Radio button
- Toggle button

You can select the type of control from the wizard when you place the option group on the form. Or you can just drag the control onto the group.

Only one control within an option group can be selected at a time. When you select one control, all others become deselected. Each control in the group has an `Option Value` property. The `Value` property of the group is assigned from the `Option` value of the selected control.

To review option groups, refer to the Round Time example we worked on in Chapter 4, "Using Built-in Functions."

→ **See** "A Conversion and Date Example," **p. 46**.

We are going to make a copy of `frmRoundTime` and modify it to illustrate how to manipulate an option group to perform these tasks:

- Display the value of the chosen option in a text box.
- Use a text box to set the value of the group.
- Clear all the options in the group.

To start, select `frmRoundTime` and then select Copy, Paste from the Home ribbon. Name the copy `frmGroupDemo`, and then open the copy in Design view. Now add a text box to the form and name it `txtTest`.

Select the group and select the `After Update` event of the group. Using the Code Builder, enter the following line of code:

```
txtTest = optType
```

To test this, place the form in Form view and select the buttons within the group. You will see the text box display either a 1 or 2 as you select either radio button (see Figure 12.18).

Figure 12.18
The selected value of the group shown in `frmGroupDemo`.

Place the form back in Design view, select the `txtTest` text box, and open the `After Update` event in the Code Builder. Enter the following code:

```
On Error Resume Next
optType = CInt(txtTest)
```

The On Error Resume Next command covers the user entering an invalid value (in this case other than a 1 or a 2). The code continues, and the Opt Group is cleared. Test this by putting the form back in Form view and typing 1, 2, or anything else in the text box.

Finally, add a button to the form (without the wizard), name it cmdDisable, and set the caption to Disable. Open the On Click event and use the Code Builder to add the following code:

```
Private Sub cmdDisable_Click()
Dim ctl As Control

For Each ctl In optType.Controls
    If ctl.ControlType = acOptionButton Then
        ctl.Enabled = False
    End If
Next ctl
End Sub
```

Because an option group contains other controls, it has its own Controls collections. This allows you to use a For...Each loop to cycle through all the controls in the group. However, because, there are controls other than the buttons (for example, labels), you need to make sure that the control has an Enabled property (which labels don't). Because each control has a ControlType property, you can test to see whether the control is a button by using a constant that the property returns, so that the control is disabled only if it's an option button.

This example is a bit impractical, because you can disable the group control in one shot by setting the group's Enabled property. However, this technique has a number of uses. For example, envision a questionnaire where different questions might have a different set of answers. This technique would allow you to alter the option group to conform to the needs of the question.

12

Working with Multiselect Controls

Just as combo boxes can do something that list boxes can't, so can a list box do some things that a combo box can't. One of those things is allow the user to select multiple items from the list. In its default setting, the list box can accept only one selection. But list boxes have a MultiSelect property. By setting its value to Simple or Extended, the user can then select more than one item from the list.

Most of the time, you set this property during your design of the form. But it can be set using VBA. The syntax is

```
listboxname.MultiSelect = setting
```

where *setting* is one of three values, identified in Table 12.2.

Table 12.2 `MultiSelect` **Property Settings**

Setting	Description	Integer Value
None	Only allows single selections (the default setting).	0
Simple	Allows for selection or deselection of multiple items by single-clicking or pressing the space bar.	1
Extended	Allows for selection or deselection of multiple items by holding down the Shift key to select a block of items, or holding down the Shift key and using the down arrow to extend the selection over a contiguous block. You also can select a noncontiguous block by holding down the Ctrl key and clicking on multiple items.	2

Because it is a violation of normalization rules to store multiple values in a single field, you won't be using a multiselect list box as a bound control. Generally, you use such a control to provide criteria to a query or report.

Determining What Is and Isn't Selected

With most controls, getting the value is simply a matter of referring to the control. For example:

```
x = Me.controlname
```

However, a multiselect list box requires more complex VBA because there are multiple values to deal with. To capture the multiple values you use a `For...Each` statement that cycles through the control's select items.

→ To review the `For...Each` statement, **see** "Using Collections," **p. 105**.

To illustrate using a multiselect list box, we are going to start by creating a new form (see Figure 12.19). This form will include a list box control so that you can select which products to display on the report `rptDailyInvTrans`.

1. From the Create ribbon, select Form Design to open a blank form in Design view.

2. From the Design ribbon, make sure the wizards are active and select the list box control.

3. Follow the wizard to create a list box that displays the item list.

4. Name the list box `lstItems`.

5. Set the `MultiSelect` property to `Extended`.

Figure 12.19
The new form with a list box and the `MultiSelect` property set to `Extended`.

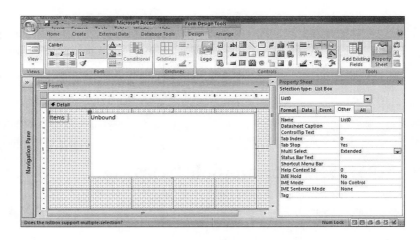

6. Take the control wizards off and add a button to the form.

7. Name the control `cmdPreview` and set the caption to `Preview`.

8. Use the Code Builder to enter the following code in the `On Click` event:

```
Private Sub cmdPreview_Click()
Dim strWhere As String
Dim varItem As Variant
Dim lst As Access.ListBox
Set lst = Me.lstitems

'Check to make sure at least one item is selected
If lst.ItemsSelected.Count = 0 Then
    MsgBox "No items selected. Please select an item.", vbOKOnly
    Exit Sub
End If

'Cycle through selected items
strWhere = ""
For Each varItem In lst.ItemsSelected
    strWhere = strWhere & "[TransactionItem] = " & lst.ItemData(varItem) & "
Or "
Next
strWhere = Left(strWhere, Len(strWhere) - 4)
DoCmd.OpenReport "rptDailyInvTrans", acViewPreview, , strWhere

End Sub
```

The `For...Each` loop builds a `Where` statement of the selected items in the list box. Return to the form in Form view. Select multiple items in the list and the click the Preview button. The report displays only the selected items. The `If` statement is used to ensure that at least one item is selected.

12

NOTE

Access 2007 has a new data type that allows you to store multiple items in a field. However, such fields are not compatible with other database engines and violate normalization rules. I will make you aware of them, but I do not recommend their use.

Case Study: Selecting Multiple Items

If you use the Form Wizard to design your forms, the first step is a screen where you select the fields to appear on the form, as shown in Figure 12.20.

Figure 12.20
In the first step of the Form Wizard you select the fields to go on the form.

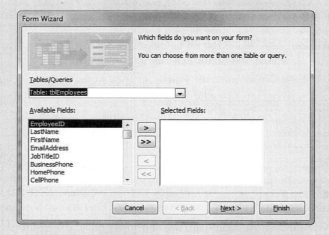

You can duplicate this functionality in your own forms to visibly show selected items. This case study illustrates how to do that, by selecting employees.

1. Open a blank form from the Create ribbon. Name it `frmSelectedEmps`.
2. Place two unbound list boxes on the form, side by side with about an inch between them. Make them 2.5 inches in width. Name the left one `lstEmps` and the right one `lstSelected`.
3. Set both list boxes to a `RowSourceType` of `Value List`. Set the Column Count to 2, and the Column Widths to `0";2.5"`. Set the `MultiSelect` property to `Extended`.
4. Place two command buttons between the two list boxes, one above the other. Name the top one `cmdSelect` and the bottom one `cmdDeselect`.
5. Set the `Caption` of `cmdSelect` to a right bracket (>) and the `Caption` of `cmdDeselect` to a left bracket (<).
6. Add a text box below the other controls and name it `txtEmployees` (see Figure 12.21). Set the `Visible` property to `No`.
7. Add a third button below the other two and name it `cmdPlace`. This is used as a placeholder for the focus.

12

Figure 12.21
The new
`frmSelectedEmps`
in Design view with the
controls added.

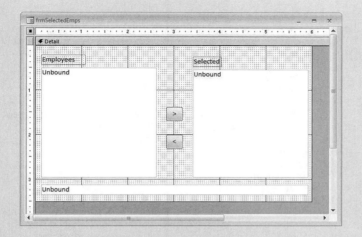

8. Add the following declarations to the `Declarations` section of the form module:

```
Dim tbox As TextBox
Dim lbox1 As ListBox
Dim lbox2 As ListBox
Dim frm As Form
```

9. Using the Code Builder add the following code to the form's On Open event:

```
Private Sub Form_Open(Cancel As Integer)
    Set frm = Forms(Me.Name)
    Set tbox = frm!txtEmployees
    Set lbox1 = frm!lstEmps
    Set lbox2 = frm!lstSelected
    SetRowSource
End Sub
```

10. Add a code procedure that populates the two list boxes. This procedure is called when the form first opens or when either of the buttons is selected. The code snippet is as follows:

```
Private Sub SetRowSource()
    Dim RowSource As String
    Dim db As Database
    Dim rs As Recordset
    Dim strSQL As String

    Set db = CurrentDb()
    'Define Employee list
    strSQL = "SELECT EmployeeID, [Lastname] & ', ' & [FirstName]"
    strSQL = strSQL & " AS FullName, [lastname], [firstname] FROM _
        tblEmployees "
    strSQL = strSQL & "WHERE ((('" & tbox & "') Not Like '*;' & _
        [employeeID] & ';*')) "
    strSQL = strSQL & "ORDER BY lastname, firstname"
    Set rs = db.OpenRecordset(strSQL)
    RowSource = ""
```

12

```
                    'Populate employee listbox
                    Do Until rs.EOF
                        RowSource = RowSource & rs!EmployeeID & ";'" & rs!FullName & "';"
                        rs.MoveNext
                    Loop
                    lbox1.RowSource = RowSource
                    RowSource = ""
                    'Define selected list
                    strSQL = "SELECT EmployeeID, [LastName] & ', ' & [FirstName] "
                    strSQL = strSQL & "AS FullName FROM tblEmployees "
                    strSQL = strSQL & "WHERE ((('" & tbox & "') Like '*;' & _
                    [EmployeeID] & ';*')) "
                    strSQL = strSQL & "ORDER BY lastname, firstname;"
                    Set rs = db.OpenRecordset(strSQL)
                    'Populate selected list
                    Do Until rs.EOF
                        RowSource = RowSource & rs!EmployeeID & ";'" & rs!FullName & "';"
                        rs.MoveNext
                    Loop
                    lbox2.RowSource = RowSource

                End Sub
```

11. Using the Code Builder add the following code to the cmdSelect button:

```
Private Sub cmdSelect_Click()
    If lbox1.ItemsSelected.Count > 0 Then
        For Each var In lbox1.ItemsSelected
            tbox = tbox & ";" & lbox1.ItemData(var)
        Next var
        tbox = tbox & ";"

        SetRowSource
        If lbox1.ListCount = 0 Then
            cmdPlace.SetFocus
            cmdSelect.Enabled = False
        End If
        cmdDeselect.Enabled = True
    End If

End Sub
```

12. Using the Code Builder add the following code to the cmdDeselect button:

```
Private Sub cmdDeselect_Click()
    Dim I As Integer

    If lbox2.ItemsSelected.Count > 0 Then
        tbox = Null
        For I = 0 To lbox2.ListCount - 1
            If lbox2.Selected(I) = False Then
                tbox = tbox & ";" & lbox2.ItemData(I)
            End If
        Next I
        tbox = tbox & ";"
        SetRowSource
```

```
        If lbox2.ListCount = 0 Then
            cmdPlace.SetFocus
            cmdDeselect.Enabled = False
        End If
        cmdSelect.Enabled = True
    End If

End Sub
```

The completed form should look similar to the one shown in Figure 12.22.

Figure 12.22
The completed
frmSelectedEmps
with two employees
selected.

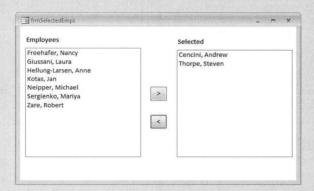

Let's now look at this code and how it works. The first snippet sets up module-level variables to be used throughout the other code snippets. The second snippet in the On Open event, populates the variables and passes control to the heart of the code, the Rowsource procedure. This procedure is where the two list boxes are populated. A key component here is the hidden text box. This text box contains a delimited string that represents the selected employeeIDs.

> **TIP**
>
> You might want to leave the text box visible initially to watch how the code works.

First, a recordset is defined for the employees to exclude any employees that have been selected according to the text box. The Where clause using the IN operator does this. The recordset is then looped through adding each selected employee to the Rowsource value list. Then the Selected list box is populated, using the employees listed in the text box.

The other two code snippets go behind the two buttons. The code for the cmdSelect button cycles through the ItemsSelected collection, adding each employeeID to the text box with a ; separator. It then calls the Rowsource procedure to repopulate the lists. The code snippet for the cmdDeselect button also cycles through the whole list, adds those not selected to the text box, and then calls the RowSource procedure.

Now there is a final piece to this. The form as constructed doesn't do anything but show selected and unselected items. You can use the list in the hidden text box to make use of the selected items by using an IN clause, as the Recordsource procedure does create a query that shows the selected records. This query can then be used as the Recordsource of a form or report.

12

Working with Other Controls

13

Working with Text Boxes

Text boxes are the most common data controls used on forms. There are a number of things you can do in VBA to manipulate text boxes. As shown in previous chapters you can ensure that the data entered is valid and appropriate. In this chapter we review some of the major properties of text box controls and some practical ways to use those properties programmatically.

Key Properties of Text Boxes

As you have designed forms and while reading through this book, you probably have already become familiar with many of the properties of text boxes. You may have set many of them manually through the Properties dialog. Most of these properties can be manipulated using VBA. However, using VBA with some of them is more practical than with others. Table 13.1 shows you some of the properties that are useful to address in your code.

Table 13.1   Key Properties of the Text Box Control

Property	Description
BackColor	The color shown as the background of the control.
BorderColor	The color of the border around the control.
ControlSource	The source of the data the control displays; this could be an expression but is usually a field in the Recordsource of the form.
Enabled	Indicates whether the control can receive focus. A Yes value indicates it can; No means it cannot.
FontBold	Indicates whether the control's text is displayed in boldface (Yes) or not (No).
FontItalic	Indicates whether the control's text is displayed in italics (Yes) or not (No).
FontName	Indicates the name of the font used by the control.
FontSize	The size in points for the font used by the control.
ForeColor	The color used to display the text within the control.
Locked	Indicates whether the control can be edited (No) or cannot (Yes).
OldValue	The previous value of the control before it was edited.
SelText	The selected text within a text box.
Tag	Used to group controls by applying a tag to each control in a group.
Text	The current text within a text box.
Value	The edited value in the control; this is the default property, so generally doesn't need to be specified.
Visible	Indicates whether a control is visible (Yes) or hidden (No).

These properties control the appearance and behavior of the text box as the user interfaces with the form. Four of these properties deal directly with the text entered into the control. Three of these properties—SelText, OldValue, and Text—refer only to the control that currently has focus. Were you to try and retrieve the Text property of a text box that doesn't have focus, the result would be an error message.

The color properties take a value that represents a color. If you know the value you can enter it, or you can click the builder button (the ellipses) to open the palette dialog to select the color. The font properties take different values depending on the property. FontName takes the name of an installed font, FontSize take a number in points (72 points = 1 inch), and the others are Boolean values. The Enabled, Locked, and Visible properties are also Boolean values.

Another property that merits special comment is the Tag property. Access does not actually use this property. Its purpose is to provide a place to store data that can be associated with the control. We discuss using the Tag property later in this chapter, in the section "Working with the Tag Property."

Many of these properties are not unique to text boxes. They can be applied and used with other controls.

Tracking the Focus

When you enter a control the only indication that the control has focus may be the flashing cursor. This cursor is not always obvious. Inexperienced users may not understand the concept of focus and that only the control that has focus can accept input of data. You can help the user along using VBA by more obviously indicating which control has focus.

To accomplish this we first must create a couple of standalone procedures. The first procedure sets the background color of the control to black and the foreground color to white; the second sets it back to black on white.

Using the `basUDFs` module add the following two procedures:

```
Public Sub HasFocus(ctl As Control)
    'Set the control's colors to white on black
    On Error Resume Next
    ctl.BackColor = RGB(255,255,255)
    ctl.ForeColor = RGB(0,0,0)
End Sub

Public Sub LoseFocus(ctl As Control)
    'Set the control's colors to black on white
    On Error Resume Next
    ctl.BackColor = RGB(0,0,0)
    ctl.ForeColor = RGB(255,255,255)
End Sub
```

Access 2007 changes the way you can assign a color to a property. In previous versions, when you select a color from the color palette that appears when you click the builder button (the ellipses), a number was entered into the property. This number could be directly assigned to the property. With Access 2007 you must use the RGB function to define the color. This function uses a value from 0–255 for each of the colors (Red, Blue, Green). You can determine what the three values are for any color using the More Colors button on the Custom tab on the palette. You can move a target over the colors to determine the RGB values. Black is represented as 0,0,0 and White as 255,255,255.

13

These two procedures accept an argument of the type `Control`. You use the generic type to refer to any type of Access control, whether it be a text box, combo box, label, and so on. This allows the procedure to be reused for any control. There is a caution here because not every control has the `BackColor` property. So you need to include the `On Error Resume Next` line to account for those instances without causing the code to stop.

> **TIP**
>
> Some examples of controls that don't have a `BackColor` property are radio buttons, check boxes, command buttons, and subforms.

The next step is to use these procedures within the Form module. Pick any form (except for those in Datasheet view) and open the form in Design view. Select a control on the form and use the Code Builder for the `GotFocus` event. Enter the following line of code:

`HasFocus` *controlname*

where *controlname* is the name of the control. Repeat the process for the `LostFocus` event with the following code line:

`LoseFocus` *controlname*

We've set an example of this using the Manufacturer control of `frmInvDetails`. As you Tab into and out of any control where you use this code, you can see the color scheme turn to white on black and then back to black on white.

Figure 13.1
The `Manufacturer` control on `frmInvDetail` has focus.

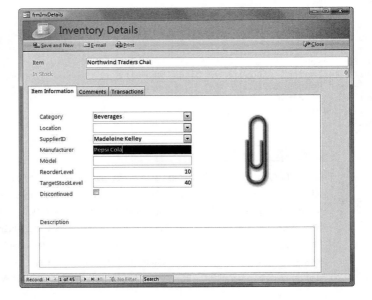

> **CAUTION**
>
> Make sure you are consistent in using this technique. Use the same color scheme and use it for all controls on all forms. Inconsistent user interfaces are difficult to use.

Working with Check Boxes, Radio Buttons, or Toggle Buttons

Check boxes, radio buttons, and toggle buttons are all Boolean controls. Such controls have three states: Yes, No, or Null. The values Yes and No are also represented by True and False or -1 and 0, so these controls are valuable when representing data that has just two values.

An example of using these controls is the Discontinued box on frmInvDetails. A checked control indicates that the item has been discontinued.

> **CAUTION**
>
> Although check boxes and radio buttons may seem an easy way to enter data, be cautious about using a lot of them. Overuse of these controls usually indicates a denormalized database structure. Do not use field names to describe data. An example of this would be if we had fields for each category and used check boxes to mark off each applicable category. A situation like that would require a child table.

One trick that you can use when dealing with Boolean controls is that the control's value can be set with an expression. To illustrate this, let's add a new field to tblemployees:

1. Open the table in Design view and add a date field named TerminationDate.
2. Open qryEmployeesExtended in Design view and add the TerminationDate field to it.
3. Open frmEmployeeDetails in Design view, add a check box control, and enter **Active** as the label.
4. In the On Current event of the form use the Code Builder to enter the following line of code:

```
Me.chkActive = IsNull([TerminationDate])
```

You can open the form in Form view, and as you cycle through the records you will see the that Active control is checked, as shown in Figure 13.2. Enter some termination dates in the table, and those records will be unchecked.

13

Figure 13.2
The Active box is
checked on
frmEmployee-
Details.

Working with Subforms

Subforms are, in themselves, another control. The contents of this control is a separate form. The subform, of course, contains its own set of controls, which may include another subform. One of the keys to working with subforms is how to reference the controls that they contain. As previously explained, you reference a control on a form using the following syntax:

```
Forms!formname!controlname
```

Because, in the case of a subform, the `controlname` only identifies the subform, you need more to reference the controls within the subform. So you need to use the following syntax:

```
Forms![mainformname].[subformcontrolname].Form![controlname]
```

Essentially the `.Form` property is telling Access that the `controlname` preceding it is a subform. For example, the form `frmInvDetails` contains a `Transactions` subform. To reference the `Quantity` control on that subform you would use

```
Forms!frmInvDetails.sfrmInvDetailTransactions.Form!txtQuantity
```

After you understand the referencing issue, working with subforms is no different from working with the main form.

13

Working with the Tag Property

The Tag property can be a bit mysterious to new VBA developers. After you learn what it does and how to use it, you may find it invaluable in designing dynamic forms. The tag property allows you to assign a value (a text string) to the control. This value can then be read from your code and used to determine an action to be taken respective to the control. Every control on a form has a Tag property. You, as developer, have full control over what is stored in it and how to use it.

To help you better understand how to use the Tag property let's revisit the HasFocus procedure we built earlier in this chapter. In its current coding, this procedure changes the foreground and background colors of the control that currently has focus to white on black. If you want to use a different color for certain controls, there isn't a property or command that does that. However, with the Tag property we can do it. To illustrate this, here's the changes you need to make:

1. Open frminvDetails in Design view.

2. Make sure the controls for Manufacturer, Model, Reorder Level, and Target Stock Level have their Got and Lost Focus events set to use the HasFocus and LoseFocus procedures.

3. Set the Tag property for the Manufacturer and Model controls to 0 and the Reorder Level and Target Stock Level controls to RGB(90,240,250).

4. Open the basUDFs module and modify the HasFocus procedure as follows:

```
Public Sub HasFocus(ctl As Control)
    'Set the control's colors to white on black
    On Error Resume Next
    ctl.BackColor = ctl.Tag
    ctl.ForeColor = RGB(90,240,250)
End Sub
```

5. Save the form and switch back to Form view.

As you Tab into and out of those four controls, you will see that a different backcolor is used for the different controls.

> **CAUTION**
>
> The Tag property is not the same as the SmartTags property. Be careful not to confuse them.

13

Case Study: An Audit Trail

Sometimes you will need to maintain a history of changes you make to your data. If you change an employee's name or title, you may need to know what the previous data was. You may also need to know when a record was changed and by whom. Doing this is usually referred to as an *audit trail*. This case study shows you one way to keep such a history of changes.

The first step in setting up the audit trail is to add a table to your database. From the Create ribbon select Table Design. Add the following fields (see Figure 13.3):

- `AuditID`—Autonumber—Primary key
- `Tablename`—Text
- `RecordID`—Number/Long Integer
- `Fieldname`—Text
- `OldValue`—Text
- `NewValue`—Text
- `EditedBy`—Text
- `EditedWhen`—Date

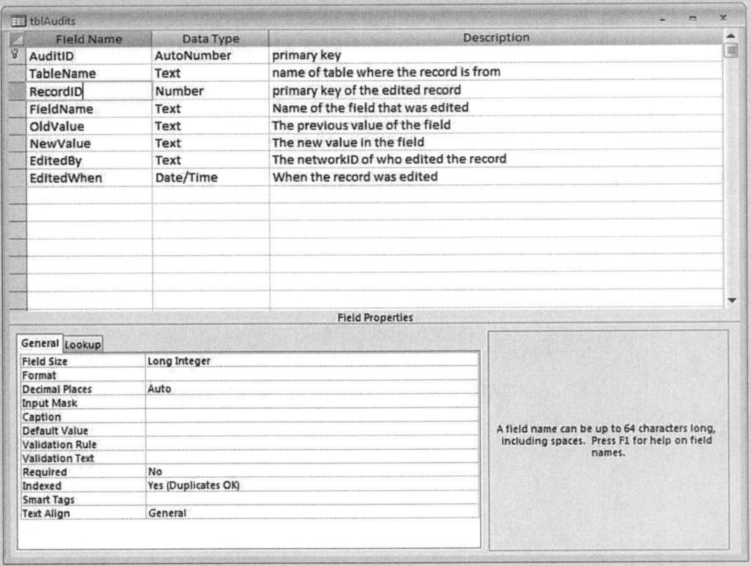

Figure 13.3
`tblAudits` in Design mode, showing the fields added.

The next step is to create a procedure that populates the table. Open `basUDFs` in Design view and enter the following code:

```
Public Sub Audit(strTable As String, strField As String, _
    strOld As String, strNew As String, lngRec As Long)

Dim strSQL As String

strSQL = "INSERT INTO tblAudits (RecordID, TableName, FieldName, "
strSQL = strSQL & "OldValue, NewValue, EditedBy, EditedWhen) "
strSQL = strSQL & "Values(" & lngRec & ", '" & strTable & "', '" & strField
strSQL = strSQL & "', '" & strOld & "', '" & strNew & "', '"
strSQL = strSQL & Environ("UserName") & "', #" & Now() & "#);"
CurrentDb.Execute strSQL

End Sub
```

Now you need to open `frmEmployeeDetails` in Design view. The first task is to add the `EmployeeID` field to the form. Open the `Field` list and drag the field onto the form under the job title. Set the `Name` property to `txtEmployeeID` and set the `Visible` property to No. Now select the `Lastname` control and select the `After Update` event. Use the Code Builder to add the following line of code:

```
Call Audit("tblEmployees", "LastName", Me.txtLastName.OldValue, _
Me.txtLastName, Me.txtEmployeeID)
```

Restore the form to Form view and change the last name of one of the employees. Open `tblAudits`, and you see a record of the change as shown in Figure 13.4.

Figure 13.4
`tblAudits` showing an edited record.

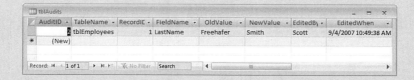

Using this method, you can select which fields you want to include in the audit by only calling the `Audit` procedure in the `After Update` event of the selected controls.

13

Working with Reports

An Introduction to the Report Module and Events

As discussed previously, your VBA code can be stored in either a standard or object module. Most of your code will be in object modules attached to a form or report. The code is saved as part of the object and supports events and properties specific to that object.

Almost all the code that you write for an object module is placed within event procedures to be triggered when some action occurs. For example, if you enter code into the report's On Open event, that code runs when the report opens. One use of this would be to maximize the report when you first open it. Following is how to do that:

1. Select the report rptinvToReorder and open it in Design view.
2. Select the On Open event and use the Code Builder to enter the following code:

```
Private Sub Report_Open(Cancel As Integer)
    DoCmd.Maximize
End Sub
```

3. Save the report.
4. Double-click the report to open it.

When the report opens, it is maximized according to your setup.

> **NOTE**
> If you have Access set to use the tabbed document interface, the report is maximized to a tab; otherwise, it covers the whole document pane.

14

Opening and Closing Reports

Part of your job as developer is to make it easy for the user to access the objects you have created for them. Many developers feel that the user should not see the Navigation pane (or the Database window in earlier versions). Instead, the user should be presented with a menu that allows him to more intuitively choose what objects to open.

Opening a Report

In previous chapters, we created a couple of forms that allow you to open reports. One such form is frmDateRange, which runs rptInvTransByDate filtered for a specific date range. The code behind the Preview button on that form is as follows:

```
Private Sub cmdPreview_Click()
    On Error GoTo cmdPreview_Click_Err
    DoCmd.OpenReport "rptInvTransByDate", acViewPreview
Exit_cmdPreview_Click:
    Exit Sub
cmdPreview_Click_Err:
    MsgBox "Error " & Err.Number & ":" & Err.Description
    Resume Exit_cmdPreview_Click
End Sub
```

Let's take a closer look at the OpenReport method. You may notice it's similar to the OpenForm method we dealt with in Chapter 10, "Working with Forms." They both are methods of the DoCmd object and have similar arguments. The syntax for the OpenReport method is as follows:

```
DoCmd.OpenReport reportname [, view] [, filtername] [, wherecondition]
[, windowmode] [, openargs]
```

where reportname is a required argument that is a string expression that names the report being opened. Table 14.1 lists the optional arguments for the OpenReport method. Tables 14.2 and 14.3 provide lists of the constants that can be used for two of the arguments.

Table 14.1 OpenReport **Optional Arguments**

Argument	Data Type	Explanation
view	Constant	Determines how the report is viewed based on one of the intrinsic constants listed in Table 14.2
filtername	Variant	A string expression that represents the name of a stored query
wherecondition	Variant	A string expression similar to a valid SQL WHERE clause excluding the WHERE keyword
windowmode	Constant	Determines the mode of the report based on one of the intrinsic constants listed in Table 14.3
openargs	Variant	A string expression or value that is then passed to the report's openargs property

Table 14.2 View **Argument Constants**

Constant	Integer Value	Explanation
acViewNormal	0	Sends the report directly to the printer
acViewDesign	1	Opens the report in Design view
acViewPreview	2	Opens the report in Print Preview view

Table 14.3 Windowmode **Argument Constants**

Constant	Integer Value	Explanation
acWindowNormal	0	Dependent on the report's properties
acHidden	1	Opens the report, but as a hidden object
acIcon	2	Opens the report, but minimizes it as an icon on the Windows taskbar
acDialog	3	Opens the report as a dialog box if the Modal and Popup properties are set to Yes

In practice, you will use only the acViewNormal and acViewpreview constants for the View argument. Generally, you will want to give the user the opportunity to preview the report before wasting paper on it. The user can then choose to print the report from the Print menu on the Office button or from a button you create for the user.

Of the Windowmode constants, you will almost always use acWindowNormal. The other three have value when dealing with forms but not with reports.

The OpenReport method in the code behind the Preview button on frmdateRange:

```
DoCmd.OpenReport "rptInvTransByDate", acViewPreview
```

opens rptInvTransByDate in Print Preview mode. Because that's all you want to do, there is no need for the other arguments. Because the report is bound to a query that uses the Date Range entered on the form to filter the results, there is no need for a *filtername* or *where-condition*. However, you could modify the code to use one of them, depending on which is better for the task.

Closing a Report

When closing a report, you use the Close method of the DoCmd object using the following syntax:

```
DoCmd.Close [objecttype] [, objectname] [, save]
```

All the arguments for the Close method are optional. If none are used, VBA closes the object that currently has focus. If you want to close a specific report, you need to explicitly reference the report name using the *objectname* argument, and you need to identify the *objecttype* using the acReport intrinsic constant. The final argument, *save* is used to save design changes to the report, not data. It uses three constants:

- acSavePrompt—Prompts the user to choose whether to save. Has an integer value of 0.

- acSaveYes—Saves any design changes made since the report was opened. Has an integer value of 1.

- acSaveNo—Ignores any design changes when closing the report. This is the default setting and has an integer value of 2.

Passing Arguments Using OpenArgs

Although the OpenForm method has long had the OpenArgs argument, it wasn't added to reports until Access 2003. In a similar way that you can pass arguments to functions and procedures, the OpenArgs argument allows you to pass values to reports (and forms).

The OpenArgs argument is part of the OpenReport method; its function is to populate the OpenArgs property of the report with the value of the argument. The property belongs to the report, and its function is to receive and store the passed value.

→   To learn more about using the OpenArgs argument and property with forms, **see** "Passing Arguments Using OpenArgs," **p. 133**.

One example of how to use this involves reports that have group totals. At times you will want to see all the detail in the report. But at other times you may want to see only the totals for each group—in other words, just a summary. You can use the OpenArgs argument to pass a value to the report that tells Access to hide or display the detail.

1. Open frmSelectedItems in Design view. Add an unbound check box to the form and name it chkDetail. Change the label caption to Detail.

2. Set the check box's Default value property to -1 so it's selected by default.

3. Select the Preview button and open the On Click event. Make sure the report name is set to rptQOHbyCategory. Add an OpenArgs argument as follows:

   DoCmd.OpenReport "rptQOHbyCategory", acViewPreview, , strWhere,,chkDetail

4. Save and close the form.

5. Open rptQOHbyCategory in Design view. Add the following line of code to the On Open event:

   Me.Detail.Visible = Me.OpenArgs

6. Save and close the report.

7. Reopen frmSelectedItems and select all the items.

8. Uncheck the Detail check box (see Figure 14.1).

Figure 14.1
`frmSelected-`
`items` is ready to run
the report.

9. Click the Preview button to run the report. Figure 14.2 shows the summarized report.

Figure 14.2
The report with the
Detail band hidden.

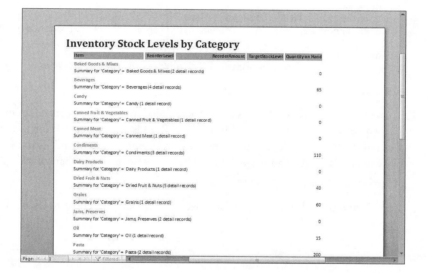

When you open the report with the check box in its checked state, the `OpenArgs` argument passes the value `True` (or `Yes`) to the report. If unchecked, the value `False` (or `No`) is passed. By setting the `Visible` property of the Detail band to the value of the `OpenArgs` property, you are telling the Detail band to be visible (`Yes`) or hidden (`No`).

Populating the Report

Reports are generally bound to a table or query to get their data. Often, however, you want to see only a partial subset of the data in the report's `RecordSource`. Rather than create several reports for each condition, you have the option of filtering the records the report uses. One way to do this is to pass criteria from a form to the report's underlying query. That method can be seen with `frmDateRange`. But an alternative is to use the *wherecondition* argument of the `OpenReport` method.

14

The form `frmSelectedItems` also illustrates use of this *wherecondition* argument. Let's review what the code behind the Preview button does:

```
Private Sub cmdPreview_Click()
Dim strWhere As String
Dim varItem As Variant
Dim lst As Access.ListBox
Set lst = Me.lstitems

'Check to make sure at least one item is selected
If lst.ItemsSelected.Count = 0 Then
    MsgBox "No items selected. Please select an item.", vbOKOnly
    Exit Sub
End If

'Cycle through selected items
strWhere = ""
For Each varItem In lst.ItemsSelected
    strWhere = strWhere & "[TransactionItem] = " & lst.ItemData(varItem) & " Or "
Next
strWhere = Left(strWhere, Len(strWhere) - 4)
DoCmd.OpenReport "rptQOHbyCategory", acViewPreview, , strWhere, , chkDetail

End Sub
```

Because the list box is set up as a multiselect list box, the user can select multiple items. The `For…Each` loop near the end of the code builds a `Where` clause for use by the `OpenReport` method. If, for example, the user chooses two items—Northwind Traders Almonds and Northwind Traders Walnuts—the loop builds a `Where` clause that looks like this:

```
[TransactionItem] = 74 Or [TransactionItem] = 14
```

This is then passed to the report and used to restrict the report to those two items (see Figure 14.3).

Figure 14.3
The report with only the two selected items.

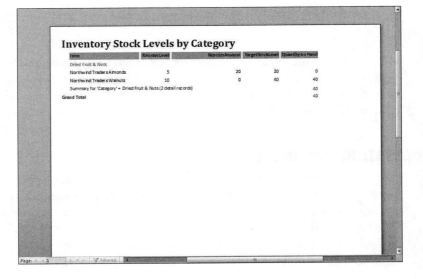

This method is a bit more complex than just passing criteria to a query from a form, but it does have its advantages. There is no correct or incorrect way here. Which method you choose depends on your requirements.

Applying a Filter and Sort Order

There is yet another method you can use to limit the records a report presents. Reports (and also forms) have properties that allow you to apply filters to the data used by the report.

- `Filter`—A string expression that contains a field name, operator, and value such as a SQL `WHERE` clause sans the `WHERE` keyword.
- `FilterOn`—Applies the filter specified in the `Filter` property.
- `OrderBy`—Determines the sort order for the records; however, the report's native sort(s) take precedence over this property.
- `OrderByOn`—Applies the sort specified in the `OrderBy` property.

Using VBA to set the `Filter` and `FilterOn` properties also allows you the flexibility to use the same report to display different sets of records.

To set a filter string, you use the following syntax:

```
Me.Filter = filterstring
```

where `filterstring` represents the expression comparing a field to a particular value. For instance, if you want to filter `rptDailyInvTrans` for a specific day, you would use the following command:

```
Me.Filter = "[TransDate] = #3/22/06#"
```

This would need to be followed by setting the `FilterOn` property:

```
Me.FilterOn = True
```

To disable the filter you would set the `FilterOn` property to `False`.

To set the sorting procedures you use syntax similar to the SQL `ORDER BY` clause by listing the fields in the order you want them sorted. You can also use the `DESC` keyword if you need the field to be sorted in reverse order. To sort `rptDailyInvTrans` by date in descending order and then by item, you would enter:

```
Me.OrderBy = "TransDate DESC, Item"
```

followed by

```
Me.OrderByOn = True
```

14

Handling Report-Level Errors

Even though reports don't do as much processing as forms, they are still subject to coding errors. You can handle these errors using a special event for reports, the On Error event. The event utilizes two arguments for passing error values to the event:

- DataErr—Contains the error code returned from the Err object.
- Response—Indicates whether the error message is displayed by using one of the following intrinsic constants: acDataErrContinue ignores the error, and acDataErrDisplay shows the default message. Using acDataErrContinue also allows you to display your own custom message.

By using the On Error event you can capture the error code and determine how you want to deal with it. We'll look at a quick example using rptDailyInvTrans:

1. Open rptDailyInvTrans in Design view and change the RecordSource to Bogus.
2. Save and close the report.
3. Run rptDailyInvTrans from the Navigation pane. This produces the error shown in Figure 14.4.

Figure 14.4
Running the report produces an error.

4. Click OK to clear the message.
5. Open the report in Design view and use the Code Builder to add the following code to the On Error event:

```
Private Sub Report_Error(DataErr As Integer, Response As Integer)
If DataErr = 2580 Then
    MsgBox "The RecordSource " & Me.RecordSource & _
    " is not valid. Please correct!", vbOKOnly, "Error"
    Response = acDataErrContinue
End If
End Sub
```

6. Run the report again. You now get the custom error message as shown in Figure 14.5.

14

Figure 14.5
The customized error message.

What to Do When There Is No Data

Previewing a report and having it open with no data to display can be embarrassing. The user may not understand why the report is blank and may be frustrated by his inability to get the data he thinks he should get. This issue can be avoided in a couple of ways depending on how the report is called. If it's being run directly, the best choice is to use the `NoData` event to cancel the report with or without a custom message.

We illustrate this using `rptInvTransByDate`. Open the report in Design view and use the Code Builder to add the following code:

```
Private Sub Report_NoData(Cancel As Integer)
    MsgBox "No records are available to print!", vbOKOnly, "No Data"
    Cancel = True
End Sub
```

Run the report directly from the Navigation pane. You first are prompted to enter the date parameters. This is because the form that normally kicks off the report is closed. Just click OK for the two dates, and you see the message box you coded (see Figure 14.6).

Figure 14.6
A message box showing no records were returned.

Working with Subreports

Just as with forms there are times when you need to deal with data from multiple tables where a multitable query doesn't do the job for you. In those instances, you can use a subreport to display the other data. Working with subreports is similar to working subforms.

→ To review how to work with subforms, **see** "Working with Subforms," **p. 182**.

The key, as with subforms, is referencing the controls on the subreport. The syntax for that is

```
Reports![mainformname].[subreportcontrolname].Report![controlname]
```

The `.Report` property is telling Access that the preceding control is a subreport that contains other controls, so Access needs to look on the subreport for the control.

14

Case Study: Product Catalog

A common aid used with sales materials is a picture catalog showing your products. Access can be used to create such a catalog, something we'll demonstrate in this Case Study.

First you need to create a report. Use the Report Wizard and create a report from qryInventoryExtended. Include the Item, Description, Category, and Company Name columns. Group on Category. Save the report as `rptCatalog`, and then go to Design. Modify the layout so it looks like Figure 14.7.

Figure 14.7
The layout for the catalog.

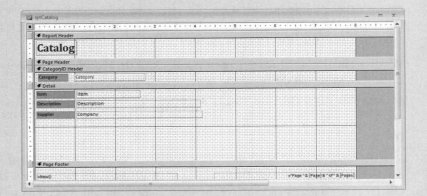

Next, add an unbound image control. When it prompts you to select a picture, use the `notavail.jpg` file in the folder for this chapter. This assigns the image file as the `Picture` property of the control. The result should look like Figure 14.8.

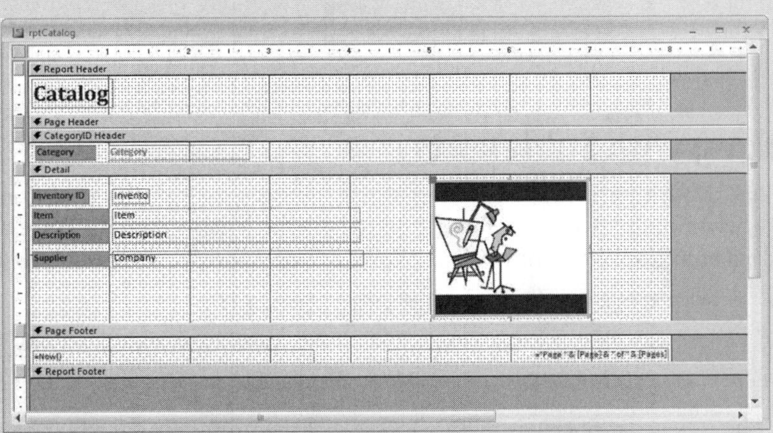

Figure 14.8
Adding the image control to the report layout for the catalog.

The next step is to use VBA to assign the correct picture for the current record to the control. For this you use the On Format event and the following code snippet:

```
Private Sub Detail_Format(Cancel As Integer, FormatCount As Integer)
Dim strPath As String

'setup full path anf file
strPath = CurrDBDir() & Me.InventoryID & ".jpg"

'Populate image control
If Dir(strPath) = "" Then
    Me.imgItem.Picture = CurrDBDir() & "notavail.jpg"
Else
    Me.imgItem.Picture = strPath
End If

End Sub
```

The images for the products are saved with the `InventoryID` as the filename. This code checks for the presence of the image and, if it's not found, it uses a default image. The next step is to view the report in Print Preview view. The result appears in Figure 14.9.

Figure 14.9
The finished catalog report.

Menus, Navigation, and Ribbons

Introducing Menus

As the developer, it's your task to make navigating around the application as easy and intuitive for the user as you can. One of the prime ways you do this is by using menus.

A *menu* is simply a list of options the user can choose from to interact with the application. With Access 2007, you have a new option, *ribbons*, which replace the custom menus of previous versions. You also have the Navigation pane, which is more customizable than the Database window of previous versions.

And, there is still the old standby of using forms to create menus by using buttons and lists on the form.

All these options are discussed in this chapter.

Creating Form-Based Menus

Form-based menus use command buttons and/or selection controls to present users with choices of functions they can select. Let's start with a simple menu to add data to the three main tables: Employees, Suppliers, and Items.

1. Open a blank form in Design view from the Form Design icon of the Create menu. Turn off the control wizards.

2. Select the Label control from the Controls section of the Design ribbon and draw a label near the top left of the form. Set the `Caption` property to `Add Data`.

3. Select the Command Button control and draw a button under the caption.

4. Set the `Caption` property to `Employees` and name the button `cmdAddEmp`.

5. Use the Code Builder to add the following code to the On Click event:

    ```
    DoCmd.OpenForm "frmEmployeeDetails", , , , acFormAdd
    ```

    By using the DataMode intrinsic constant acFormAdd, the form is opened in Add mode with a blank record.

6. Repeat steps 3–5 to add buttons for Suppliers (frmSupplierDetails) and Items (frmInvDetails).

7. Set the Record Selectors and Navigation Buttons properties of the form to No and the Scroll Bars property to Neither. Set the Caption property of the form to Main Menu.

The finished form looks like the one shown in Figure 15.1.

Figure 15.1
The form as a main menu with three buttons.

You can test each of the buttons, and you will see it opens each form to a new, blank record. The next thing we want to do is expand our menu to open forms for editing existing data.

1. Expand the form to the right a couple of inches.

2. Add a label with the caption Edit Data.

3. Add three more command buttons; name them **cmdEditEmps**, **cmdEditSupps**, and **cmdEditItems**.

4. Open the On Click event for each button and add the following code:

    ```
    DoCmd.OpenForm "frmEmployeeDetails"
    ```

In this case, we don't need the DataMode because we are using the default, which is Edit mode (see Figure 15.2).

Figure 15.2
The main menu with the
added Edit section.

You can continue this way and add buttons for every form or report you want to edit. But if you do that, your form gets awfully crowded. Under these circumstances you may need to use multiple forms to organize your menu options. So, let's start a new form but make it more flexible.

1. Open a blank form in Design view from the Form Design icon of the Create menu. Turn off the control wizards.

2. Add a label to the form with the caption `Main Menu`.

3. Add an option group (using the wizard) with two options: `Add` and `Edit` and a caption of `Add/Edit`. Name it **optAction**.

4. Add another option group (using the wizard) with three options: `Employees`, `Items`, and `Suppliers`, using the caption `Data`. Name it **optData**.

5. Use the Command Button Wizard to add a button that opens a form (any form will do). Use the default picture instead of a text description.

6. Delete the embedded macro created by the wizard and open the `On Click` event using the Code Builder. Enter the following code:

```
Private Sub cmdForm_Click()
Dim strDocument As String

Select Case optData
    Case 1
        strDocument = "frmEmployeeDetails"
    Case 2
        strDocument = "frmInvDetails"
    Case 3
        strDocument = "frmSupplierDetails"
    Case Else
        MsgBox "No data type selected!", vbOKOnly, "Error"
        GoTo ExitSub
End Select

Select Case optAction
    Case 1
        DoCmd.OpenForm strDocument, , , , acFormAdd
```

15

```
        Case 2
            DoCmd.OpenForm strDocument
        Case Else
            MsgBox "No action selected", vbOKOnly, "Error"
            GoTo ExitSub
    End Select

    ExitSub:
    End Sub
```

Figure 15.3 shows a more advanced menu setup.

Figure 15.3
A more advanced main
menu.

Now select an action and a data type and click the Form button on the bottom. This opens the appropriate form in the appropriate data mode. This menu provides more flexibility because you can simply add a data type to the Data option group and modify the one code snippet.

The next modification we will make to this menu form deals with reports. We will add a facility to select and run a report. The first thing we need to do to prepare for this functionality is to create a table for reports.

1. Open Table Design view from the Create ribbon.
2. Add three text fields: `Reportname` (set as primary key), `Description`, and `Formname`. The `Formname` is used if you need to open the report through a form that provides criteria to the report. Figure 15.4 shows the table in Design view.
3. Save the table, naming it `tblReports`.
4. Add records for `rptDailyInvTrans`, `rptEmployeePhoneList`, `rptinvStockLevels`, `rptInvTransByDate`, and `rptQOHbyCategory`. Figure 15.5 shows the completed records for those reports.
5. Save the table.
6. Return to `frmMainMenu` in Design mode.
7. Add a combo box to the form (at the bottom) using the wizard. Select to look up from a table and select `tblReports` as the table. Add all three fields and sort by `Description`. Check to hide the key column; expand the `Description` field and contract the `Formname` field so that it doesn't show. Use Reports as the label and finish the wizard.

Figure 15.4
The Reports table in Design view.

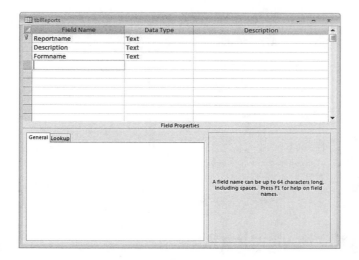

Figure 15.5
The Reports table with some records.

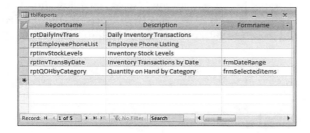

8. Name the combo box **cboReports** and use the Code Builder to add the following code to the After Update event:

```
Private Sub cboReports_AfterUpdate()
Dim varForm As Variant

varForm = Me.cboReports.Column(2)
If Len(varForm) = 0 Then
    DoCmd.OpenReport Me.cboReports, acViewPreview
Else
    DoCmd.OpenForm varForm
End If
End Sub
```

Figure 15.6 offers a look at the completed main menu.

Now test the menu, by selecting a report from the combo. If a form is needed the form will open; otherwise, the report opens in Preview mode. You could add a number of other things to the menu. For example, you could add a check box to print or preview the report. Or you could add criteria such as a date range if multiple reports allow for that.

15

Figure 15.6
The completed
main menu.

Managing the Navigation Pane

The Navigation pane is a new feature for Access 2007. It replaces the Database window of previous versions but does a lot more than the Database window did. The NavPane, as it's referred to, can be customized as to how it displays objects in your database. If you right-click on top of the NavPane and select Navigation Options, you get the dialog box shown in Figure 15.7.

Figure 15.7
The Navigation Options
dialog.

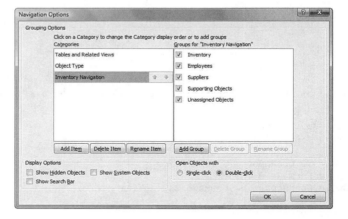

There are two levels of grouping objects within the NavPane: Categories and Groups. A category refers to the whole pane, whereas the groups are the divisions within the pane. Access gives you two preprogrammed categories:

- Tables and Related Views—Groups objects by the tables and the objects related to that table. For example, under `tblEmployee` are all the forms, queries, and reports related to that table (see Figure 15.8).

Figure 15.8
The `tblEmployees` category of the NavPane.

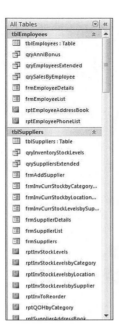

15

- Object Type—Groups objects by their object type—for instance, tables, queries, reports, and so on.

In addition to these two you can add your own custom categories. We're going to create a simple category just for data entry purposes. Follow these steps:

1. Right-click on the top of the NavPane and select Navigation Options. Or click the Office button, and select Access Options, Current Database, and the Navigation Options button.

2. In the Navigation Options dialog, click Add Item and name it **Data Entry**.

3. Click the Add Group button and name it **Employees**. Repeat the process for groups named **Items** and **Suppliers**.

4. Click OK to close the Options window and get back to the database.

5. Pull down the list at the top of the NavPane and select the Data Entry category. The three groups we added along with the default Unassigned group are displayed.

6. Right-click on `frmEmployeeDetails` and select Add to Group, Employees (see Figure 15.9).

Figure 15.9
Add `frmEmployee-Details` to the Employees group.

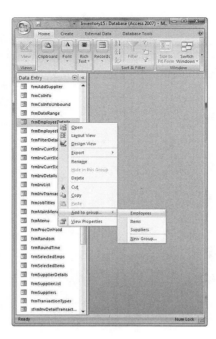

7. Repeat the process for `frminvDetails` and `frmSupplierDetails`.

8. Right-click on the Unassigned group header and select Hide.

The result is the menu shown in Figure 15.10, a menu just for the three main data entry forms.

But this book is about using VBA, so now that we have created the NavPane, let's see how to use it to customize how the application can appear to certain users.

Three new methods of the `DoCmd` object deal with the Navigation pane. Table 15.1 explains them.

Table 15.1   Navigation Pane Methods

Method	Arguments	Description
NavigateTo	*Category, Group*	Opens the specified category and group.
LockNavigationPane	*T/F*	A `True` value locks the NavPane preventing the user from deleting objects and shortcuts.
SetDisplayedCategories	*T/F, Category*	A `False` value hides the specified category.

With these three methods you can prevent the user from making some modifications to the NavPane, navigate to a specific category and group, and hide or display specific categories.

Figure 15.10
The finished Data Entry
NavPane category.

In addition to these, the command in prior versions that would hide the Database window hides the Navigation pane:

```
DoCmd.Runcommand acCmdWindowHide
```

The first thing we need to do is create a module that sets up the NavPane. Open the basUDFs module in Design view and add a procedure named DataEntryUsers with the following code:

```
Public Sub DataEntryUsers()
Dim lngTitle As Long

'Retrieve JobtitleId based on logon ID
lngTitle = Nz(DLookup("[JobtitleID]", "tblEmployees", "[EmailAddress] = '" & _
Environ("username") & "@NorthwindTraders.com'"),0)

'Setup NavPane according to Job title
Select Case lngTitle
    Case 10
        DoCmd.NavigateTo "Data Entry", "Suppliers"
    Case 17
        DoCmd.NavigateTo "Data Entry", "Employees"
    Case 18
        DoCmd.NavigateTo "Data Entry", "Items"
    Case Else
        DoCmd.NavigateTo "Inventory Navigation"

End Select

End Sub
```

15

Next, we need to add some code to the On Close event of rptInvtoReorder to set up the Navigation pane when the report closes. Open the report in Design view and use the Code Builder to add the following code line to the On Close event:

```
Call DataEntryUsers
```

Finally, to test this, you need to enter an employee with an email address of your username and @northwindtraders.com. if you want to see a specific group of the Data Entry category, set the JobTitle to either Marketing Assistant (Suppliers), HR (Employees), or Data Entry (Items). Then close Access and reopen the application.

If you don't use one of those three titles, you will see the Inventory Navigation category as shown in Figure 15.11.

Figure 15.11
The Inventory Navigation NavPane category.

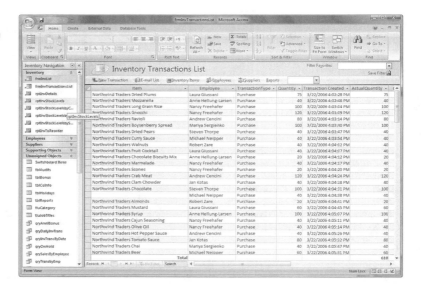

You might also want to create NavPanes specific to what the user is currently doing, such as working on a specific form. To call such a pane you would use the SetDisplayed-Categories method like so:

```
DoCmd.SetDisplayedCategories True, "Inventory Navigation"
```

You might use such code in the On Open event of a form to open the particular pane with the form.

Using Custom Ribbons

The most obvious new feature of Office 2007 is the "ribbon." The ribbon gives a more consistent interface to all the Office applications. Microsoft maintains that the ribbon presents a more coherent and intuitive user interface than the former collection of menus and toolbars, not to mention it's easier to use. Microsoft refers to the ribbon as the Microsoft Office Fluent user interface (UI). This new interface uses the new RibbonX API. Ribbon UI objects are defined by creating XML documents that declare the objects within the ribbon.

Creating custom ribbons is really beyond the scope of this book. Following are some resources you can use to learn more about creating custom ribbons.

Microsoft provides a three-part series of articles that describe, in detail, the process. These articles can be viewed and downloaded for free at the following locations:

- "Customizing the Office (2007) Ribbon User Interface for Developers" (Part 1 of 3): http://msdn2.microsoft.com/en-us/library/ms406046.aspx

- "Customizing the Office (2007) Ribbon User Interface for Developers" (Part 2 of 3): http://msdn2.microsoft.com/en-us/library/aa338199.aspx

- "Customizing the Office (2007) Ribbon User Interface for Developers" (Part 3 of 3): http://msdn2.microsoft.com/en-us/library/aa722523.aspx

Another article that you should look at is "Customizing the Office Fluent User Interface in Access 2007," which can be found at http://msdn2.microsoft.com/en-us/library/ bb187398.aspx. This article also has a link to a sample accdb file, Marketing Projects, which has samples of customized ribbons.

> **NOTE** Patrick Schmid, an Office 2007 UI expert, has authored a utility named RibbonCustomizer Professional, an add-in that eases the process of making custom ribbons for Access and other Office 2007 applications. You can download a 30-day free trial and learn more about the utility at http://pschmid.net/office2007/ribboncustomizer.

To use the ribbons you customize, they have to be made available to Access using a VBA module. The syntax of the command to load the ribbon info is

```
expression.LoadCustomUI(customUIname, customUIXML)
```

Both arguments are required. The `customUIname` identifies the custom ribbon. The `customUIXML` contains the XML markup code that defines the customized ribbon. You can call several ribbons using multiple `LoadCustomUI` statements. You need to use different XML markup code, unique ribbon names, and unique ID attributes of the ribbon tabs for each ribbon loaded.

The following line of code loads a ribbon named MyRibbon:

```
Application.LoadCustomUI "MyRibbon", "MyRibbonXML"
```

Application Collections

16

Understanding Application Collections

We have explained how Access is an object-oriented development platform and that much of your application design is involved with manipulating objects via their properties. In previous chapters we worked with many different objects, such as tables, forms, reports, and queries. You learned how to assign values to many of the properties of these objects and to open and close these objects. You can also utilize Access objects with the built-in applications collections. Figure 16.1 shows part of the Access object model displaying some of the collections.

There are two main ways to navigate through the `Application` collection to the individual objects that are a part of them. First is the `CurrentProject` object, which contains collections for each of the objects that make up the user interface, such as `AllForms`, `AllReports`, and so on. The other is the `CurrentData` object, which contains collections for the data-related objects, for instance, `AllQueries` and `AllTables`. These collections then lead down to the Access objects that correspond to the individual items within each collection.

Figure 16.1
Part of the
`Application`
object and its associated
collections and objects.

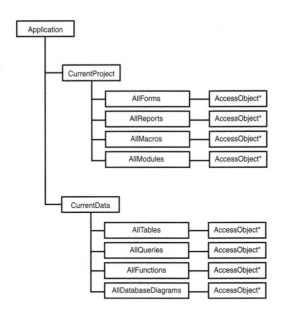

16

> **NOTE**
> The `CurrentData` object contains objects that relate to the data engine used by your applica-
> tion. In some cases this may be a SQL Server. Other objects specific to SQL Server won't be dis-
> cussed here.

> **CAUTION**
> The collections prefixed with `All` refer to all the objects within the application. There are corre-
> sponding collections, such as the `Forms` and `Reports` collections, that refer only to objects cur-
> rently open. Be careful not to confuse them.

In this chapter we demonstrate some ways you can use these collections and objects. With
these objects you can use VBA code to manipulate information listed in the default
NavPane categories. Four properties support each of the object collections:

- `Application`—Used to determine the parent `Application` object
- `Count`—Returns a count of the `AccessObject` objects within the collection
- `Item`—Indicates the position of the `AccessObject` within the collection, used to return
  individual objects
- `Parent`—A pointer to the parent object

Retrieving Lists of Objects

A frequent use of these collections is in compiling lists of all the objects within your database. For ease of use and security reasons you will often not want to expose all the objects to the user. One key of a good user interface is not showing the user any more than she needs to see to accomplish tasks. So the ability to work with lists of objects in your VBA code is important in creating a good user-friendly interface.

One example of this is using the AllForms collection to populate a list box of forms to select which form to open. We modify the frmMainMenu we built in Chapter 15 to replace the option group used to select a form with a new list box of forms. Follow these steps:

1. Open frmMainMenu in Design view.

2. Delete the Data option group.

3. Unselect the wizards and draw a list box in the place the option group was. Name it **lstForms**.

4. Using the Code Builder, add the following code to the On Load event:

```
Private Sub Form_Load()
Dim AO As AccessObject

'Populate the listbox with the names of the
'Forms you want the user to see
For Each AO In CurrentProject.AllForms
        Me.lstForms.AddItem (AO.Name)
Next
End Sub
```

5. Finally, use the Code Builder to open the On Click event of the button cmdForm. Modify the code so it uses the value from lstForms, like so:

```
Private Sub cmdForm_Click()
Dim strDocument As String

'Set form to open
strDocument = Me.lstForms

'Setup whether to open in Add or Edit mode
Select Case optAction
    Case 1
        DoCmd.OpenForm strDocument, , , , acFormAdd
    Case 2
        DoCmd.OpenForm strDocument
    Case Else
        MsgBox "No action selected", vbOKOnly, "Error"
        GoTo ExitSub
End Select

ExitSub:
End Sub
```

Figure 16.2 shows the revised menu form with the addition of a list box to select the form to open.

Figure 16.2
The new
frmMainMenu with a
list box showing all the
forms in the application.

16

Open the form in Form view and select a form from the list. Select an action and click the Form button to test that the correct form opens.

Working with Object Properties

We've now shown you how each of the objects in any of the object collections corresponds to an AccessObject object. Such an object has a set of properties that provide information about the object. For example; the code to populate the list box uses the Name property. Table 16.1 lists the properties.

Table 16.1   Object Properties

Property	Description
CurrentView	A constant that indicates the current view of the object (for example: Design view or Datasheet view) if the object is currently open.
DateCreated	When the object was initially created.
DateModified	When the object was last modified.
FullName	The full name (including path) for the object (only applicable to Data Access pages stored as separate files).
IsLoaded	Returns a True value if the object is currently open; otherwise, it returns a False value.
Name	The name you assigned to the object.
Parent	The collection that contains the object.
Properties	A list of the custom properties of the object.
Type	A constant indicating the type of the object; for example, form, report, table, and so on.

Another advantage of using the AccessObject object is that you have the ability to create properties of your own for each object. This can be used similarly to how the Tag property can be used on a form. You can use custom properties to store information about an object that you can use in your code.

→ To review the Tag property, **see** "Working with the Tag Property," **p. 183**.

You might have noticed that the Form list we just added to frmMainMenu includes all forms in the application, including ones you would not want the user to open separately like subforms. This really makes the list more confusing to the user. Creating a custom property provides a way to deal with this issue.

16

The first thing you need to know is how to add your own custom properties to the object and set it to indicate whether it should be displayed in the list. This is typically something you do once when you design your application. Let's open the module basUDFs in Design mode and add the following procedure:

```
Public Sub ShowOnMainMenu(strFormname As String)
Dim AO As AccessObject

'Define what object to the code
Set AO = CurrentProject.AllForms(strFormname)
'Set the new property to True
AO.Properties.Add "ShowOnMainMenu", True

'Display confirmation in the Immediate window
Debug.Print "Property added to " & strFormname
End Sub
```

The Properties collection of an AccessObject lists the custom properties that have been added to it. The first task of this code is to retrieve the AccessObject object and set the AO variable to that object. The next task is to use the Add method of the Properties collection to append the new custom property. The arguments for the Add method are the property name (as a string) and its initial value (which can be any variant type). So this code adds a new property named ShowInMainMenu and initializes it as True. Because you are going to set this property as part of your development, you can trigger this procedure from the Immediate window to set the property (see Figure 16.3).

Figure 16.3
Adding the new custom
property to your form.

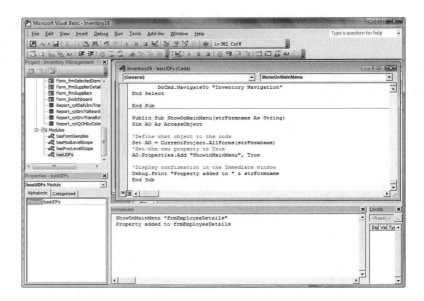

You want to go through the process of adding the new property to the following forms:
`frmEmployeeDetails`, `frmSupplierDetails`, and `frminvDetails`. You can add any other forms
you think pertinent. Some others you might want to add are `frmCoInfo`, `frmProcOnHold`, and
`frmTransactionTypes`.

The next step is to go back to the `On Load` event of `frmMainMenu` and modify the code you
entered there to add only forms that you have selected to appear in the menu. Following is
the modified code:

```
Private Sub Form_Load()
Dim AO As AccessObject
'Continue with code if property missing
On Error Resume Next
'Populate the listbox with the names of the
'Forms you want the user to see
For Each AO In CurrentProject.AllForms
    'Check if Property is True
    If AO.Properties.Item("ShowOnMainMenu").Value = True Then
        If Err = 0 Then
            Me.lstForms.AddItem AO.Name
        Else
            Err.Clear
        End If
    End If
Next

End Sub
```

If you try to retrieve the value of a property and that property doesn't exist for an object,
Access causes an error. You need to be aware of that when working with custom properties.
Provide error trapping in your code to make sure it doesn't bomb if the property doesn't

exist. The code we used illustrates one alternative for dealing with this. By setting the error handler to On Error Resume Next, you make sure that if an error is encountered it's not fatal and it doesn't stop the code from processing. The code attempts to retrieve the custom property for each form in the collection. One of three things can occur when it tries to retrieve the property:

- If the property does not exist for that object, the code continues processing the next line of code. Because the built-in Err variable will still be set to some number other than zero, the next line causes the line adding the item to be skipped. The Err Variable needs to be cleared if an error occurs because it retains its value until another error occurs.

- If the property exists, but its value is set to False, the check for True fails and the line adding the item also is skipped.

- If the property does exist and its value is set to True, the line adding the item is processed.

Figure 16.4 shows the form after making the modifications to the On Load code. The list box now displays only the forms you want it to.

Figure 16.4
Adding the new custom property to your form.

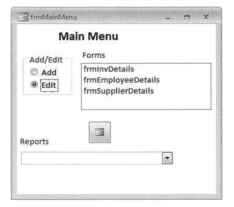

Programmatically Determining Dependencies

Although many Access objects stand by themselves, many are dependent on other objects. The prime example is a form that depends on a query as its Recordsource. That query, in turn, depends on at least one, maybe several, tables for its data. The form, then, is directly dependent on that query; it's also indirectly dependent on the table or tables that make up the query. New in Access 2003 was the capability to determine these dependencies both through the Access user interface and also by using VBA.

To find this information through the user interface, select an object in the Navigation pane; then open the Database Tools ribbon. Select Object Dependencies on that ribbon. If this is the first time you are viewing dependencies, or if they have been updated since the last time you generated them, the messages shown in Figures 16.5 and 16.6 display.

Figure 16.5
Dependency information may need to be updated.

Figure 16.6
All other objects must be closed to generate dependencies.

When the dependencies are finished generating, the Object Dependencies pane as shown in Figure 16.7 is displayed. You can view the dependencies in one of two ways: either by showing the objects that depend on the selected object or by showing the objects on which the selected object depends. Which view you use is determined by which radio button at the top of the pane is selected.

Figure 16.7
The Object Dependencies pane showing objects that depend on `tblInventory`.

CAUTION _____

To allow object dependencies to work, Name AutoCorrect must be turned on for Access. This is turned on by clicking the Office button and then selecting Access Options. Under the Current Database options, scroll down and check the Track Name AutoCorrect Info box. Access 2007 automatically checks this box if you respond Yes to the message displayed in Figure 16.6.

Being able to track these dependencies is a powerful tool for developers to troubleshoot problems in applications.

You can also use VBA to track the dependencies. This is done utilizing the `DependencyInfo` object of the `AccessObject` object. Following is some code to demonstrate how this is done:

```
Public Sub DisplayDependencies(intObjType As AcObjectType, _
    strObjName As String)

'Display dependency info for the named object
Dim AO1 As AccessObject
Dim AO2 As AccessObject
Dim DI As DependencyInfo

    On Error GoTo DisplayDependencyError

    'Retrieve the AccessObject
    Select Case intObjType

        Case acTable
            Set AO1 = CurrentData.AllTables(strObjName)
            Debug.Print "Table: ";
        Case acQuery
            Set AO1 = CurrentData.AllQueries(strObjName)
            Debug.Print "Query: ";
        Case acForm
            Set AO1 = CurrentProject.AllForms(strObjName)
            Debug.Print "Form: ";
        Case acReport
            Set AO1 = CurrentProject.AllReports(strObjName)
            Debug.Print "Report: ";
    End Select
    Debug.Print strObjName

    'Retrieve Dependency Info
    Set DI = AO1.GetDependencyInfo()

    'Show results
    If DI.Dependencies.Count = 0 Then
        Debug.Print "This object doesn't depend on others"
    Else
        Debug.Print "This Object depends on: "
        For Each AO2 In DI.Dependencies
            Select Case AO2.Type
                Case acTable
                    Debug.Print "   Table: ";
                Case acQuery
                    Debug.Print "   Query: ";
                Case acForm
                    Debug.Print "   Form: ";
                Case acReport
                    Debug.Print "   Report: ";
            End Select
            Debug.Print AO2.Name
        Next AO2
    End If
```

16

```
        If DI.Dependencies.Count = 0 Then
            Debug.Print "No objects depend on this one"
        Else
            Debug.Print "These Objects depends on this one: "
            For Each AO2 In DI.Dependants
                Select Case AO2.Type
                    Case acTable
                        Debug.Print "    Table: ";
                    Case acQuery
                        Debug.Print "    Query: ";
                    Case acForm
                        Debug.Print "    Form: ";
                    Case acReport
                        Debug.Print "    Report: ";
                End Select
                Debug.Print AO2.Name
            Next AO2
        End If

ExitHere:
Exit Sub

DisplayDependencyError:
    MsgBox " Error " & Err.Number & ": " & _
        Err.Description, vbCritical
    Resume ExitHere

End Sub
```

That code may seem intimidating, but if you take it in small chunks, you should be able to get a handle on it. The first task the code needs to perform is retrieving the AccessObject on which you want to check dependencies. Two required arguments are needed by the procedure: a constant indicating the object type and a string showing its name. In the first Select Case statement, the object collection to use is determined and then a message is printed in the Immediate window, displaying the object's name and type.

The next process retrieves the DependencyInfo object using the GetDependencyInfo method of the AccessObject. This object has two collections of its own, both containing their own AccessObject objects. The first is the Dependencies collection, which contains an AccessObject for each object on which the current object depends. The second is the Dependants collection, which does the same for objects that depend on the current object.

The rest of the sample code performs a loop through each of these two collections printing their contents to the Immediate window. Figure 16.8 displays the Immediate window with the results of running this code for tblInventory.

Figure 16.8
The Immediate window with the list of `tblinventory`'s object dependencies.

```
Immediate                                                    ×
DisplayDependencies acTable, "tblInventory"
Table: tblInventory
This Object depends on:
    Table: tblSuppliers
    Table: tblTransactions
    Table: tluCategory
These Objects depends on this one:
    Table: tblSuppliers
    Table: tblTransactions
    Table: tluCategory
    Query: qryDailyInvTrans
    Query: qryInventoryExtended
    Query: qryInventoryTransactionsExtended
    Query: qryInvTransByDate
    Form: frmInvDetails
    Form: frmInvTransactionsList
    Form: frmProcOnHold
    Form: frmSelectedItems
    Form: sfrmInvDetailTransactions
    Form: sfrmInvSupplierItems
    Report: rptDailyInvTrans
    Report: rptDiscontinuedInventory
    Report: rptInvDetails
    Report: rptInvTransByDate
    Report: srptInvTransactions
```

CASE STUDY

Case Study: Version Control

In addition to the ability to create custom properties for the `AccessObject` objects, you can also create custom properties for the database. This is one of the standard routines I use to create and display version numbers for my applications.

The first part of this is to manually create the properties. These steps are summarized in the dialog box shown in Figure 16.9.

1. Click the Office button.
2. Select Manage, Database Properties.
3. Go to the Custom tab.
4. Enter the name of the first property: `appVersion`.
5. Set the Type to Number.
6. Set the initial value to 1.
7. Click the Add button.
8. Enter the name of the second property: `appBuild`.
9. Set the Type to Number.
10. Set the initial value to 0.

16

Figure 16.9
The Custom properties tab with the `appVersion` property added and the `appBuild` property ready to add.

11. Click the Add button, and the two properties are now added.

Next we need to create a function that reads those properties. The code for that is as follows:

```
Public Function CustomDBProp(PropName As String) As String
    Dim dbs As Database
    Dim cnt As Container
    Dim doc As Document
    Dim strret As String

    On Error GoTo CustomDBProp_err

        'navigate thru collections to assign property
        Set dbs = CurrentDb
        Set cnt = dbs.Containers("databases")
        Set doc = cnt.Documents("UserDefined")
        strret = doc.Properties(PropName)
CustomDBProp_end:
    CustomDBProp = strret
    Exit Function
CustomDBProp_err:
    If Err = 3270 Then
        strret = "Property Not Found"
    Else
        MsgBox Err & ": " & Err.Description
    End If
    Resume CustomDBProp_end
End Function
```

This function uses the `Documents` collection of the `Containers` collection, which is where the custom properties are stored. The `Properties` property of the document is the value you assigned to the property. So this function returns the assigned value of the named property.

The final step is to create a subform to display these values:

1. From the Create ribbon use the Form Design icon to open a blank form in Design view.

2. Open the Properties sheet and set the following properties as indicated:

    Record Selectors: No

    Navigation Buttons: No

    Border Style: None

3. Add a text box to the form named `txtVersion`.

4. Set the `Controlsource` for the text box to `=CustomDBprop("appVersion")`

5. Add a text box to the form named `txtBuild`.

6. Set the `Controlsource` for the text box to `=CustomDBprop("appBuild")`

7. Size the form down to just the two controls and save it as **sfrmVersion**.

Now, we add that subform to the main menu, and the result is shown in Figure 16.10.

Figure 16.10
The revised main menu with the version subform showing the version and build.

Working with Data

III

Object Models for Working with Data

What They Are and Why We Need Them

Data entered into a Microsoft Access database is often thought of as being stored in a table. Although that is true from a user and practical perspective, from a lower level point of view, much more is involved than just data and a table. Data is stored in a specific format within your MS Access file, or possibly, even externally. Microsoft Access performs a bit of data exchange between the raw data structures and the user interface objects. The *user interface (UI) objects* are the forms, reports, and the Datasheet view of tables and queries you use to manipulate your data. The data structures of your database are commonly referred to collectively, or individually, as the *schema*.

The schema is the set of rules, definitions, and configurations (in other words, table definitions, query definitions, and relationships) to which your data adheres as it is stored and retrieved from the file where the raw data is stored, which is otherwise known as the *data source*. The bit of data exchange is the process by which the data, within the specifications of the schema, is provided to, and consumed by, the user interface objects. Fortunately, Microsoft Access handles the exchange of information transparently when interacting with data through the user interface objects. To illustrate this concept take a look at Figure 17.1.

17

Figure 17.1
Data exchange.

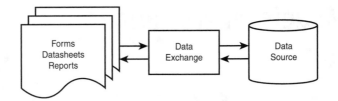

As you get more comfortable using VBA to calculate values, open forms, and print out reports, you may find yourself wanting to use VBA to interact with your data, without the use of your user interface objects. You may also want to manipulate the schema of your database programmatically. That is where the object models for working with data, which I also refer to as the *data interface object models*, come in to the scope of what is needed to accomplish those tasks. The data interface object models that will be discussed offer the programming language, or *syntax*, you will use to manipulate data and manage your databases, as well as their objects and structure (see Figure 17.2).

Figure 17.2
Data exchange with data interface object models.

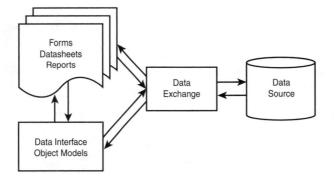

From a user and practical point of view, we think of data as being stored in tables (noted earlier). I make a specific point of this because the terminology used in dialog concerning databases reflects that concept. You will hear descriptions such as this: *"My data is stored in the table named tblEmployees of the database Inventory.accdb."* Also, as alluded to earlier, the data exchange process is often described as being an exchange between a *data provider* and a *data consumer*. From a simple standpoint, a data provider opens the door, or exposes, the data from the data source to the consumer. The consumer then has the ability to manipulate the data. With respect to the data interface object models that will be discussed, Data Access Objects (DAO) acts as a data provider, as well as a data consumer; ActiveX Data Objects (ADO) and ActiveX Data Objects Extensions (ADOX) are data consumers.

NOTE The programming language used to interface with the object models is made available to VBA through the use of libraries that are referenced in the Microsoft Access VBA Editor. To examine the libraries in use, go to Tools, References. The dialog box that opens indicates the reference libraries in use. Most programmers tend to not distinguish between the interface library and the object model the library is exposing to VBA. In other words, when it is said to use the DAO object model, that encompasses the object model and the interface library that exposes the object model to VBA.

Data Access Objects

Data Access Objects (DAO) is the default object model for Microsoft Office Access 2007. With the introduction of Access 2007, Microsoft introduced the Access Connective Engine (ACE). ACE brings with it several enhancements, such as multivalued fields, also called *complex data fields*, and *attachment* fields. DAO has been enhanced as well to expose those capabilities to the VBA environment.

With the new features, the implementation of DAO for use with the new database engine is titled Microsoft Office 12 Access Database Engine Object Library and is generically defined as a programming interface to access and manipulate database objects. DAO can fill the roles of both a data provider as well as a data consumer, at least from a conceptual point of view. The key benefits of the DAO object library are

- Tight integration with Microsoft Access
- Stable
- Fast

NOTE The database engine that powers Microsoft Access is referred to by many phrases or synonyms: Access database engine, Access Connectivity Engine, ACE, the ACE database engine. Please understand that these phrases all refer to the same entity.

Earlier versions of Access used the Joint Engine Technology (JET) database engine, also referred to as the JET database engine or just JET. JET is the predecessor of ACE, thus the JET acronym is often present in ACE properties and documentation.

Like any other object model, DAO has a specific hierarchy to build syntax for referring to all the collections of objects and object types within the database. The top of the DAO hierarchy is the DBEngine object. Figure 17.3 shows the full object hierarchy.

Figure 17.3
Microsoft Office 12.0
Access database engine
object model (DAO).

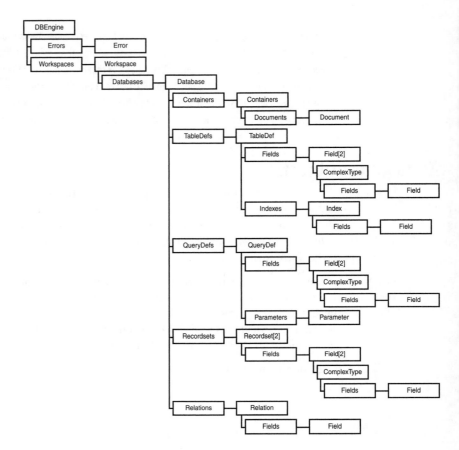

As you examine Figure 17.3, you will see some items that are plural; those items are the object collections. The items that are singular represent a single item within the parent collection. Also, as you follow the hierarchy, you will see the Field[2] and Recordset[2] objects. They are identified in such a way as to represent two objects for each representation; Field and Field2 as well as Recordset and Recordset2. The objects and collections beneath the Field[2] and Recordset[2] objects are associated with the Field2 and Recordset2 objects. Those objects are represented this way because the Field2 and Recordset2 objects contain all the same properties and methods as the Field and Recordset objects. The collections and objects of the DAO object model are explained further in Table 17.1.

Table 17.1 Data Access Objects

Collection/Object	Explanation
DBEngine	Top-level object that contains all other objects in the hierarchy of DAO objects.
Errors	Collection that contains all the errors generated for a DAO operation.
Error	Object that contains details about the last VBA error.
Workspaces	Collection that contains all the active Workspace objects.
Workspace	Represents the area for each database that a user has open. A default Workspace is automatically created when you open any database. That Workspace can be loosely interpreted as the navigation pane and the Access desktop.
Databases	Collection that contains all the Database objects you have open.
Database	Object that represents an open database.
Containers	Collection that contains all the Container objects.
Container	A holding place for the description of similar types of "documents" (that is forms, reports, queries, macros, and so on)
Documents	Collection that contains a group of Document objects of the same type, such as forms.
Document	Object that stores information about one instance of a created object, such as a form, report, or query.
TableDefs	Contains all the stored table definition objects in a database.
TableDef	Definition of either a local table or a linked table. A linked table is simply a shortcut to a table that is stored in an external database file. A linked table provides the conduit for data to pass between the current database and the external database.
Indexes	Collection that contains all the Index objects for a particular TableDef.
Index	The listing of how records of a TableDef are ordered, as well as overriding constraints, such as the prevention of duplicating data in a Field.
QueryDefs	Collection that contains all the query definition objects in a database.
QueryDef	Object that holds the description and SQL statement that will be executed against a table or set of tables. A QueryDef can show, modify, insert, or delete data.
Recordsets	Collection that holds all the Recordset objects that have been opened. This collection is automatically maintained.
Recordset	Object that represents records that are the result of opening a TableDef, QueryDef, or SQL statement.

17

continues

Table 17.1   Continued

Collection/Object	Explanation
Recordset2	Object identical to the `Recordset` object but also has the additional capability to understand the new features of the ACE database engine (that is, multivalue and attachment data types).
Relations	Collection that contains the `Relation` objects of your database.
Relation	Object that is the definition of how `TableDefs` or `QueryDefs` relate to each other through one or more `Field` objects.
Fields	Collection that contains all the `Field` objects of a `TableDef`, `QueryDef`, `Recordset`, `Relation`, or `ComplexType`.
Field	Object that represents a column of data within a `TableDef`, `QueryDef`, or `Recordset` and has the same data type and data definition for each record.
Field2	Object identical to a `Field` object except it has additional capabilities to handle the new features of the ACE database engine (that is, multivalue and attachment data types).
ComplexType	The object that represents a multivalue field.
Parameters	Collection that contains all the `Parameter` objects of a `QueryDef` object.
Parameter	The holding place for information that will be supplied to a `QueryDef` or SQL statement. It is analogous to a variable in Visual Basic.

ActiveX Data Objects

Microsoft ActiveX Data Objects (ADO) is another object model (like DAO) by which we can programmatically connect to and manipulate data stored in a database that Access can use. ADO is not referenced by default in Access 2007; to use the ADO object model, you will have to select the reference library named Microsoft ActiveX Data Object 2.x Library.

> **TIP**
> To reference the Microsoft ActiveX Data Object 2.x Library, use the VBA interface and follow the menu path Tools, References. In the dialog box that appears, scroll through the list and place a check mark by the appropriate line item.

ADO enables your application to manipulate information from various data sources and is more generic in nature than DAO. ADO has the capability to actually bypass the Access Connectivity Engine and have a direct exchange of information stored on a database server, such as SQL Server or in another application such as Microsoft Excel. ADO and DAO have a large degree of overlap with respect to their functionality; however, each has unique capabilities, and it is not uncommon to use both object models in database projects. ADO is considered to be a data consumer only, and thus when connecting to a data source, the data provider information must be known to successfully connect to that data. ADO's key benefits are

- Ease of use
- Portability

It is important to note that ADO supports key features for building client/server and web-based applications. It is also important to know that some features of ADO might not be supported by a particular data provider.

As with all object models, the ADO object model is hierarchical in structure and consists of collections of specific object types. You might notice, as shown in Figure 17.4, that the physical size of the ADO object model is considerably smaller than the DAO object model. This is because ADO is a data consumer only, and as such is focused solely on the retrieval and manipulation of data.

Figure 17.4
ADO object model.

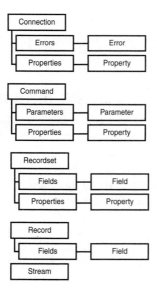

Similar in format to the DAO object model hierarchy, the plural items in the model are collections; singular items are the individual objects that are contained by the indicated parent. The items in the hierarchy shown in Figure 17.4 are explained in Table 17.2.

Table 17.2   ActiveX Data Objects

Collection/Object	Explanation
Connection	Object that describes a communication channel to the source of the data.
Command	Object used to specify and execute a SQL statement against a data source. The object is temporary but can be appended to the Views or Procedures collection of the ADOX object model to preserve the object.
Recordset	Object that represents records that are the result of opening a table, query, or SQL statement.
Record	Represents a single row of data.
Stream	A constant binary stream of data or text.
Errors	Collection that contains all the Error objects.
Error	Object that contains details about an error, such as the error number and description.
Properties	Collection that holds properties of an ADO object.
Property	Object that is characteristic of an ADO object.
Fields	Collection that contains all the Field objects of a Recordset.
Field	Object that is column of data with the same data type within a Recordset.

ActiveX Data Objects Extensions for Data Definition

The name for this object model is *ActiveX Data Objects Extensions for Data Definition Language and Security*, but it is definitely easier to say ADOX! I removed the "and Security" from the heading simply due to the fact that the Microsoft Access 2007 file format does not support user-level security. ADOX can be thought of as a helper library to ADO. ADO, as you know, is highly centered on data and its retrieval and modification. From that perspective, developers utilizing the ADO library exclusively did not have a programmatic interface to manipulate the schema of a database. From that need, ADOX was created to expose the additional schema objects to the programmer. ADOX is not referenced by default in Access 2007; to use the ADOX object model, you will have to select the reference library named Microsoft ADO Ext. 2.x for DDL and Security.

> **TIP**
> To reference the Microsoft ADO Ext. 2.x for DDL and Security library, use the VBA interface and follow the menu path Tools, References. In the dialog box that appears, scroll through the list and place a check mark by the appropriate line item.

As mentioned in the official title, ADOX does include security objects to maintain users and groups and other security information; however, those features are not supported by the MS Access 2007 file format and will not be discussed in the book. ADOX is lumped into the data consumer category with its sibling ADO. With that in mind it is important to understand the data provider information while working with ADOX, because some features of ADOX may not be supported by a particular data provider. Figure 17.5 illustrates the hierarchy for the ADOX object model.

Figure 17.5
ADOX object model.

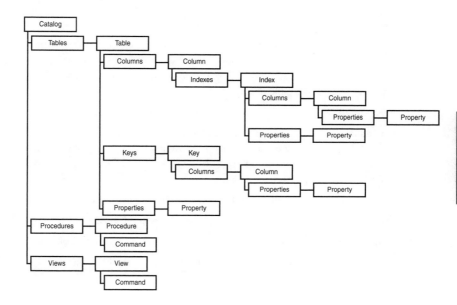

As with the other object model hierarchies being discussed in this chapter, the plural items in the model are collections. Singular items are the individual objects that are contained by the indicated parent. The items in the hierarchy shown in Figure 17.5 are explained in Table 17.3.

Table 17.3   ActiveX Data Objects Extensions

Collection/Object	Explanation
Catalog	Contains the objects that describe the schema of a data source.
Tables	Collection that contains all the `Table` objects of a `Catalog`.
Table	Object that is the description of a table in a data source.
Columns	Collection that contains a group of columns.
Column	Object that describes a column of data of the same data type within a table, index, or key.
Indexes	Collection that contains all the index objects of a table.

continues

Table 17.3   Continued

Collection/Object	Explanation
Index	The description of how the records of a table are ordered as well as overriding constraints, such as the prevention of duplicating data in a column.
Keys	Collection that contains all the Key objects of a table.
Key	A column or group of columns that can be used to uniquely identify a record (primary or unique key) or provide the information required to relate a record or group of records to a primary or unique key of a record in another table (foreign key).
Procedures	Collection that contains all the Procedure objects of a Catalog.
Procedure	An object (also called a *stored procedure*) that is code, such as SQL statements and control-of-flow statements. The series of statements is stored under a name and processed as one unit. The capability of stored procedures depends on your data provider.
Views	Collection that contains all the view objects of a Catalog.
View	Object that represents a filtered set of records.
Properties	Collection that holds a property of an ADOX object.
Property	Object that is characteristic of an ADOX object.

Object Model Selection

Now that you have all this information, you might be asking yourself, "Okay…which object model should I use?" The quick answer to that question is, "That one!" In all honesty, some tasks can only be accomplished in one model or the other. For example, you can modify the input mask on a field with DAO; however, ADOX does not offer that functionality. On the flip side, ADO has the capability to provide a recordset of all the users who are connected to an MS Access database file, whereas DAO does not have this functionality. In addition, ADO cannot handle the new features added to DAO, such as the multivalued fields.

> **NOTE**
>
> For this discussion I lump ADO and ADOX together as one model because the ADOX library is an extension of ADO that expands the capabilities of ADO.

In general, DAO is more efficient than ADO when working with ACE data (which includes linked tables) simply because DAO was designed for and around the JET (Joint Engine Technology) database engine, which is the predecessor to the ACE database engine, used by MS Access 2007. The ACE database engine and its interface library (DAO) incorporate connectivity that makes the back-end providers look as much like the native ACE engine as possible, thus the reason I say DAO acts like a data provider and consumer. ADO spends much of its time retrieving the schema information from the ACE data provider (Microsoft.ACE.OLEDB.12.0). This inefficiency is exaggerated when recordsets have a large number of fields.

Even with that generalization, if speed is a constraint that you are programming with, each object model deserves its own test in the configuration in which your code will be implemented. I have found that DAO objects open faster, and ADO objects navigate faster. Armed with that general knowledge, I tend to fill my TreeViews (an ActiveX control populated by looping a recordset) with ADO and perform my lookup type operations with DAO; this is a generalized conclusion and should not be taken as being absolutely true in all cases.

Ultimately, you will be a better programmer if you know both object models and use the most appropriate tool for the task at hand.

17

> **NOTE** For more information on the differences between DAO and ADO I recommend the following Internet links:
>
> INFO: Issues Migrating from DAO/JET to ADO/JET:
>
> http://support.microsoft.com/kb/225048
>
> Choosing ADO or DAO for Working with Access Databases:
>
> http://msdn2.microsoft.com/en-us/library/aa164825(office.10).aspx
>
> While investigating the differences, understand that many of the articles were written at a time in which ADO was viewed as a viable replacement for DAO. However, as time has progressed, both object models have developed a large base of support, which solidifies the presence of both object models well into the future.

Creating Schema

18

Overview

Chapter 17, "Object Models for Working with Data," introduced the concept of a database schema. To review, the *schema* is the set of rules, definitions, and configurations that your data adheres to as it is stored and retrieved from the file (or files) where the raw data is stored, the data source. Rules and definitions can be compared to table definitions and relationships. Configurations can be compared to queries.

At times, we may find ourselves in a situation that requires us to create the schema objects outside the tools provided within the user interface. For example, you may need to create a table to hold some values while your code is executing. Also, you may find that as your applications grow or your user base increases a mechanism is needed to implement changes in the schema that does not involve the user. The mechanism of choice for these tasks is user-defined procedures created in Visual Basic for Applications.

When creating schema objects often more than one method can be used to arrive at the same result. Typically schema objects, which are members of collections, are created by using the methods and commands provided by the DAO and ADOX object models, as well as execution of a *Data Definition Language (DDL)* statement.

DDL is basically a subset of SQL in which statements that create schema can be formulated and sent to the database engine with the `Execute` method available in the DAO or ADO models via the `Database` or `Connection` objects, respectively.

This chapter focuses on the methods used by the DAO and ADOX object models. Chapter 20, "Advanced Data Operations," will have some examples of DDL for you to examine but is by no means a complete reference. The sequence in which the material is presented loosely represents the sequence used to create the schema for an application: Create the database, and then create tables, fields, indexes, relationships, and queries.

While reading this chapter you will see that, in general, creating objects that belong to a collection, regardless of the object model used, follows a simple pattern:

1. Instantiate (or create) the object in memory.

2. Set the properties and attributes of the object (if applicable).

3. Append the object to the collection to which it belongs.

→ For more information on collections, **see** "Using Collections," **p. 105**, and "Understanding Application Collections" **p. 211**.

However, the implementation of the pattern might not look exactly the same between object models, or between programmers for that matter. With that in mind, I have made the sample code for each task from each technique similar in structure for you to see a direct correlation between the different methods for creating schema.

My intent is also to provide you with a foundation for creating schema. This chapter provides several tables of information detailing the arguments, properties, and attributes pertaining to the creation of the schema objects and the methods used to create them. With this reference information in hand, the Microsoft Access help system and the Intellisense feature of VBA can be used to expand on the information provided in this chapter to give you additional information on all the properties and methods of the objects being creating. To access this plethora of information, place your cursor on a keyword, method, property, or object variable data type and press the F1 key!

> **NOTE**
> The ADO `Connection` object is NOT part of the ADOX object model. However, the ADOX and ADO object models interface with each other through a `Connection` object.

> **TIP**
> You might find it handy to place a bookmark on Figure 17.3 and Figure 17.5, the object models for DAO and ADOX, respectively. Viewing the hierarchy of objects is often helpful when creating schema.
>
> In addition, you might want to keep in mind that deleting an item from a collection is easily accomplished with one line of code:
>
> ```
> expression.Delete strObjectName
> ```
>
> where *expression* is a collection object and *strObjectName* is the name of the object (or item) in the collection you want to delete.

Creating Databases

The database is the object used to store all your schema definitions. For Microsoft Office Access, the file used to store all the information regarding a Database object is called a database file, which is also called the data source. Access needs that file to store the schema as well as the data. When creating a Database object, we also create the database file.

Using the DAO Object Model

To create a database with the DAO object model, the CreateDatabase method is used. The CreateDatabase method saves the database to disk and returns an opened Database object.

The following is the syntax of the CreateDatabase method:

`expression.CreateDatabase(filename, locale[, options])`

where *expression* is a DBEngine or Workspace object. Table 18.1 lists the arguments of the method.

Table 18.1	**Arguments for** CreateDatabase **Method**	
Argument	**Data/Type**	**Explanation**
filename	String	Required; a valid filename and path of the database file you are creating, often called the fully qualified name. The fully qualified name can use the Universal Naming Convention (UNC) path, such as \\Server\Share\Folder\My_Database, if your network supports it. The extension of the filename is not required.
locale	String	Required; an expression that specifies how text is sorted (collating order) for creating the database. Typical value is dbLangGeneral; see Table 18.2 for more constants. You also can use this argument to create a database password for the new Database object by concatenating the password string to the desired *locale*. The password must be preceded with ;pwd= and is concatenated into the *locale* argument like this: dbLangSpanish & ";pwd=NewPassword" If you want to use the default locale but specify a password, simply enter a password string for the *locale* argument: ";pwd=NewPassword" It is suggested to use strong passwords that combine upper- and lowercase letters, numbers, and symbols. An example of a strong password would be Bk7M@%67.
options	Variant	Optional; a constant or combination of constants that indicates one or more options. If you want to use more than one option, you sum up the constants with a simple addition expression.

18

The *locale* argument can be one of the following constants from Table 18.2. Note that the values returned from these constants have a String data type.

Table 18.2   Constants Available for the *locale* Argument of the CreateDatabase Method

Constant	Collating Order
dbLangGeneral	English, German, French, Portuguese, Italian, and Modern Spanish
dbLangArabic	Arabic
dbLangChineseSimplified	Simplified Chinese
dbLangChineseTraditional	Traditional Chinese
dbLangCyrillic	Russian
dbLangCzech	Czech
dbLangDutch	Dutch
dbLangGreek	Greek
dbLangHebrew	Hebrew
dbLangHungarian	Hungarian
dbLangIcelandic	Icelandic
dbLangJapanese	Japanese
dbLangKorean	Korean
dbLangNordic	Nordic languages (Microsoft Jet database engine version 1.0 only)
dbLangNorwDan	Norwegian and Danish
dbLangPolish	Polish
dbLangSlovenian	Slovenian
dbLangSpanish	Traditional Spanish
dbLangSwedFin	Swedish and Finnish
dbLangThai	Thai
dbLangTurkish	Turkish

The *options* argument can be one, or a combination of, the constants from Table 18.3.

Table 18.3   Constants Available for the *option* Argument of the CreateDatabase Method

Constant	Description
dbEncrypt	Creates an encrypted database
dbVersion10	Creates a database that uses the Microsoft Jet database engine version 1.0 file format.

Constant	Description
`dbVersion11`	Creates a database that uses the Microsoft Jet database engine version 1.1 file format
`dbVersion20`	Creates a database that uses the Microsoft Jet database engine version 2.0 file format
`dbVersion30`	Creates a database that uses the Microsoft Jet database engine version 3.0 file format (compatible with version 3.5)
`dbVersion40`	Creates a database that uses the Microsoft Jet database engine version 4.0 file format
`dbVersion120`	Creates a database that uses the Microsoft Access database engine version 12.0 file format

In VBA code, not much else is needed other than the core syntax already shown. The procedure shown in Listing 18.1 creates an encrypted `Database` object and file with the password `mypassword` and returns the object reference of the newly created `Database`.

Listing 18.1 `DAO_CreateDatabase`

```
Public Function DAO_CreateDatabase(strFilename As String) As DAO.Database
'This procedure will create/open an encrypted, password protected
'database file and return to the caller a database object.

    'Execute the method and return the object
    Set DAO_CreateDatabase = DBEngine.CreateDatabase(strFilename, _
                             dbLangGeneral & ";pwd=mypassword", _
                             dbEncrypt + dbVersion120)

End Function
```

> **TIP**
>
> To create databases for a previous version of Access, just use the appropriate *options* constant.

Using the ADOX Object Model

To create a database with the ADOX object model, the `Create` method is used. In ADOX the `Catalog` object represents a database. The `Create` method creates a database file and returns a `Catalog` object. The syntax for the `Create` method is fairly simple:

expression.`Create` *ConnectString*

where *expression* is a `Catalog` object, and *ConnectString* is a connection string that defines the settings that Microsoft Access utilizes to connect to and create the data file.

The connection string is the item that provides you the flexibility of creating a database via code. Each setting of the connection string is separated by a semicolon (;). The connection string contains, at minimum, a *Provider* and *Data Source* setting. A typical connection string may look something like this:

```
Provider=Microsoft.ACE.OLEDB.12.0;
Data Source=C:\Inventory.accdb;
Jet OLEDB:Database Password=thedbpassword;
```

Two other common keywords of a connection string are the *User ID* and *Password*. Table 18.4 explains what each one is.

Table 18.4   Keywords of a Connection String

Keyword	Description
Provider	The OLE DB provider. The sample given is the provider for the Access Connective Engine (ACE) version 12.
Data Source	Indicates the name of the database. The sample shows the full path and name to the Inventory.accdb database.
User ID	The user ID that will be used for authentication. In the sample, this keyword was not used. This is an optional keyword.
Password	The password associated with the indicated user. This is an optional keyword.

The connection string can contain many pieces of information that define several properties when creating or connecting to a database. Most of the settings are not required and have a default value that is appropriate. Settings that are not part of ADO, but used in connection strings are often called *provider-specific* settings. Table 18.5 lists some of the common settings used when connecting to the ACE provider (that is, Microsoft Access database).

Table 18.5   JET ADOX Provider-Specific Connection String Settings

Setting	Description
Jet OLEDB:Database Password	Indicates the database level password.
Jet OLEDB:Engine Type	Indicates the database engine level to create a database to or read the data with. Valid numbers and what they mean are 1—JET10 2—JET11 3—JET2X 4—JET3X 5—JET4X 6—ACE12 (Note: JET stands for Joint Engine Technology, the predecessor to ACE.)

Setting	Description
`Jet OLEDB:Database Locking Mode`	Indicates either row-level locking (1), or page-level locking (0).
`Jet OLEDB:Encrypt Database`	On creation of a database, setting this to `True` yields an encrypted database; `False` does not implement encryption. On existing data sources, this setting reveals the status of encryption.

The ADOX equivalent of the DAO function in Listing 18.1 is shown in Listing 18.2. Please remember that before ADOX can be used in VBA, you must create a reference to the library named *Microsoft ADO 2.x Ext. library for DDL and Security*.

> **TIP**
>
> To reference the *Microsoft ADO 2.x Ext. Library for DDL and Security*, use the VBA Editor's interface and follow the menu path Tools, References. In the dialog box that appears, scroll through the list and place a check mark by the appropriate line item.

The procedure in Listing 18.2 creates an encrypted `Database` object and files with the password `mypassword` and returns the object reference of the newly created catalog (database).

Listing 18.2 `ADOX_CreateCatalog`

```
Public Function ADOX_CreateCatalog(strFilename As String) As ADOX.Catalog
'This procedure will create/open an encrypted, password protected
'database file and return to the caller a catalog object.

    Dim cat As ADOX.Catalog

    'Instantiate the object
    Set cat = New ADOX.Catalog

    'Create an A2007 db (.accdb) ... Note the extension IS NOT
    'AUTOMATICALLY appended, so you must include the extension
    'in the passed argument
    cat.Create "Provider=Microsoft.ACE.OLEDB.12.0;" & _
               "Data Source=" & strFilename & ";" & _
               "Jet OLEDB:Database Password=mypassword;" & _
               "Jet OLEDB:Encrypt Database=True;"

    Set ADOX_CreateCatalog = cat

End Function
```

> **TIP**
>
> To create databases of a previous version, just specify the appropriate value for the provider-specific setting of `"Jet OLEDB:Engine Type"`. Also, you may be able to change the provider. For example: Microsoft.JET.OLEDB.4.0 will create the database in Microsoft Access 2003 format.

18

> **CAUTION**
>
> When creating a database with the ADOX object model, you *must* provide the extension of the file that is created. The extension for a Microsoft Access database is ACCDB for Access 2007 and MDB for prior versions.

Creating Tables

Now that we have learned how to create a database, the next step is adding additional schema to a database. The first logical schema object to add is a table, because all your data is stored in them. Additionally, all other schema objects are based on tables or more specifically, the fields within them. To create a table you need to have at least one field for the table in which to hold data. Because you are creating two pieces of schema (a table and a field), the standard process of creating tables becomes nested but still adheres to the general practice mentioned earlier:

1. Instantiate (create) the table in memory.
2. Instantiate at least one field in memory.
3. Set the properties of the field.
4. Append the field to the collection to which it belongs.
5. Set the properties of the table.
6. Append the table to the collection to which it belongs.

Using the DAO Object Model

When using the DAO object model to create a table, please refer to the DAO object model in Figure 17.3. The `Database` object has a collection named TableDefs (for Table Definitions). The TableDefs collection is where we append a `TableDef` object. The following is the core method we use to create a `TableDef` object is `CreateTableDef`, which returns a `TableDef` object, where *expression* is a `Database` object, and the optional arguments are defined as listed in Table 18.6:

```
expression.CreateTableDef([Name][, Attributes][, SourceTableName][, Connect])
```

The arguments, which are also `TableDef` properties, are indeed optional at the time of the execution of the line of code; however, the *Name* and the other properties should be specified before the object is appended to the collection. Table 18.6 lists the `TableDef` properties that are relevant during the creation process.

Table 18.6 `TableDef` **Properties**

Property	Description
Attributes*	Number (Long) representing one or more characteristics of a `TableDef` object. Each attribute has a numeric value. If more than one attribute is needed, the attributes are added together. See Table 18.7 to learn more about the attributes available for this method.
Connect*	String to store the location (or data source) of the `SourceTableName` as well as other settings needed for a *Linked* table. This property takes a form similar to `;database=C:\SomeFolder\SomeDatabase.accdb` which represents a `Connect` property for a linked table connected to a Microsoft Access database.
Fields	The Fields collection.
Indexes	The Indexes collection.
Name*	The name of the table.
Properties	The Properties collection.
SourceTableName*	The name of a table in a remote data source that is bound to the local `TableDef` object.
ValidationRule	Table-level validation rule.
ValidationText	Message shown to the user if the validation rule is violated.

*Optional argument for the `CreateTableDef` method.

As noted in Table 18.6, the `Attributes` property (or argument) is a value that represents several characteristics of a `TableDef` object. The constants that can be used to provide the value are listed in Table 18.7.

Table 18.7 `TableDef` **Attributes**

Attribute	Description
dbAttachExclusive	Opens a linked table's database for exclusive use
dbAttachSavePWD	Saves the password used to open the remote database of a linked table
dbSystemObject	Indicates the table is a "System" level object
dbHiddenObject	Setting this attribute hides the table from the Access user interface
dbAttachedTable	Indicates the table is a linked table from a non-ODBC source, such as Microsoft ACE/JET (Read-Only)
dbAttachedODBC	Indicates the table is a linked table from an ODBC source, such as SQL Server (Read-Only)

The example in Listing 18.3 illustrates the process for creating a table in VBA.

> **NOTE**
>
> The code in Listing 18.3 contains the creation of a `Field` and `Index`, which are discussed later in this chapter.

Listing 18.3   `DAO_CreateTable`

```
Public Sub DAO_CreateTable(strTableName As String, _
                           strPrimaryKeyField As String, _
                           Optional db As DAO.Database)
'Create a table and the primary key field and index. The primary key
'field is created as an Autonumber field. If a database object is
'passed, then the table is created in the passed
'database, if no database is passed then the current database is used.

    Dim tdf As DAO.TableDef
    Dim fld As DAO.Field
    Dim idx As DAO.Index

    'Set the database if it was not passed
    If db Is Nothing Then Set db = CurrentDb

    With db

        'Instantiate the table
        Set tdf = .CreateTableDef(strTableName)

        'Instantiate, set up, and append at least one field
        'to the table
        Set fld = tdf.CreateField(strPrimaryKeyField, dbLong)
        fld.Attributes = dbAutoIncrField
        tdf.Fields.Append fld

        'Instantiate, set up, and append the PrimaryKey
        'index to the table
        Set idx = tdf.CreateIndex("PrimaryKey")
        idx.Fields.Append idx.CreateField(fld.Name)
        idx.Primary = True
        tdf.Indexes.Append idx

        'Append the table to the collection
        .TableDefs.Append tdf

    End With

    'Refresh the User Interface
    RefreshDatabaseWindow

End Sub
```

> **TIP**
>
> You can add more than one `Field` or `Index` to a table before appending the table to the `TableDefs` collection. Just remember that the fields specified while building your `Index` must be appended to the `tdf.Fields` collection prior to use in your `idx.CreateField` line, where *tdf* and *idx* are `TableDef` and `Index` objects, respectively.

Using the ADOX Object Model

Using the ADOX object model to create a table is not that much different than using DAO. From a generic perspective they are pretty much identical. Remember that the ADOX terminology is different, so refer to Figure 17.5 (p. 235), the ADOX object model. Note that the `Table` object is part of the `Tables` collection of a `Catalog`. The core method we use to create a `Table` object is not really a method at all; we just instantiate the declared object variable as a `New` item of the `Table` type:

```
Set tbl = New ADOX.Table
```

where *tbl* is an object variable with the `ADOX.Table` type. After instantiating the object, it is in memory, just like with DAO, and you can set the properties, including provider-specific properties, `columns` and `indexes` on the instantiated object.

To set provider-specific properties of the ADOX `Table` and `Column` objects, you must first indicate where (which `catalog`) to get the properties from by using the `ParentCatalog` property of the object in question. Setting the `ParentCatalog` property does not `Append` the object to the collection. Examine Table 18.8 for a the ADOX `Table` properties.

18

Table 18.8   ADOX Table Properties

Property	Description
`Columns`	The `Columns` collection.
`Indexes`	The `Indexes` collection.
`Keys`	The `Keys` collection.
`Name`	Name of table.
`ParentCatalog`	Specifies the parent catalog to provide access to provider-specific properties.
`Properties`	The `Properties` collection, including provider-specific properties when `ParentCatalog` is specified.
`Temporary Table*`	Boolean. A setting of `True` indicates the table is a temporary table, which is not appended to the `Tables` collection.
`Jet OLEDB:Table Validation Text*`	String. A message that displays if the validation rule is not met.

continues

Table 18.8 Continued

Property	Description
Jet OLEDB:Table Validation Rule*	String. A validation rule, in string form that resembles an expression. This rule can span multiple columns within the table, allowing for more complicated restrictions than individual column validations.
Jet OLEDB:Cache Link Name/Password*	Boolean. Indicates whether the username and password will be saved.
Jet OLEDB:Remote Table Name*	String. The table name in which to link to, which does not have to correspond to the name used in the Access user interface.
Jet OLEDB:Link Provider String*	String. The provider of a linked table.
Jet OLEDB:Link Datasource*	String. The data source of a linked table.
Jet OLEDB:Exclusive Link*	Boolean. If set to True, the remote data store is opened exclusively.
Jet OLEDB:Create Link*	Boolean. Indicates whether to create the table as a linked table or a native table.
Jet OLEDB:Table Hidden In Access*	Boolean. Indicates whether to display the table user interface (that is, the Navigation pane).

Provider-specific property, accessed through the Properties collection.

Listing 18.4 provides example code for creating a Table using the ADOX object model.

> **NOTE** The VBA code in Listing 18.4 contains the creation of columns and indexes that will be discussed later in this chapter.

Listing 18.4 ADOX_CreateTable

```
Public Sub ADOX_CreateTable(strTableName As String, _
                            strPrimaryKeyField As String, _
                            Optional cat As ADOX.Catalog)
'Create a table and the primary key field and index. The primary key
'field is created as an Autonumber field. If a catalog object is
'passed, then the table is created in the passed
'catalog, if no catalog is passed then the current project is used.

    Dim tbl As ADOX.Table
    Dim col As ADOX.Column
    Dim idx As ADOX.Index
```

```
'Set the catalog if one was not passed
If cat Is Nothing Then
    Set cat = New Catalog
    cat.ActiveConnection = CurrentProject.Connection
End If

'Instantiate the table
Set tbl = New ADOX.Table
With tbl

    'Set up the table
    .Name = strTableName

    'Instantiate, set up, and append at least one field
    'to the table
    Set col = New ADOX.Column
    col.ParentCatalog = cat    'ParentCatalog exposes provider
                               'specific properties, like autoincrement
    col.Name = strPrimaryKeyField
    col.Type = adInteger
    col.Properties("Autoincrement") = True
    .Columns.Append col

    'Instantiate, set up, and append the PrimaryKey
    'index to the table
    Set idx = New ADOX.Index
    idx.Name = "PrimaryKey"
    idx.Columns.Append strPrimaryKeyField, adInteger
    idx.PrimaryKey = True
    tbl.Indexes.Append idx

End With

'Append the table to the collection
cat.Tables.Append tbl

'Refresh the User Interface
RefreshDatabaseWindow

End Sub
```

18

Creating Fields

In prior examples (Listings 18.3 and 18.4), you have seen the creation of fields, also known as `Columns` in ADOX. To review, fields are the columns of a table that identify and store data for an attribute of the entity represented by the table. In short, a field or column is where we store descriptive data for the subject matter we are tracking with the table. The process for creating a `Field` remains true to the general concept of adding an item to a collection.

> **TIP**
>
> Many Field properties, such as the Name and Type, become read-only after the Field is appended to the *tdf*.Fields collection, where *tdf* is a TableDef object. However, you can still modify many of those properties programmatically through the execution of a properly formed DDL statement.

Using the DAO Object Model

A Field object is part of the Fields collection. The Fields collection belongs to the TableDef object. This hierarchy can be seen by referring to Figure 17.3. The object method used to create a field in the DAO object model is CreateField, which returns a Field object:

*expression.*CreateField([Name][, Type][, Size])

where *expression* is a TableDef object, and the arguments, which are also Field object properties, are defined in Table 18.9.

Table 18.9   DAO Field Properties

Property	Description
AppendOnly	(Field2 object only) If True the field for appending data only.
AllowZeroLength	Allow a zero-length string (ZLS) to be stored.
Attributes	Characteristics. See Table 18.10.
DefaultValue	The default value for new records.
ForeignName	Foreign table field name that corresponds to the primary table field name in a relationship.
Name*	Name of the field.
OrdinalPosition	The ordinal position of the field.
Properties	The Properties collection.
Required	Indicates whether a value is required for records.
Size*	The size in bytes.
Type*	The type of data the field will hold.
ValidateOnSet	If set to True, the data is validated upon set, instead of upon record save.
ValidationRule	The validation rule.
ValidationText	The text to show whether validation rule is violated.

*Optional argument used by the CreateField *method*

Table 18.10 describes the constants that can be added to characterize a field with the Attributes property.

Table 18.10   DAO Field Attributes

Attribute	Description
dbAutoIncrField	The field of Long Integer data type is automatically incremented for new records.
dbDescending	The field of the collection of Fields of an Index object is sorted in descending order (100 to 0, Z to A).
dbFixedField	The field size is fixed.
dbHyperlinkField	The field of Memo data type contains hyperlink information.
dbSystemField	The field is marked to store replication information. System fields cannot be deleted.
dbUpdatableField	The field data is updatable.
dbVariableField	The field of Text data type can store variable lengths of text.

Table 18.11 provides a list of the valid values for the Type property. Table 18.1 indicates the user interface type in correlation with a VBA constant. The user interface type is the type that is listed in the drop-down selection box while creating a field in table design mode in the user interface.

Table 18.11   DAO Data Types for the CreateField Method

User Interface Type	Constant	Description
Attachment	dbAttachment	Variant data
N/A	dbBigInt	Big Integer data
N/A	dbBinary	Binary data
Yes/No	dbBoolean	Boolean; 2 bytes; True/False
Number:Byte	dbByte	Byte; 1 byte; 0–255
N/A	dbChar	Text data (fixed width)
Number:Byte	dbComplexByte	Multivalued byte data
Number:Decimal	dbComplexDecimal	Multivalued decimal data
Number:Double	dbComplexDouble	Multivalued double-precision floating-point data
Replica	dbComplexGUID	Multivalued GUID data
Number:Integer	dbComplexInteger	Multivalued integer data
Number:Long	dbComplexLong	Multivalued long integer data
Number Single	dbComplexSingle	Multivalued single-precision floating-point data
Text	dbComplexText	Multivalued text data (variable width)

18

continues

Table 18.11   Continued

User Interface Type	Constant	Description
Currency	dbCurrency	Currency (scaled integer); 8 bytes; –922,337,203,685,477.5808 to 922,337,203,685,477.5807
Date/Time	dbDate	Date/Time; 8 bytes; dates are stored as a Double with a *day* unit of measure. The number stored is the number of days and fraction of day, past the base date (a value of 0.0) of December 30, 1899 12:00 AM.
Number:Double	dbDouble	Double-precision floating-point; –1.79769313486231E308 to –4.94065645841247E-324 for negative values; 4.94065645841247E-324 to 1.79769313486232E308 for positive values
Replica	dbGUID	Global Unique Identifier (GUID); 16 bytes
Number:Integer	dbInteger	Integer; 2 bytes; –32,768 to 32,767
Number:Long	dbLong	Long Integer; 4 bytes; –2,147,483,648 to 2,147,483,647
Auto Number	dbLong	The Auto Number data type uses the dbLong data type with an additional setting on the field.
OLE Object	dbLongBinary	Binary data. Often used by images.; 1GB
Memo	dbMemo	Memo; an extended block of text. For example, a text block that can contain more than 255 characters; 65,535 characters, if manipulated through a text box control; limited by the size of the database, if manipulated through DAO.
Hyperlink	dbMemo	A memo field, with additional setting to indicate hyperlink data.
Number:Single	dbSingle	Single-precision floating-point data; 4 bytes –3.402823E38 to –1.401298E-45 for negative values; 1.401298E-45 to 3.402823E38 for positive values
Text	dbText	Text, numbers, and symbols; 255 characters

The procedure in Listing 18.5 shows how to add a `Field` to an existing table.

Listing 18.5 DAO_AddField

```
Public Sub DAO_AddField(strTable As String, _
                        strFieldName As String, _
                        lngFieldType As DAO.DataTypeEnum, _
                        Optional blIsRequired As Boolean = False)
'Add a field to an existing table. Note the the Size property is not passed
'and therefore the Size property will be set at the default for the type of
'field being created.

    Dim db As DAO.Database
    Dim tdf As DAO.TableDef
    Dim fld As DAO.Field

    'Point to the Current Database and passed table
    Set db = CurrentDb
    Set tdf = db.TableDefs(strTable)

    'Create the field, and add it to the collection
    With tdf

        'Instantiate and set properties
        Set fld = .CreateField(strFieldName, lngFieldType)
        fld.Required = blIsRequired

        'Append to the collection
        .Fields.Append fld

    End With

End Sub
```

Using the ADOX Object Model

The `Column` object is part of the `Columns` collection of a `Table` object (refer to Figure 17.5 on p. 235). The `Column` object is synonymous with the `Field` object from DAO. The technique for adding a `Column` follows the same pattern of creating objects within a collection. Also, as with creating a table in ADOX, the core step of creating a `Column` object does not really have a method associated with it; you simply instantiate the object:

```
Set col = New ADOX.Column
```

where *col* is an object variable with the ADOX.column type. Similar to the Table object, after instantiation of the Column object, properties can be set before being appended to the Columns collection.

As noted when creating an ADOX table, to set provider-specific properties of an ADOX Column object, you must first indicate where (which catalog) to get the properties by using the ParentCatalog property of the object in question. Setting the ParentCatalog property does not append the object to the collection. Table 18.12 lists the properties commonly used in the creation of a column.

Table 18.12   ADOX Column Properties

Property	Description
Attributes	Characteristics of a column (adColNullable, adColFixed).
DefinedSize	Size, in bytes of the column.
Name	Name of the column.
ParentCatalog	Specifies the parent catalog to provide access to provider-specific properties.
Properties	The Properties collection, including provider-specific properties when ParentCatalog is specified.
RelatedColumn	The column name of the foreign table that participates in a key with the column.
SortOrder	The sort order of the Column object in an Index object.
Type	The data type of the column.
Autoincrement*	Boolean. Is the column an automatically incremented column?
Default*	Variant. The default value that new records will assume if no value is otherwise specified.
Fixed Length*	Boolean. True: Fixed Length; False: Variable Length.
Nullable*	Boolean. True: Value is NOT required, thus has the capability to contain a Null; False: A value IS required, thus shall not contain a Null.
Jet OLEDB:Allow Zero Length*	Boolean. True indicates the column CAN accept zero-length strings.
Jet OLEDB:AutoGenerate*	Boolean. True indicates that a Globally Unique Identifier (GUID) should be automatically generated for the column. Used for replication, which is not supported in Access 2007.
Jet OLEDB:Compressed UNICODE Strings*	Boolean. True indicates to compress UNICODE characters for storage. Only valid with JET 4.0 or higher.

Property	Description
`Jet OLEDB:Hyperlink*`	Boolean. `True` indicates the column is storing a hyperlink location. Used with the data type `adLongVarWChar` (Memo in Access).
`Jet OLEDB:One BLOB per Page*`	Boolean. `True` indicates that Binary Large Objects (BLOB) CANNOT share database pages on the disk. `False` indicates that BLOBs can share pages and thus save on disk space.
`Jet OLEDB:Column Validation Rule*`	Text. An expression to be evaluated before a record is saved. If the expression returns `False`, the record is not saved.
`Jet OLEDB:Column Validation Text*`	Text. Message displays to the user if the validation rule returns `False`.

*Accessed through the `Properties` collection

Table 18.13 lists the data types for the ADOX object model and their corresponding data type used in the table design view of creating a table.

> **CAUTION**
>
> Be careful when adding columns through ADOX. The column defaults may be different from what occurs when adding columns/fields through the user interface or through the DAO object model.

18

Table 18.13   ADO Data Types for `ADOX.Columns`

User Interface Type	Constant	Description
Yes/No	`adBoolean`	Boolean (true/false) data.
Text (Fixed Length)	`adChar`	Fixed-length text.
Currency	`adCurrency`	Currency data. (Currency is a fixed-point type.)
Date/Time	`adDate`	Date/time data.
Number:Double	`adDouble`	Double data.
Replica	`adGUID`	Global Unique Identifier (GUID).
Long	`adInteger`	Integer data.
Auto Number	`adInteger`	Long data type with an additional property set. (Refer to Table 18.11 for more detail on the Auto Number user interface type.)
OLE Object	`adLongVarBinary`	Binary data. Usually used by images.

continues

Table 18.13 Continued

User Interface Type	Constant	Description
Memo	adLongVarWChar	Memo data, which is extended text. For example, a text block with more than 255 characters.
Hyperlink	adLongVarWChar	A Memo data type with an additional property set. (Refer to Table 18.11 for more information on the Hyperlink user interface type.)
Number: Decimal	adNumeric	Decimal data.
Number: Single	adSingle	Single-precision floating-point data.
Number: Integer	adSmallInt	Integer data.
Number: Byte	adUnsignedTinyInt	Byte data.
Attachment	adVarBinary	Variant.
Text	adVarWChar	Text, numbers, and symbols.
Text (Fixed Length)	adWChar	Fixed-length text.

→ **See** Table 18.14 for additional details related to the user interface type indicated.

> **NOTE**
> ADO is independent of Microsoft Access and ACE, and thus has several other data type constants. However, those constants are not listed as they are outside the scope of this book. The entire list of ADO data type constants is available in the Microsoft Access VBA Editor help system. A search for "DataTypeEnum" will yield the location of the entire list of data types.

The procedure in Listing 18.6 shows how to add a column to an existing table.

Listing 18.6 ADOX_AddColumn

```
Public Sub ADOX_AddColumn(strTable As String, _
                          strColumnName As String, _
                          lngColumnType As ADODB.DataTypeEnum, _
                          Optional blIsRequired As Boolean = False)
'Add a column to an existing table. Note the the Size property is not passed
'and therefore the Size property will be set at the default for the type of
'column being created.

    Dim cat As ADOX.Catalog
    Dim tbl As ADOX.Table
    Dim col As ADOX.Column

    'Point to the Current Connection and passed table
    Set cat = New ADOX.Catalog
```

```
cat.ActiveConnection = CurrentProject.Connection
Set tbl = cat.Tables(strTable)

'Create the field, and add it to the collection
With tbl

    'Instantiate and set properties
    Set col = New ADOX.Column
    col.Name = strColumnName
    col.ParentCatalog = cat
    col.Type = lngColumnType
    col.Properties("Nullable") = Not blIsRequired

    'Append to the collection
    .Columns.Append col

End With

End Sub
```

Creating Indexes

Indexes specify the order in which records are accessed. They can also be set up to constrain a field in such a way to prevent duplication of data. Indexes provide an efficient mechanism to search for data in a particular field. Despite these advantages of having indexes, it is also possible to have too many indexes. Indexes are automatically updated by the database engine for each update (including insertions and deletions) to the set of records stored in the table. As a general guideline, an index should be created for fields that are commonly searched or that participate in a relationship. Other considerations for creating an index are

- Frequent sorting on a field
- Many different values are stored in the field
- A multifield index can be created for a group of fields that are used together often to search and sort; for example, first and last names.

> **CAUTION**
>
> By default, Microsoft Access automatically creates an index for field names that begin or end with a specified sequence of characters. By default, the following prefix/suffix values ID, key, code, or num are used. This feature has the capability to create many indexes that are not necessarily needed. You can modify the prefix/suffix values in the Access Options dialog box. To get there, follow this path: Microsoft Office button, Access Options button, Object Designers, Table Design. There you can add, edit, or remove values in the AutoIndex on Import/Create section. A semicolon (;) must be used to separate the values. If you want to disable this feature, leave the setting blank.

18

Using the DAO Object Model

The Index object is part of the Indexes collection of a TableDef object. Also note from Figure 17.3 (p. 230) that an Index is the parent of a Fields collection. The Fields collection of the Index object can only be appended to with a Field from a Fields collection of a TableDef. An Index can't exist with out at least one Field. The creation of a DAO Index has already been seen earlier in this chapter (refer to Listing 18.3), and once again follows the generic process that has been evident throughout this chapter. The object method to use to create an index is CreateIndex, which returns an Index object:

expression.CreateIndex([*Name*])

where *expression* is a TableDef object and *Name* is an optional argument that adheres to the constraints of a valid name in Microsoft Access. As with other objects, the optional arguments might not be required on instantiation; however, they might be required to be appended. Table 18.14 lists the properties of an Index object that may be used to further define the index.

Table 18.14 DAO Index Properties

Property	Description
Fields	The Fields collection.
IgnoreNulls	Indicates whether records with Null values in the index fields have index entries.
Name*	The name of the index.
Primary	Indicates whether the Index is the primary index of the table.
Properties	The Properties collection.
Unique	Does each entry of the index key have to be unique?

Optional argument when used with CreateIndex

Listing 18.7 demonstrates how to create an Index object.

Listing 18.7 DAO_CreateIndex

```
Public Sub DAO_CreateIndex(strTablename As String, _
                           strIndexName As String, _
                           strWithField As String, _
                           Optional blDescending As Boolean, _
                           Optional blIsUnique As Boolean)
'Create an index for the passed table, using the passed name and settings

    Dim db As DAO.Database
    Dim tdf As DAO.TableDef
    Dim idx As DAO.Index
    Dim fld As DAO.Field
```

```
    Set db = CurrentDb
    Set tdf = db.TableDefs(strTablename)

    With tdf

        'Instantiate the index
        Set idx = .CreateIndex(strIndexName)

        'Set the fields and properties of the index
        Set fld = idx.CreateField(strWithField)
        If blDescending Then fld.Attributes = dbDescending
        idx.Fields.Append fld
        idx.Unique = blIsUnique

        'Append the index to collection
        .Indexes.Append idx

    End With

End Sub
```

Using the ADOX Object Model

Just as with the DAO index, the creation of an ADOX index has already been seen earlier in this chapter (refer to Listing 18.4). Also, similar to DAO, and referring to Figure 17.5 (p. 235), the `Index` object contains a `Columns` collection; the `Columns` collection of an `Index` object can only be appended to with a column from a `Columns` collection of a table. Like the other objects of a collection, the ADOX index once again follows the generic process that has become evident. In ADOX, as seen in the creation of other ADOX objects, an object method is not used to create an index; you just instantiate the `Index` object:

```
Set idx = New ADOX.Index
```

where *idx* is an object variable with the `ADOX.Index` type. Similar to the `Table` object, after instantiation of the `Index` object, the index properties and columns that define the index are set before being appending to the `Tables` collection. Table 18.15 lists the properties used to define an ADOX index.

Table 18.15   ADOX Index Properties

Property	Description
Columns	The `Columns` collection of the `Index` object
IndexNulls	Specifies whether records with null values are indexed
Name	Name of the column
PrimaryKey	Indicates whether the index represents the primary key on the table
Properties	The `Properties` collection of the `Index` object
Unique	Indicates whether the index keys must be unique

For an example of a technique that creates an index through ADOX, see Listing 18.8.

Listing 18.8   `ADOX_CreateIndex`

```
Public Sub ADOX_CreateIndex(strTablename As String, _
                            strIndexName As String, _
                            strWithField As String, _
                            Optional blDescending As Boolean, _
                            Optional blIsUnique As Boolean)
'Create an index for the passed table, using the passed name and settings

    Dim cat As ADOX.Catalog
    Dim tbl As ADOX.Table
    Dim idx As ADOX.Index

    Set cat = New ADOX.Catalog
    cat.ActiveConnection = CurrentProject.Connection.ConnectionString
    Set tbl = cat.Tables(strTablename)

    With tbl

        'Instantiate the index
        Set idx = New ADOX.Index

        'Set the Columns and properties of the index
        idx.Name = strIndexName
        idx.Columns.Append strWithField
        idx.Unique = blIsUnique
        If blDescending Then
            idx.Columns(strWithField).SortOrder = adSortDescending
        End If

        'Append the index to collection
        .Indexes.Append idx

    End With

End Sub
```

Creating Relationships

Relationships are a crucial element in a Relational Database Management System
(RDBMS). Relationships enable the prevention of redundant data and can be used to
ensure that related data is kept in sync by enforcing *referential integrity* between tables par-
ticipating in the relationship.

A relationship works by matching data from one table, called the *primary* (parent) table to
data from another table, which is called the *foreign* (child) table. The data from each table is
called the *key*. The key can be generated from one or more fields. The key in the primary
table is called the *primary key*. The primary key must be a unique value for each record in
the table. An Auto Increment field is commonly chosen as the primary key of a table.
Similarly the key from the foreign table is called the *foreign key;* which is not required to be

unique for each record in the foreign table. However, if referential integrity is enforced, the foreign key value must exist in the set of primary keys to append data to the foreign table. Note, however, that a foreign key can be set to Null without hindering the addition of records to the foreign table, barring any field constraints in the foreign table.

Assuming you are an experienced Access user, which you should be by this point, you probably are already familiar with these relationships. I reviewed the relationship details simply because the terminology used when creating relationships through VBA can get confusing!

Using the DAO Object Model

In DAO, a relationship is represented by the `Relation` object as shown in Figure 17.3 (p. 230) of the DAO object model. The `Relation` object has a collection of fields. The `Fields` collection of the `Relation` object can only be appended to with a field from a `Fields` collection of a `TableDef`. The object method used to create a `Relation` object is the `CreateRelation` method of the `Relations` collection, which returns a `Relation` object:

`expression.CreateRelation([Name][, Table][, ForeignTable][, Attributes])`

where *expression* is a `Database` object, and the optional arguments are as listed as marked properties in Table 18.16.

Table 18.16   DAO Relation Properties

Property	Description
Attributes*	Characteristics of the relation. See Table 18.17.
Fields	The `Fields` collection of the relation.
ForeignTable*	The foreign table of this relation.
Name*	The name of the relation.
Properties	The `Properties` collection.
Table*	The primary table in the relation.

*Optional argument of the `CreateRelation` method

Table 18.17   DAO Relation Attributes

Attribute	Description
dbRelationDeleteCascade	Deletions of the primary key record cascade, meaning that matching foreign key records are deleted also
dbRelationDontEnforce	Relationship not enforced (no referential integrity)
dbRelationInherited	Relationship exists in the database containing the two linked tables

continues

Table 18.17 Continued

Attribute	Description
dbRelationLeft	Show a LEFT JOIN as the default join type
dbRelationRight	Show a RIGHT JOIN as the default join type
dbRelationUnique	One-to-one relationship, which occurs when the foreign key is unique
dbRelationUpdateCascade	Updates cascade

Listing 18.9 shows you how to create a Relation object using VBA.

Listing 18.9 DAO_CreateRelation

```
Public Sub DAO_CreateRelation(strPrimaryTable As String, _
                              strPrimaryField As String, _
                              strForeignTable As String, _
                              strForeignField As String)
'Create a relationship based on the passed informaton. Referential integrity
'is enforced and a On Delete Cascade bit is set.

    Dim rel As DAO.Relation
    Dim fld As DAO.Field

    With CurrentDb

        'Instantiate the relation
        Set rel = .CreateRelation(strPrimaryTable & strForeignTable)

        'Set the properties to create the relation, and
        'set the Primary and Foreign tables
        rel.Table = strPrimaryTable
        rel.ForeignTable = strForeignTable

        'Append a primary key to the fields collection
        rel.Fields.Append rel.CreateField(strPrimaryField)

        'Set the ForeignName (Foreign Key) of the PrimaryKey field.
        rel.Fields(strPrimaryField).ForeignName = strForeignField

        'Enforce RI with a cascading delete
        rel.Attributes = dbRelationDeleteCascade

        'Append to the relation and refresh the db window
        .Relations.Append rel

    End With

End Sub
```

Using the ADOX Object Model

ADOX represents relationships using the `Key` object. As shown in Figure 17.5 (p. 235) the `Key` object is part of the `Keys` collection of a `Table` object. This structure is slightly different from that found in the DAO object model with analogous objects. Ultimately the result is the same; two tables become related through some criteria. While creating code, these slight nuances of each model force us to put ourselves in the appropriate mindset because it is easy to get turned around. In following the process of item (or object) creation within a collection, the instantiation of an ADOX `Key` object is similar to other ADOX objects. You just set an object variable to a `New` object of the appropriate type.

```
Set expression = New ADOX.Key
```

where *expression* is a declared object with a variable type of `ADOX.Key`. The properties in Table 18.18 are used to define the key before it is appended to the `Keys` collection.

Table 18.18   Properties

Property	Description
Columns	The columns related by the `Key` object.
DeleteRule	Enumerated value that indicates the action performed when a primary key is deleted. See Table 18.19 for a list of values.
Name	The name of the `Key` object.
RelatedTable	Indicates the name of the related table.
Type	The type of `Key` object. See Table 18.20 for a list of values.
UpdateRule	Enumerated value that indicates the action performed when a `PrimaryKey` is updated. See Table 18.19 for a list of values.

Table 18.19   ADOX Referential Integrity Rules (Used with `UpdateRule` and `DeleteRule` Properties)

Constant	Description
adRICascade	Cascade changes.
adRINone	No action is taken. (Default if not specified.)
adRISetDefault	Foreign key value is set to the default.
adRISetNull	Foreign key value is set to null.

18

Table 18.20   ADOX Key Types

Constant	Description
adKeyPrimary	The key is a primary key. (Default if not specified.)
adKeyForeign	The key is a foreign key.
adKeyUnique	The key is unique.

Using the properties and techniques discussed, Listing 18.10 is offered for you to examine the process for creating a Key through ADOX.

Listing 18.10   ADOX_CreateKey

```
Public Sub ADOX_CreateKey(strPrimaryTable As String, _
                          strPrimaryField As String, _
                          strForeignTable As String, _
                          strForeignField As String)
'Creates a relationship (aka: Key) using ADOX and the arguments specified.

    Dim cat As ADOX.Catalog
    Dim keyForeign As ADOX.Key

    'Connect to the catalog that is holding the Schema
    Set cat = New ADOX.Catalog
    cat.ActiveConnection = CurrentProject.Connection

    'Instantiate the Key
    Set keyForeign = New ADOX.Key

    'Define the Key (Creating a Foreign Key key)
    With keyForeign

        .Name = strPrimaryTable & strForeignTable
        .Type = adKeyForeign
        .Columns.Append strForeignField
        .RelatedTable = strPrimaryTable
        .Columns(strForeignField).RelatedColumn = strPrimaryField
        .UpdateRule = adRINone
        .DeleteRule = adRICascade

    End With

    'Append the Foreign Key to the Foreign Table
    cat.Tables(strForeignTable).Keys.Append keyForeign

End Sub
```

Creating Queries

Queries in Microsoft Access provide the capability of selecting certain data and specifying how it is to be sorted, or updating, adding, or deleting a group of records at the same time.

With a query you can JOIN your tables together to produce many different ways to view your data.

Queries are really pretty simple when looking at them from an object level. They basically do one thing, store a SQL statement. The SQL statement being stored supplies most of the properties of a Query object. In short, the SQL statement is the heart of a Query object.

> **TIP**
>
> Here is basic SQL syntax to select data:
>
> ```
> SELECT fieldlist
> FROM tablename
> IN anotherdatabase.mdb
> WHERE conditions
> GROUP BY fieldlist
> HAVING conditions for fields that are grouped
> ORDER BY fieldlist;
> ```
>
> The *italicized* arguments are inputs expected from you, and the monospaced terms are SQL keywords, not all of which are required.

The depth of information regarding construction of a SQL statement is outside the scope of this section, so I encourage you to search the Access Help system for the "Microsoft JET SQL Reference." In that topic I recommend the sections on Data Definition Language (DDL) and Data Manipulation Language (DML) to become more familiar with proper construction of SQL statements.

18

Using the DAO Object Model

As noted in Figure 17.3 (p. 230) an Access query is represented in the DAO object model as a QueryDef object. A QueryDef object is an item in the QueryDefs collection of the Database object. So with that hierarchy, I bet by this time you know the process by which we are going to create a QueryDef object! If you need a refresher, review the "Overview" section of this chapter. The method used to create a QueryDef object is CreateQueryDef, which returns a QueryDef object.

expression.CreateQueryDef([*Name*][, *SQL*])

Here, *expression* is a Database object. The optional *Name* and *SQL* arguments are also QueryDef properties. Table 18.21 contains the properties and their descriptions that can be used to define a QueryDef object.

Table 18.21 `QueryDef` **Properties**

Property	Description
CacheSize	The number of records retrieved from an ODBC data source that will be cached locally. The default value is 100. Setting to 0 turns it off.
Connect	A string that defines where the `QueryDef` gets its data. Typically set to an ODBC connect string when the data is stored remotely and not exposed through linked tables. This setting is also used for pass-through queries. The value is an empty string for queries that will execute against a local `TableDef` object.
MaxRecords	The maximum number of records returned by the `QueryDef` when connecting to a remote data source.
Name*	The name of the `QueryDef` and consequently the `Query` object it represents.
ODBCTimeout	The number of seconds MS Access waits for a response from a remote data source before raising a timeout error. The default is the value specified by the `QueryTimeout` property of the `Database` object, which has a default value of 60. If a value of 0 is specified, no timeout occurs.
Properties	The collection of properties.
ReturnsRecords	Indicates whether a pass-through query returns records.
SQL*	The SQL statement the `QueryDef` executes.

Optional arguments of the `CreateQueryDef` method

As you read the table of properties you will see that most of them deal with the situations involving remote data access. The `QueryDef` object is simple to create via code as shown in Listing 18.11.

Listing 18.11 `DAO_CreateQuery`

```
Public Sub DAO_CreateQuery(strName As String, strSQL As String)
'Creates a Query via a DAO QueryDef object and the passed SQL statement.

    Dim qdf As DAO.QueryDef

    With CurrentDb

        'Instantiate the object
        Set qdf = .CreateQueryDef

        'Set the object properties
        qdf.Name = strName
        qdf.SQL = strSQL
```

```
        'Append the object to the collection
        .QueryDefs.Append qdf

    End With

    'Refresh the User Interface
    RefreshDatabaseWindow

End Sub
```

Using the ADOX Object Model

The ADOX object model uses the `View` object to facilitate the creation of `Query` objects in the Microsoft Access user interface. A `View` is an item in the `Views` collection; however, in this case, that `View` is *not* created with the standard process of creating an item in a collection. The reason for this is that a `View` object cannot be instantiated. That's where the ADO `Command` object comes in. As you may recall from Table 17.3, the `Command` object is temporary and thus cannot be stored. So now we have a `View` that can't be temporary, and a `Command` that can't be permanent, so ADO and ADOX work together to allow us to store the temporary `Command` as a permanent `View` within the `Views` collection. Now that the `Command` object has been brought into the mix, we can follow the standard process for creating a `View`. The method used to instantiate a `Command` is simple; we just set an object variable to a `New` instance of that object:

```
Set cmd = New ADODB.Command
```

where *cmd* is a declared object as an `ADODB.Command` type. The `Command` object has many properties that resemble a `QueryDef` object. Table 18.22 lists the properties of a command. Table 18.23 lists the `View` item's properties.

Table 18.22   ADO Command **Properties**

Property	Description
ActiveConnection	Defines where the command gets the data from using a connection string.
CommandText	The SQL statement that will be executed against the data source.
CommandTimeout	The time, in seconds, that the command waits before returning a timeout error. Default is 30.
CommandType	Indicates the type of Command object. See Table 18.24.
Name	The name of the command.
Properties	The properties collection of the Command object.

18

Table 18.23 ADOX `View` Properties

Property	Description
Command	An ADO `Command` object that is stored in the `Views` collection.
Name	The name of the view or procedure, which becomes the name of the Microsoft Access `Query` object.

Table 18.24 ADO `Command` Types

Constant	Description
adCmdUnspecified	If the `CommandText` type is not specified, the provider then attempts to resolve the type of command issued.
adCmdText	Evaluates `CommandText` as a textual definition of a command or stored procedure call—for example, a SQL statement.
adCmdTable	Evaluates `CommandText` as a table name.
adCmdStoredProc	Evaluates `CommandText` as a stored procedure name.
adCmdUnknown	Indicates that the type of command in the `CommandText` property is not known (default).
adCmdFile	Evaluates `CommandText` as the filename of a persistently stored `Recordset`. Used with `Recordset.Open` or `Requery` only.
adCmdTableDirect	Evaluates `CommandText` as a table name.

Follow the pattern exhibited by storing other items into collections; it is simple to store a command into the `Views` collection. Listing 18.12 shows a simple procedure for performing such a task.

Listing 18.12 `ADOX_CreateView`

```
Public Sub ADOX_CreateView(strName As String, strSQL As String)
'Creates a Query with the name and SQL passed in the arguments

    Dim cmd As ADODB.Command
    Dim cat As ADOX.Catalog

    'Point to the data
    Set cat = New ADOX.Catalog
    cat.ActiveConnection = CurrentProject.Connection

    'Instantiate the Command
    Set cmd = New ADODB.Command

    'Set the properties
    cmd.CommandText = strSQL
```

```
'Append to the collection
cat.Views.Append strName, cmd

'Refresh the User Interface
RefreshDatabaseWindow

End Sub
```

CASE STUDY

Case Study: Updating an Existing Database Installation

To demonstrate the power of using VBA to create database schema, consider a scenario that is likely to happen if you develop several databases.

Suppose that you have an application used by three or four distinct clients. All use your program and all have the ability to customize the application to a small degree (that is, add their own reports). Over time, you decide to add a table to your application to accommodate some of the requests that have been coming in from users.

The normal upgrade path of just replacing the user's application with the updated one is not an option, due to the fact that your users have added customizations they want to keep. At this point it becomes apparent that creating a small piece of code to perform the following steps is the quickest method of implementation:

1. Create a new table (`tluSalaryRanges`).
2. Add fields to that table (`SalaryRange, Minimum, Maximum`).
3. Create an index on the table to prevent duplication in the `SalaryRange` field.
4. Add the foreign key field to the table that shares an alliance with the new table (`tluJobTitles`).
5. Create the relationship between the two.

The procedure in Listing 18.13 executes the Case Study steps using the DAO object model.

Listing 18.13   Case Study: `DAO_UpdateDatabase`

```
Public Sub DAO_UpdateDatabase()

    'First Create the new table
    DAO_CreateTable "tluSalaryRanges", "SalaryRangeID"

    'Next Add the Fields we need
    DAO_AddField "tluSalaryRanges", "SalaryRange", dbText, True
    DAO_AddField "tluSalaryRanges", "Minimum", dbCurrency, True
    DAO_AddField "tluSalaryRanges", "Maximum", dbCurrency, True

    'Next Create an Index on on the SalaryRange
    DAO_CreateIndex "tluSalaryRanges", "srUnique", "SalaryRange", , True
```

continues

Listing 18.13   Continued

```
'Next Add the Foreign Key field to the JobTitles table
DAO_AddField "tluJobTitles", "SalaryRangeID", dbLong, False

'Next Create the Relationship between the two tables
DAO_CreateRelation "tluSalaryRanges", "SalaryRangeID", _
                   "tluJobTitles", "SalaryRangeID"

'Refresh the User Interface
RefreshDatabaseWindow

End Sub
```

The procedure in Listing 18.14 executes the Case Study steps using the ADOX object model.

Listing 18.14   Case Study: ADOX_UpdateDatabase

```
Public Sub ADOX_UpdateDatabase()

    'First Create the new table
    ADOX_CreateTable "tluSalaryRanges", "SalaryRangeID"

    'Next Add the Fields we need
    ADOX_AddColumn "tluSalaryRanges", "SalaryRange", adVarWChar, True
    ADOX_AddColumn "tluSalaryRanges", "Minimum", adCurrency, True
    ADOX_AddColumn "tluSalaryRanges", "Maximum", adCurrency, True

    'Next Create an Index on on the SalaryRange
    ADOX_CreateIndex "tluSalaryRanges", "srUnique", "SalaryRange", , True

    'Next Add the Foreign Key field to the JobTitles table
    ADOX_AddColumn "tluJobTitles", "SalaryRangeID", adInteger, False

    'Next Create the Relationship between the two tables
    ADOX_CreateKey "tluSalaryRanges", "SalaryRangeID", _
                   "tluJobTitles", "SalaryRangeID"

    'Refresh the User Interface
    RefreshDatabaseWindow

End Sub
```

On execution of DAO_UpdateDatabase or ADOX_UpdateDatabase, the new table is added and fully implemented in the schema in a short amount of time.

Data Manipulation

19

Connecting to a Data Source

To manipulate data, we must first connect to a data source. Those words sound a lot like ADO object model terminology, but the intent is not to focus your attention on ADO but on the concept that to manipulate data, we need to be able to see it.

We look at data through the object models discussed in Chapter 17, "Object Models for Working with Data." In the ADO object model visibility of data is gained through opening a `Connection` object. In the DAO object model visibility of data is gained through opening a `Database` object. The process of opening a `Connection` or `Database` object is commonly referred to as *connecting to a data source*.

After we successfully connect to a data source, we can perform the task of manipulating data. In Chapter 18, "Creating Schema," we used object variables set to the current database opened in the Access environment. The current database is referenced with DAO's `CurrentDb` method as well as the ADO `Connection` property of the `CurrentProject` object (`CurrentProject.Connection`). The exciting thing is that we are not limited to just using the current database. Using the objects mentioned we can connect to databases stored remotely as well as data sources in different formats, such as SQL Server, text files, and other database formats.

Using the DAO Object Model

When using the DAO object model to connect to an existing data source, the `OpenDatabase` method is used, which returns a DAO `Database` object. The syntax for this method is

```
expression.OpenDatabase(Name[, Options] _
[, ReadOnly][, Connect])
```

where *expression* is a DBEngine or Workspace object. If *expression* is not specified the default Workspace is used. Table 19.1 lists the arguments of the method.

Table 19.1 **Arguments for** OpenDatabase **Method**

Argument	Data/Type	Explanation
Name	String	Required. A valid filename and path of the database file you are opening, often called the fully qualified name. The fully qualified name can use the Universal Naming Convention (UNC) path, such as \\Server\Share\Folder\My_Database.mdb, if your network supports it. This argument may also be the data source name (DSN) of an ODBC data source. Also, this argument may be a Zero Length String (ZLS). If the *Name* argument is an empty string (""), the Connect argument must contain information sufficient to fully connect to a database.
Options	Variant	Optional. Options that can be invoked while opening a database. For Microsoft Access, if set to True, the database opens in exclusive mode; False, and the database opens in shared mode.
ReadOnly	Boolean	Optional. True if you want to open the database with read-only access, or False (default) if you want to open the database with read/write access.
Connect	String	Optional. Connection information, including passwords. The Connect argument is typically expressed in two parts: the database type, followed by a semicolon (;) and the optional arguments. The optional arguments follow in no particular order but must be separated by semicolon. If the remote database is a Microsoft Access database type, the database type does not need to be specified. Here are a couple of examples: ";pwd=Mydbpassword" "ODBC;DATABASE=pubs;DSN=Publishers"

Using this expression in VBA is straightforward. Listing 19.1 illustrates the usage of the OpenDatabase method.

Listing 19.1 DAO_OpenDatabase

```
Public Sub DAO_OpenDatabase()
'Illustrate a couple of ways to connect to (or open) a remote database.

    Dim db As DAO.Database
    Dim strFullpath As String

    'Get the full path and name of the current database
    strFullpath = CurrentDb.Name

    'Open the current database, as if it were a remote database.
    Set db = OpenDatabase(strFullpath)
    Debug.Print "There are " & db.TableDefs.Count & _
```

```
                     " table definitions (including system tables) in " & _
                CurrentProject.Name

     'Open the current database, as read only.
     Set db = Workspaces("#DEFAULT WORKSPACE#") _
                         .OpenDatabase(strFullpath, , True)
     Debug.Print "There are " & db.TableDefs.Count & _
                " table definitions (including system tables) in " & _
                CurrentProject.Name

     'Clean up a bit
     db.Close
     Set db = Nothing

End Sub
```

Using the ADO Object Model

The ADO object model can be used to connect to an existing data source. In ADO the process is similar to creating objects with ADO methods. For this process of connecting to an existing data source, the Open method of the Connection object is used and follows this general process:

1. Instantiate the object.

2. Set properties for the object as needed.

3. Open the object for use.

The syntax for opening the Connection object for use is

```
cnn.Open [ConnectionString][, UserID][, Password][, Options]
```

where *cnn* is an instantiated Connection object. Table 19.2 describes the remaining arguments.

19

Table 19.2   Open **Method Arguments of the** Connection **Object**

Argument	Data Type	Explanation
ConnectionString	String	Optional. A string that indicates the information needed to successfully connect to a data source. ADO interprets the following arguments specified in Table 19.3. If other arguments are contained in the string, they are passed to the data provider. If this string is not passed the ConnectionString property of an instantiated Connection object must be specified prior to the execution of the Open method.
UserID	String	Optional. The user ID to be passed to the data source.
Password	String	Optional. The password of the user ID that allows access to the data source.

continues

Table 19.2 Continued

Argument	Data Type	Explanation
`Options`	Numeric	Optional. A value that indicates whether the code should halt until the connection is established (synchronously) or continue, regardless of whether the connection is established (asynchronously). See Table 19.4 for the constants that can be used for this argument.

The `ConnectionString` argument can have several arguments within it. The form of the string is `argument1=value1;argument2=value2;...` (continue as needed). ADO interprets the arguments specified in Table 19.3, while any other arguments specified are passed on to the data provider with which ADO is communicating.

Table 19.3 ADO-Specific Connection String Arguments

Argument	Explanation
`Provider=`	The provider that ADO uses to access the data
`File Name=*`	File containing connection information
`Remote Provider=*`	Provider when opening a client-side connection (Remote Data Service only)
`Remote Server=*`	Path name of the server when opening a client-side connection (Remote Data Service only)
`URL=*`	An absolute universal resource location (URL) identifying a resource, such as a file or directory

*Not commonly used with Microsoft Access Applications

> **TIP**
>
> The website http://www.connectionstrings.com is recommended as an excellent source of information with respect to properly formed connection strings.

The `Options` argument accepts the `ConnectOptionEnum` constants as indicated in Table 19.4.

Table 19.4 `ConnectOptionEnum` Constants

Constant	Description
`adAsyncConnect`	Opens the connection in an asynchronous manner, thus allowing code to continue while ADO works on opening the connection.
`adConnectUnspecified`	(Default) Opens the connection in a synchronized manner, thus halting the code progression until the connection is opened.

ADO's Open has many options that can be specified when connecting to a data source. This helps ADO support a wide array of data sources. When connecting to Microsoft Access data sources you can rely on the default value for most of the settings, which aids in creating easy-to-follow code.

In addition to the options of the Open method, the Connection object itself has several properties that control its behavior. Table 19.5 lists the more common Connection properties. Note that the values of these properties must be set before the connection is opened.

Table 19.5 Common Connection Object Properties

Property	Description
ConnectionString	A string that has information used to connect to a data source. This property can be passed as an argument in the Open method.
ConnectionTimeout	Indicates the number of seconds to wait for a data source to respond. The default value for this is 15 seconds.
CursorLocation	Sets the location of the cursor provided by the data provider. Two choices are available, and each can affect the connection as a whole. The two constants are adUseServer and adUseClient. A cursor is basically a pointer to a record in a set of records. With adUseServer the cursor is managed by the data provider. The adUseClient cursor location indicates that the application examining the data will manage the cursor.
Provider	Specifies the OLE DB provider that ADO will be interfacing with to get data.

Table 19.5 is not a complete listing of all the properties of a connection. As I have encouraged you to do previously, I suggest you utilize Intellisense and the help system to further your knowledge of the Connection object and its properties.

The code in Listing 19.2 illustrates connecting to a data source.

Listing 19.2 ADO_OpenConnection

```
Public Sub ADO_OpenConnection()
'Illustrate a couple of ways to connect to (or open) a remote database.

    Dim cnn As ADODB.Connection
    Dim strFullpath As String
    Dim x As Integer

    'Get the full path and name of the current database
    strFullpath = CurrentProject.FullName

    'Open the current database, as if it were a remote database.
    Set cnn = New ADODB.Connection
```

continues

19

Listing 19.2 Continued

```
cnn.Open "Provider=Microsoft.ACE.OLEDB.12.0;" & _
        "Data Source=" & strFullpath

'Open a Schema recordset of all the tables and count them
With cnn.OpenSchema(adSchemaTables, Array(Empty, Empty, Empty, "TABLE"))
    Do Until .EOF
        x = x + 1
        .MoveNext
    Loop
End With

'Show the results
Debug.Print "There are " & x & " Local tables in " & _
        CurrentProject.Name

'Close the connection and reset x
cnn.Close
x = 0

'Open the current database, as read only.
cnn.Mode = adModeRead
cnn.Open "Provider=Microsoft.ACE.OLEDB.12.0;" & _
        "Data Source=" & strFullpath

'Open a Schema recordset of all the tables and count them
With cnn.OpenSchema(adSchemaTables, Array(Empty, Empty, Empty, "TABLE"))
    Do Until .EOF
        x = x + 1
        .MoveNext
    Loop
End With

'Show the results
Debug.Print "There are " & x & " Local tables in " & _
        CurrentProject.Name

'Clean up a bit
cnn.Close
Set cnn = Nothing

End Sub
```

Opening a Recordset

After you are connected to a data source, manipulating data can be accomplished by opening a Recordset. A Recordset can be conceptualized as a set of records such as a table or query visualized in a Datasheet view; however a Recordset is typically not visualized. You can also manipulate data directly with Action queries or SQL statements that tell the database engine what you want to have done to the data. In those cases you do not need to have a Recordset open. To invoke an Action query or SQL statement, you can use the Execute method of a Database, Connection, or Command object.

All `Recordset` objects have a *cursor*, which marks the current record. The functionality of the `Recordset`, as well as the visibility of record modifications, is affected by what type of cursor your `Recordset` has (or was opened with). The influence of the cursor type is so heavy, that the type of `Recordset` you are working with is determined by the type of cursor it has. Table 19.6 lists the four core types of cursors (or `Recordsets`).

Table 19.6   Types of Cursors (or `Recordsets`) and Their VBA Constants

ADO Name (`CursorTypeEnum` Constant)	DAO Name (`RecordsetTypeEnum` Constant)	Description
Keyset (`adOpenKeyset`)	Dynaset (`dbOpenDynaset`)	Allows you to add, change, or delete records. Additions by other users are not visible. You are denied access to records that have been deleted by other users. Updates by other users are visible to you. Movement is unrestricted.
Static (`adOpenStatic`)	Snapshot (`dbOpenSnapshot`)	Provides a static copy of a set of records. Additions, updates, and deletions are not visible to you. In ADO, you can update and add records. In DAO, the `Recordset` is not updatable. Movement is unrestricted.
Forward-only (`adOpenForwardOnly`)	Forward-only (`dbOpenForwardOnly`)	Behaves like a Static or Snapshot `Recordset`, except you can only move forward through the `Recordset`.
Dynamic (`adOpenDynamic`)	Dynamic (`dbOpenDynamic`)	Behaves like the Keyset or Dynaset type, except additions and deletions by other users are visible to you. Note that ACE does not support this type of cursor. With ADO, you can request this type; however, Access automatically reverts you back to a Keyset cursor. With DAO you get an error if you request this cursor type because ACE does not support this type.

The four types of cursors (or `Recordsets`) in Table 19.6 allow you to work with multiple tables, joined together to create the records contained within a `Recordset`. With DAO there is one other type of `Recordset`; it is referred to as the *Table type* recordset represented by the `dbOpenTable` constant, which is part of the `RecordsetTypeEnum` enumeration. With the Table type `Recordset`, you are restricted to working with just one table. The interaction of a Table typed `Recordset` is similar to a Dynaset type.

In ADO, no type relates to opening a table directly as in DAO. However, in ADO, when opening a `Recordset` you have the ability to set an option with opening the recordset to indicate your intent to work with the table directly. The constants for that option are `adCmdTable` or `adCmdTableDirect` (see Table 19.12).

19

TIP The performance of the cursor is affected by the capabilities the cursor type has. The Forward-only cursor type is the most efficient; it opens and navigates fast but has the fewest capabilities. Conversely, the Dynamic cursor is the most burdensome; however, because ACE does not support that cursor, the Keyset cursor is considered the most taxing type of cursor in Microsoft Access. The Keyset cursor does, however, provide the most capability.

Using the DAO Object Model

To open a `Recordset` with the DAO object model, the `OpenRecordset` method is used. This method has two separate syntax configurations. The syntax that you choose is relative to the DAO object that is invoking the `OpenRecordset` method.

For `Database` objects:

```
expression.OpenRecordset(source[, type][, options][, lockedits])
```

where *expression* is a `Database` object.

For `QueryDef`, `TableDef`, and `Recordset` objects:

```
expression.OpenRecordset([type][, options][, lockedits])
```

where *expression* is a `QueryDef`, `TableDef`, or `Recordset` object. Table 19.7 describes the remaining arguments.

Table 19.7 `OpenRecordset` **Method Arguments**

Argument	Data Type	Description
source	String	Required for use with a `Database` object; this argument is not present when using a `QueryDef`, `TableDef`, or `Recordset` object. The source of the records for the `Recordset`. The source can be a table name, query name, or a SQL statement the returns records. If using a Table type recordset, the *source* argument must be a table name.
Type	Variant	Optional. A value from the `RecordsetTypeEnum` constants in the DAO column of Table 19.6. If not specified, the `dbOpenTable` is attempted. If that type is not applicable, DAO iterates the different types in this order: `dbOpenDynaset`, `dbOpenSnapshot`, and `dbOpenForwardOnly`, and chooses the first type that is valid.
Options	Variant	Optional. A combination of the constants from `RecordsetOptionEnum` that specify characteristics of the `Recordset`. (See Table 19.8.)
Lockedits	Variant	Optional. A constant from DAO `LockTypeEnum` (see Table 19.9) that specifies how to lock a record when edits are performed.

The *options* argument is a combination (summation) of `RecordsetTypeEnum`, which is expanded in Table 19.8.

Table 19.8 `RecordsetOptionEnum` **Constants**

Constant	Description
dbAppendOnly	Allows the user to add new records to the dynaset but prevents the user from reading existing records
dbConsistent	Applies updates only to those fields that will not affect other records in the dynaset (Dynaset and Snapshot types only)
dbDenyRead	Prevents other users from reading `Recordset` records (Table type only)
dbDenyWrite	Prevents other users from changing `Recordset` records
dbFailOnError	Rolls back updates if an error occurs
dbForwardOnly	Creates a forward-only scrolling Snapshot type `Recordset` (Snapshot type only)
dbInconsistent	Applies updates to all dynaset fields, even if other records are affected (Dynaset and Snapshot type only)
dbReadOnly	Opens the `Recordset` as read-only
dbSeeChanges	Generates a runtime error if another user is changing data you are editing (Dynaset type only)
dbSQLPassThrough	Sends a SQL statement to an ODBC database (Snapshot type only)

CAUTION

Inconsistent updates are those that violate the referential integrity of multiple tables represented in a multitable dynaset. If you need to bypass referential integrity, use the dbInconsistent option, and ACE will allow you to do so. This capability is useful but can easily be misused to create records that are invalid with respect to the schema of your database.

19

Table 19.9 lists the different constants that can be used in the *lockedits* argument during the execution of the OpenRecordset method that affect the way records are locked.

Table 19.9 **DAO** `LockTypeEnum` **Constants**

Constant	Description
dbOptimistic	The record being edited is not locked until the record is saved.
dbPessimistic	The record is locked immediately on the first edit, thus preventing others from editing the record simultaneously.

19

> **TIP**
>
> To find out the value of a constant: Open the Visual Basic Editor and view the Immediate window. Place your cursor inside the Immediate window and type out a "?" followed by the constant in question, like this:
>
> ```
> ? dbOptimistic
> ```
>
> On pressing the Enter key, the value appears immediately below the line that was just typed.

As you work with `Recordset` objects, you can extract information about the `Recordset` by examining the properties of the `Recordset` object. Some of the more common properties used are listed with brief descriptions in Table 19.10.

Table 19.10   Common DAO Recordset Properties

Property	Description
AbsolutePosition	The relative position of the current record. Zero-based (starts from zero).
BOF	Indication (`True` or `False`) of your position in the `Recordset` with respect to the beginning of the file. If `True`, you are at the beginning.
Bookmark	System-generated value that uniquely identifies a particular record in the `Recordset`. Bookmarks are created on the opening of the `Recordset`.
EditMode	Indicates the recordset's editing state.
EOF	Indication (`True` or `False`) of your position in the `Recordset` with respect to the end of the file (or `Recordset`). If `True`, you are at the end.
Filter	Expression that can be used to filter records from a `Recordset`.
LastModified	Bookmark pointing to the most recently modified record.
LockEdits	The type of locking in effect when editing.
NoMatch	Indication (`True` or `False`) whether a search (using `.FindFirst`, or similar method) was successful. `True` means no matching record was found.
RecordCount	Number of records in the `Recordset`. For this property to return an accurate result, you must navigate to the last record in order to fully populate the `Recordset`. If you do not fully populate the `Recordset`, this property, if available to the type of `Recordset` being used, will be >= 1 if the `Recordset` has records in it.
Sort	Expression defining the sort order of records.
Type	The recordset (or cursor) type.
Updatable	Indicates whether the recordset can be updated.

> **TIP**
>
> To test for an empty `Recordset` you can test for a `True` condition for both the `EOF` and `BOF` properties simultaneously:
>
>   If (rst.BOF And rst.EOF) = True Then ...

It is important to note that a `Recordset` property may not be available for every type of `Recordset`. For example, the `AbsolutePosition` property, which indicates the position of a record with in the `Recordset`, is not available in a `dbOpenForwardOnly` or `dbOpenTable` typed `Recordset`.

Listing 19.3 shows a simple example of opening a `Recordset`. A message box appears that displays the `RecordCount` of the source table.

Listing 19.3 DAO_OpenRecordset

```
Public Sub DAO_OpenRecordset()
'Open a recordset using DAO

    Dim rst As DAO.Recordset
    Dim db As DAO.Database
    Dim x As Long

    'Point the database and open a recordset
    Set db = CurrentDb
    Set rst = db.OpenRecordset("SELECT * FROM tblEmployees", dbOpenSnapshot)

    'Fully populate the recordset
    If Not (rst.BOF And rst.EOF) Then
        rst.MoveLast
        x = rst.RecordCount
    End If

    'Display the record count
    MsgBox "There are " & x & " records in the tblEmployees table."

    'Clean up
    rst.Close
    Set db = Nothing

End Sub
```

19

Using the ADO Object Model

> **CAUTION**
>
> Note that many objects, methods, and properties are named identically between the ADO, ADOX, and DAO object models. With that in mind, be aware of the context in which the terms are being used. In VBA code, the distinction is often made clear by *fully qualifying* an object type. For example:
>
> ```
> Dim rst As ADODB.Recordset
> ```
>
> Identifies the *rst* variable as a Recordset object from the ADO object model exposed by the ADODB object library reference used by VBA.

When using the ADO object model to open a Recordset you follow the general process shown earlier in this chapter. For review, that process is

1. Instantiate the object.
2. Set properties for the object as needed.
3. Open the object for use.

To open a Recordset object, the Open method of the ADO Recordset object is used. The syntax for opening the Recordset object is

```
rst.Open [Source][, ActiveConnection][, CursorType][, LockType][, options]
```

where *rst* is an ADO *Recordset* object variable. The arguments of the Open method, except for *options*, are Recordset properties. Table 19.11 shows common Recordset properties.

Table 19.11   ADO Recordset Properties

Property	Description
AbsolutePosition	The relative position of the current record. Starts from 1.
ActiveConnection*	The Connection object the Recordset belongs to.
BOF	Indicates whether the current record position is before the first record. The position is called the Beginning Of File.
Bookmark	A unique identifier for a record, generated by the system. The value is not static and thus changes with each opening of the Recordset.
CursorLocation	Sets the location of the *cursor* provided by the data provider. Two choices are available, and each can affect the connection as a whole. The two constants are adUseServer and adUseClient. A cursor is basically a pointer to a record in a set of records. With the adUseServer the cursor is managed by the data provider. The adUseClient cursor location indicates that the application examining the data will manage the cursor.

Property	Description
CursorType*	A value from the CursorTypeEnum constants listed in Table 19.6. The default is adOpenForwardOnly.
EditMode	Editing status of the current record. EditModeEnum constants are adEditNone—No edits in progress. adEditInProgress—Edits in progress, but not saved. adEditAdd—New record is being edited. adEditDelete—Record has been deleted.
EOF	Indicates whether the current record position is before the first record.
Fields (Collection)	A collection of Field objects.
Filter	A filter for the data in the Recordset. This value can be a criteria string or an array of Bookmarks.
Index	The index in use. Only valid on a recordset opened with the acCmdTableDirect characteristic set in the *options* argument.
LockType*	The lock type as specified by an ADO LockTypeEnum constant: adLockBatchOptimistic—Optimistic batch updates adLockOptimistic—Optimistic locking adLockPessimistic—Pessimistic locking adLockReadOnly—Read-only adLockUnspecified—No locking specified
MaxRecords	The maximum amount of records returned by the Recordset. A value of indicates unlimited.
Properties (Collection)	Provider-specific properties.
RecordCount	The quantity of records. Unlike DAO, an ADO recordset is fully populated and thus will return the full count immediately following the Open statement.
Sort	Sort criteria string.
Source*	Indicates the source of the Recordset. A valid Command object, SQL statement, table name, query name, URL, or even a filename.
State	The state of the Recordset as indicated by the ObjectStateEnum constants: adStateClosed—Object is closed. adStateOpen—Object is opened. adStateConnecting—Object is connecting. adStateExecuting—Object is executing a command. adStateFetching—Object is retrieving rows.

19

*Property can be passed as an argument in the Open method.

The *options* argument, like many other arguments that share the same name, is a value comprised of constants. The *options* argument of the Open method specifies how the provider is to interpret the Source property (or argument), if the Source is not a Command. The constants available for this argument come from two sets of enumerations: CommandTypeEnum or ExecOptionEnum, which are represented by Table 19.12 and Table 19.13, respectively. Both tables represent the constants relevant to opening a Recordset and valid with the ACE data provider.

Table 19.12 CommandTypeEnum **Constants**

Constant	Description
adCmdStoredProcedure	Evaluates Source as a stored procedure name. With ACE/JET providers, this is not a valid option when using the Open method. However, with the Execute method, the option indicates that the Source is the name of an Action query.
adCmdTable	Evaluates Source as a table name (or name of a Select type query with the ACE/JET data providers).
adCmdTableDirect	Evaluates Source as a table name (or name of a Select type query with the ACE/JET data providers). This option must be specified to use the Seek method of the opened Recordset. Cannot be combined with the ExecuteOptionEnum value adAsyncExecute.
adCmdText	Evaluates Source as a textual definition of a command or stored procedure call—in other words, a SQL statement.
adCmdUnknown	Default. Indicates that the type of command in the Source argument is not known. The data provider determines what the Source is to the best of its ability.
adCmdUnspecified	Does not specify the command type argument.

Table 19.13 ExecOptionEnum **Constants**

Constant	Description
adAsyncExecute	Indicates that the Source (or command) should execute asynchronously. This means that the next line of your VBA code can execute even though the opening of the Recordset is not complete. This value cannot be combined with the CommandTypeEnum value adCmdTableDirect.
adAsyncFetch	The remaining rows after the quantity specified by the CacheSize property are to be retrieved asynchronously.
adAsyncFetchNonBlocking	Indicates that the main thread never blocks while retrieving. If the requested row has not been retrieved, the current row automatically moves to the end of the file.
adOptionUnspecified	Indicates that the command is unspecified.

Listing 19.4 illustrates the opening of an ADO `Recordset` object and displaying the number of records in the resultant `Recordset`.

Listing 19.4   ADO_RecordsetOpen

```
Public Sub ADO_RecordsetOpen()
'Open a recordset using ADO

    Dim rst As ADODB.Recordset
    Dim cnn As ADODB.Connection
    Dim x As Long

    'Point the database and open a recordset
    Set cnn = CurrentProject.Connection
    Set rst = New ADODB.Recordset
    rst.Open "SELECT * FROM tblEmployees", cnn, _
            adOpenStatic, adLockReadOnly, adCmdText

    'Record the record count
    If Not (rst.BOF And rst.EOF) Then x = rst.RecordCount

    'Display the record count
    MsgBox "There are " & x & " records in the tblEmployees table."

    'Clean up
    rst.Close
    Set cnn = Nothing

End Sub
```

ADO recordsets, by default, fully populate on opening. If your `Source` argument (or property) returns a large number of records, you may experience an unacceptable delay in your code. To help alleviate this delay, you may want to use the `adAsyncExecute` or the `adAsyncFetch` constant in the *options* argument. By doing this you allow your code to continue, while your records are gathered by the `Open` method. Another option is to consider reducing the amount of records you are retrieving from your `Source`. Listing 19.5 illustrates the opening of a `Recordset` in asynchronous form.

19

Listing 19.5   ADO_AsyncRecordsetOpen

```
Public Sub ADO_AsyncRecordsetOpen()
'Open a recordset using ADO, asynchronously

    Dim rst As ADODB.Recordset
    Dim cnn As ADODB.Connection
    Dim x As Long

    'Point the database and open a recordset
    Set cnn = CurrentProject.Connection
    Set rst = New ADODB.Recordset
```

continues

Listing 19.5   Continued

```
    rst.Open "SELECT * FROM tblEmployees", cnn, _
            adOpenStatic, adLockReadOnly, adCmdText + adAsyncExecute

    ''''''''''''''''''
    'Put code that is not dependent on the rst here
    ''''''''''''''''''

    'Wait till the recordset is fully populated
    Do Until rst.State = adStateOpen
        Echo True, "Waiting for recordset to open ... "
        DoEvents
    Loop

    'Record the record count
    If Not (rst.BOF And rst.EOF) Then x = rst.RecordCount

    'Display the record count
    MsgBox "There are " & x & " records in the tblEmployees table."

    'Clean up
    rst.Close
    Set cnn = Nothing

End Sub
```

Inserting Data

Inserting records, via code, into a table (or Recordset) can be done in a couple of ways:

- The Execute method as it applies to DAO's Database and QueryDef objects, as well as ADO's Connection and Command objects.
- The AddNew method as it applies to the DAO and ADO Recordset objects.

DAO'S Execute Method

The Execute method runs an action query or executes a SQL statement on a specified Database object. Because the behavior of the Execute method is to run an action query or SQL statement, it is up to you to specify a query or SQL statement that performs the task at hand. The Execute method can be called in VBA with two syntax forms.

For Database objects:

db.Execute *CommandText*[, *options*]

For QueryDef objects:

qdf.Execute [*options*]

where *db* is a DAO Database object and *qdf* is a DAO QueryDef object whose SQL property setting specifies an action type SQL statement. The remaining arguments are presented in Table 19.14

Table 19.14   Arguments of DAO's `Execute` **Method**

Argument	Description
`CommandText`	A `String` that is a SQL statement or the `Name` property value of a `QueryDef` object.
`Options`	Optional. A constant or combination of `RecordsetOptionEnum` constants that determines the characteristics you want in place while the data is acted on (refer to Table 19.8).

C A U T I O N

The `Execute` method issues the query or SQL directly to the Access database engine (ACE), which means the Access user interface is bypassed, which is good for speed. However, if your SQL statement or SQL property of the `QueryDef` references an Access object such as a form control:

```
UPDATE sometable SET field1 = [Forms]![MainForm]![txtTextBox]
```

an error that is worded like this—"Too few parameters..."— is raised.

One technique to avoid this error and keep your Access references in your SQL statement is to use the `DoCmd.RunSQL` or `DoCmd.OpenQuery` methods, which resolve any Access user interface parameters before issuing the SQL statement to the database engine.

```
DoCmd.RunSQL strSQL
```

where `strSQL` is the SQL statement to be run.

Another technique is to wrap your Access user interface reference with the `Eval()` function:

```
UPDATE sometable SET field1 = _
Eval('[Forms]![MainForm]![txtTextBox]')
```

The `Eval()` function is "understood" by ACE and resolves the Access user interface reference when using the `Execute` method.

In Listing 19.6, the `Execute` method is used to insert a record into a table.

Listing 19.6   `DAO_InsertRecordExec()`

```
Public Sub DAO_InsertRecordExec()
'Insert a record into tblEmployees

    Dim strSQL As String

    'Build SQL command text
    strSQL = "INSERT INTO tblEmployees" & _
             " (FirstName, LastName)" & _
             " VALUES ('Brent', 'Spaulding')"

    'Execute the SQL command statement and display message
        With CurrentDb
```

continues

Listing 19.6 Continued

```
            .Execute strSQL, dbFailOnError
            MsgBox "Inserted " & .RecordsAffected & " records."
        End With
End Sub
```

> **TIP**
>
> The `Execute` method, with both DAO and ADO object models, can be used to invoke an action type (`INSERT INTO`, `DELETE FROM`, `UPDATE`, `ALTER TABLE`, and others) SQL statement.

ADO's `Execute` Method

The ADO `Execute` method does the same task as the `Execute` method in DAO in that it runs an action type SQL statement on a connected data source; the action must be defined in the resultant SQL statement. However, ADO's `Execute` returns a `Recordset` object. Like DAO, two syntax forms can be used.

For the `Connection` object:

`cnn.Execute CommandText[, RecordsAffected][, Options]`

For the `Command` object:

`cmd.Execute RecordsAffected[, Parameters][, Options]`

where *cnn* is a `Connection` object, and *cmd* is a `Command` object. Table 19.15 describes the remaining arguments.

Table 19.15 Arguments of ADO's `Execute` Method

Argument	Description
CommandText	A `String` that is a SQL statement or the `Name` property value of a `QueryDef` object.
RecordsAffected	A variable of the `Long` data type that will be set to the number of records affected by the action invoked. If the `adAsyncExecute` option is used, the value will not be accurate.
Parameters	An array of parameter values used in SQL statement set in *CommandText* or the *cmd* object.
Options	A value of combination of values from `CommandTypeEnum` or `ExecOptionEnum`. (See Tables 19.12 and 19.13, respectively.)

Listing 19.7 illustrates the use of ADO's `Execute` method.

Listing 19.7 ADO_InsertRecordExec()

```
Public Sub ADO_InsertRecordExec()
'Insert a record into tblEmployees

    Dim strSQL As String
    Dim lngRecordsAffected As Long

    'Build SQL command text
    strSQL = "INSERT INTO tblEmployees" & _
            " (FirstName, LastName)" & _
            " VALUES ('Scott', 'Gem')"

    'Execute the SQL command statement and display message
    CurrentProject.Connection.Execute strSQL, lngRecordsAffected, adCmdText

    MsgBox "Inserted " & lngRecordsAffected & " records."

End Sub
```

DAO'S AddNew **Method**

The AddNew method is easy to understand; it adds a new record to a table. The syntax and typical usage of the AddNew method is

```
rst.AddNew
rst.Fields(fieldname) = somevalue
rst.Update
```

where *rst* is an updatable Recordset object, *fieldname* is the name of a field, and *somevalue* is an appropriate value for the field specified by *fieldname*.

When modifying a DAO Recordset, which is what the AddNew method enables, there are some things to keep in mind. The most important is the fact that your modifications will *not* be saved until you have executed the Update method. That behavior is different from modifications in an ADO Recordset. If you close the DAO Recordset or navigate off the new (or modified) record before you Update, your record values will be discarded without warning. Another nuance of DAO and the AddNew method is that the newly added record does not become the current record; the current record remains as it was before you issued the AddNew method. To navigate to the newly added record, use the LastModified method of the DAO Recordset object. Listing 19.8 illustrates the DAO's AddNew method and programming techniques to handle the behaviors mentioned.

19

Listing 19.8 DAO_InsertRecordAddNew()

```
Public Sub DAO_InsertRecordAddNew()
'Insert a record into tblEmployees

    Dim rst As DAO.Recordset
    Dim strSQL As String
```

continues

Listing 19.8   Continued

```
'Build SQL statement that will return an empty
'recordset, since we are inserting data.
strSQL = "SELECT * FROM tblEmployees WHERE 1=0"

'Open the recordset
Set rst = CurrentDb.OpenRecordset(strSQL, dbOpenDynaset, dbPessimistic)

'Add the record
With rst
    .AddNew
    .Fields("FirstName") = "Eric"
    .Fields("LastName") = "Covington"
    .Update
End With

'Display message
rst.Bookmark = rst.LastModified
MsgBox "Just added " & rst.Fields("FirstName")

'Clean up
rst.Close

End Sub
```

> **CAUTION**
>
> You must execute the `Update` method of a DAO `Recordset` to save your new or modified record. Your changes will be discarded without warning if you `Close` the `Recordset` or navigate off the new (or modified) record.

ADO'S AddNew **Method**

The `AddNew` method in ADO can behave similarly to its DAO counterpart; it adds a new record to a table. However, with ADO, you get the benefit of a more flexible syntax, which is

```
rst.AddNew [FieldList][, Values]
```

where *rst* is an updatable `Recordset` object, *FieldList* is an array of field names, or ordinal positions, from *rst*, and *Values* is a variant array of values that correspond to the fields in *FieldList*.

Like DAO, modification of an ADO `Recordset`, requires you to keep some behaviors in mind. One of the most relevant is the fact that your modifications *will* be saved, even without an `Update` method call, when you navigate away from the new (or modified) record, which is a different from the behavior of a DAO `Recordset`. If you choose to add records using the *FieldList* and *Values* arguments, the new record is saved immediately, with no need to call the `Update` method. In addition, attempting to `Close` an ADO `Recordset` before the modified record is saved yields an error.

Another behavior of an ADO `Recordset` that is different from that of a DAO `Recordset` is the fact that after a new record has been saved (or committed), that record becomes the current record. Listing 19.9 illustrates ADO's `AddNew` method.

> **TIP**
>
> Even though the behavior of an ADO `Recordset` automatically saves your record modifications on navigation, it is a typical practice and the recommendation is that you invoke the `Update` call to control the saving of your modifications. The one exception is when adding new records via the optional arguments of the `AddNew` method.

Listing 19.9 `ADO_InsertRecordAddNew()`

```
Public Sub ADO_InsertRecordAddNew()
'Insert a record into tblEmployees

    Dim rst As ADODB.Recordset
    Dim strSQL As String
    Dim strNewNames As String

    'Build SQL statement that will return an empty
    'recordset, since we are inserting data.
    strSQL = "SELECT * FROM tblEmployees WHERE 1=0"

    'Open the recordset
    Set rst = New ADODB.Recordset
    rst.Open strSQL, CurrentProject.Connection, adOpenKeyset, _
            adLockPessimistic, adCmdText

    'Add a record
    With rst
        .AddNew
        .Fields("FirstName") = "Rob"
        .Fields("LastName") = "Covington"
        .Update

        strNewNames = .Fields("FirstName") & ", "
    End With

    'Add another record
    With rst
        .AddNew Array("FirstName", "LastName"), _
                Array("Tony", "McCoy")

        strNewNames = strNewNames & .Fields("FirstName")
    End With

    'Display message
    MsgBox "Just added " & strNewNames

    'Clean up
    rst.Close

End Sub
```

19

Finding Data

After you go through the process of adding data, you often need to find a particular record or a group of records in your database! Finding data in an ADO or DAO `Recordset` is conceptually the same: You find the data that matches your criteria. As with most actions you perform in VBA and Access, there are more than a couple of ways to accomplish the task. The discussion in this section focuses on

- Limiting the records of a `Recordset` with a SQL statement
- The `FindFirst`, `FindNext`, `FindLast`, `FindPrevious`, `Seek`, and `Filter` methods of a DAO `Recordset`
- The `Find`, `Seek`, and `Filter` methods of an ADO `Recordset`

> **TIP**
>
> I recommend that you investigate the DAO and ADO `Move` methods: `Move`, `MoveFirst`, `MoveNext`, `MovePrevious`, and `MoveLast`. They move the current record position; however, no criteria is applied in the move. These methods are often used in looping type scenarios.

Limiting Records Retrieved

By far the most effective and efficient way to work with data is to retrieve what you need in your `Recordset`. For example, if you intend to work with all transactions with a creation date after a specified date, construct your SQL statement (the *source* argument as referenced in the "Opening a `Recordset`" section earlier in this chapter) in such a way to retrieve only those records of interest:

```
SELECT tblTransactions.*
FROM tblTransactions
WHERE CreatedDate >= #April 4 2006#
```

This returns only those records where the creation date is greater than or equal to, April 4, 2006. Another example might be the need to work with only one record that matches specific criteria. For example, you may want to find the most recent transaction by a particular employee. Again construct your SQL statement to reflect your criteria:

```
SELECT TOP 1 tblTransactions.*
FROM tblTransactions
WHERE Employee = 7
ORDER BY CreatedDate DESC
```

The `ORDER BY` clause sorts the records by descending creation date. The `WHERE` clause indicates the retrieval of those records with an `Employee` field value of 7. The `TOP 1` predicate tells Microsoft Access to stop looking for records after one has matched the criteria, so that only one record is fully retrieved from the table to populate your `Recordset`.

This chapter is not a SQL syntax reference; however, it is important to understand the effects of proper, and improper, construction of the *source* argument in the context of opening a Recordset. Listing 19.10 illustrates the building and use of a limiting SQL statement.

→ For a brief overview of SQL statements see the appendix, **p. 373**.

Listing 19.10 GetLastTransactionDate()

```
Public Function GetLastTransactionDate(lngEmployeeID As Long) As Variant
'Returns the last transaction date (CreateDate) for a passed lngEmployeeID.
'If no transactions exist, then a Null is returned.

    Dim strSQL As String

    'Build SQL to Retrieve information
    strSQL = "SELECT TOP 1 tblTransactions.CreatedDate" & _
             " FROM tblTransactions" & _
             " WHERE Employee = " & lngEmployeeID & _
             " ORDER BY CreatedDate DESC"

    'Open a recordset that retrieves the informaton
    With CurrentDb.OpenRecordset(strSQL, dbOpenForwardOnly)
        'Return the information
        If (.BOF And .EOF) Then
            GetLastTransactionDate = Null
        Else
            GetLastTransactionDate = .Fields("CreatedDate")
        End If
    End With

End Function
```

DAO's FindFirst, FindNext, FindLast, and FindPrevious **Methods**

The Find methods of a DAO Recordset are concerned with doing one thing, finding one record. As a programmer you may search an entire recordset using FindNext, and then with each successful match of the initial criteria, you test the record against additional criteria. But even with that, the Find methods find only one record at a time. The syntax, which is valid for all the Find methods of the DAO Recordset is

```
rst.FindFirst criteria
```

where *rst* is a DAO Recordset that is unrestricted with respect to navigation (dbOpenSnapshot or dbDynaset), and *criteria* is a string that forms a WHERE clause, except without the "WHERE."

When using the Find methods, the `NoMatch` property of the DAO `Recordset` is used to test for a successful match. If a record is found, it becomes the current record. If a record is not found, the current record becomes unknown. Although the current record is officially unknown, typically the current record remains the same as it was before the Find method of choice was invoked, with the exception of `FindFirst`, which typically leaves the first record as the current record.

The Find methods start searching from and in the direction of, as follows:

- `FindFirst`—From the first record to the end of the `Recordset`
- `FindLast`—From the last record to the beginning of the `Recordset`
- `FindNext`—From the current record to the end of the `Recordset`
- `FindPrevious`—From the current record to the beginning of the `Recordset`

Listing 19.11 illustrates the usage of the DAO `FindFirst` method. The other Find methods are used similarly.

Listing 19.11 DAO_GetItemRank()

```
Public Function DAO_GetItemRank(lngInventoryID As Long, _
                                dtDateInMonth As Date) As Long
'Finds where the passed inventory item ranked with respect to
'volume for the month passed. Returns a 0 if no transactions
'occurred for the passed item.

    Dim rst As DAO.Recordset2
    Dim strSQL As String
    Dim dtMonthBegin As Date
    Dim dtMonthEnd As Date

    'Calc the month boundaries
    dtMonthBegin = DateSerial(Year(dtDateInMonth), Month(dtDateInMonth), 1)
    dtMonthEnd = DateSerial(Year(dtDateInMonth), Month(dtDateInMonth) + 1, 0)

    'Build a SQL statement to retreive the data
    strSQL = "SELECT TransactionItem, Sum(Quantity) As TotalTransactions" & _
            " FROM tblTransactions" & _
            " WHERE CreatedDate Between" & _
                " #" & dtMonthBegin & "# And #" & dtMonthEnd & "#" & _
            " GROUP BY TransactionItem" & _
            " ORDER BY Sum(Quantity) DESC"

    'Open the recordset and find the rank of the passed item
    Set rst = CurrentDb.OpenRecordset(strSQL, dbOpenSnapshot)
```

19

```
'Get the rank of the passed item. Note that the function is
'declared as a Long, which defaults to 0, so only return
'a result if a record is found.
With rst
    If Not (.EOF And .BOF) Then
        .FindFirst "TransactionItem = " & lngInventoryID
        If Not .NoMatch Then
            DAO_GetItemRank = .AbsolutePosition + 1 'Zero based
        End If
    End If
End With

'Clean Up
rst.Close

End Function
```

DAO's Seek **Method**

The Seek method is an efficient method to find records in a Recordset when an Index name and value (or key) of the Index is known. Many times, a table's primary key is named "PrimaryKey" and is based on an AutoNumber data type. Before you can invoke the Seek method, you must specify the Index you want to use. The syntax for DAO's Seek method is

rst.Seek *comparison*, *key1*[, *key2*][, *key3*],…[, *key13*]

where *rst* is a DAO Recordset. The other arguments are as follows:

- *comparison* is passed as a string, required, and must be one of the following comparison operators: <, <=, =, >=, or >.
- *key1* is a value of the Index in use and is required.
- *key2* ... *key13* are subsequent values of a multifield Index. The number of keys required for input is depends on the number of fields in the Index.

The success of the Seek operation is indicated by the NoMatch property, just as in the Find methods. If the Seek operation is successful, the record found becomes the current record; if unsuccessful, the current record is unknown, just as in the Find methods. To see the usage of the Seek method, examine Listing 19.12.

19

Listing 19.12   DAO_SeekTransaction

```
Public Sub DAO_SeekTransaction(lngTransactionID As Long)
'Seek the passed transaction id

    Dim rst As DAO.Recordset2

    'Open a Table
    Set rst = CurrentDb.OpenRecordset("tblTransactions", dbOpenTable)

    'Seek a Record
```

continues

Listing 19.12   Continued

```
With rst

    'Set up and seek for the passed value
    .Index = "PrimaryKey"
    .Seek "=", lngTransactionID

    'Indicate the result
    If .NoMatch Then
        MsgBox "Transaction not found!"
    Else
        MsgBox "Transaction found!"
    End If

End With

End Sub
```

> **TIP**
>
> The Seek method cannot be used on linked tables. You can, however, open the remote database into a DAO.Database typed object variable, and then use the tables through that object variable.

Using DAO's Filter Method

The Filter property of a DAO Recordset can be used to identify a subset of records within a Recordset. The Filter property is conceptually like a WHERE clause in a SQL statement without the keyword "WHERE." The Filter property can be used to find a single record but is more commonly used to find a subset of records. The syntax for the Filter property is

```
rst.Filter = criteria
```

where *rst* is a DAO Recordset object, and *criteria* is a string that creates an expression that a record must satisfy to be included in the resultant Recordset. The Filter property is used with the OpenRecordset method discussed earlier in this chapter in the section "Opening a Recordset." To illustrate the Filter property in VBA, examine Listing 19.13.

Listing 19.13   DAO_FilterRecordset

```
Public Sub DAO_FilterRecordset()
'Displays the effect of applying a filter to a Recordset

    Dim rst As DAO.Recordset
    Dim rstFiltered As DAO.Recordset
    Dim strSQL As String

    'Build the SQL statement
    strSQL = "SELECT * FROM tblTransactions"
```

```
'Open a Recordset
Set rst = CurrentDb.OpenRecordset(strSQL, dbOpenSnapshot)

If Not (rst.EOF And rst.BOF) Then

    'Display a message
    rst.MoveLast
    MsgBox "There are " & rst.RecordCount & " in the original Recordset"

    'Set the Filter
    rst.Filter = "Employee = 8"

    'Apply the Filter
    Set rstFiltered = rst.OpenRecordset

    'Display message
    If Not (rstFiltered.EOF And rstFiltered.BOF) Then
        rstFiltered.MoveLast
        MsgBox "There are " & rstFiltered.RecordCount & _
               " records in the filtered recordset"
    End If

    'Clean up a bit
    rstFiltered.Close

End If

'Clean up some more
rst.Close

End Sub
```

TIP

It is more efficient to construct your SQL statement with a WHERE clause when opening the origi-
nating Recordset when compared to opening a Recordset, setting the Filter, and then
opening the filtered Recordset.

19

Using ADO's Find **Method**

ADO's Find method behaves similarly to the DAO Find methods in that it finds a single
record based on the criteria you specify. Unlike DAO, ADO only has one Find method; the
arguments of the method determine the search direction and the start location. The syntax
for ADO's Find method is

```
rst.Find Criteria[, SkipRows][, SearchDirection][, Start]
```

where *rst* is an ADO Recordset that is unrestricted with respect to navigation. The other
arguments are defined in Table 19.16.

Table 19.16 Arguments of ADO's `Find` Method

Argument	Description
`Criteria`	Required. A `String` that defines the expression a record must satisfy to be found. The string is similar to a `WHERE` clause without the word "WHERE."
`SkipRows`	Optional. The offset from the current record, or the bookmark specified in the `Start` argument in which to begin the search.
`SearchDirection`	Optional. A value from `SearchDirectionEnum`. adSearchBackward—Searches toward the BOF. adSearchForward—Searches toward the EOF.
`Start`	Optional. A bookmark that is the starting point for the search.

The `Find` method of an ADO `Recordset` is an efficient operation; however, ADO's `Find` can search only one column (or field) at a time.

The current record is the first record that satisfies the criteria. The BOF or EOF, depending on search direction, will be True if the `Find` does not yield a match. Listing 19.14 gives a simple example that mimics its DAO counterpart listed earlier in this chapter.

Listing 19.14 `ADO_GetItemRank`

```
Public Function ADO_GetItemRank(lngInventoryID As Long, _
                                dtDateInMonth As Date) As Long
'Finds where the passed inventory item ranked with respect to
'volume for the month passed. Returns a 0 if no transactions
'occurred for the passed item.

    Dim rst As ADODB.Recordset
    Dim strSQL As String
    Dim dtMonthBegin As Date
    Dim dtMonthEnd As Date

    'Calc the month boundaries
    dtMonthBegin = DateSerial(Year(dtDateInMonth), Month(dtDateInMonth), 1)
    dtMonthEnd = DateSerial(Year(dtDateInMonth), Month(dtDateInMonth) + 1, 0)

    'Build a SQL statement to retrieve the data
    strSQL = "SELECT TransactionItem, Sum(Quantity) As TotalTransactions" & _
        " FROM tblTransactions" & _
        " WHERE CreatedDate Between" & _
            " #" & dtMonthBegin & "# And #" & dtMonthEnd & "#" & _
        " GROUP BY TransactionItem" & _
        " ORDER BY Sum(Quantity) DESC"

    'Open the recordset and find the rank of the passed item
    Set rst = New ADODB.Recordset
    rst.Open strSQL, CurrentProject.Connection, _
             adOpenStatic, adLockReadOnly, adCmdText
```

```
    'Get the rank of the passed item. Note that the function is
    'declared as a Long, which defaults to 0
    With rst
        If Not (.EOF And .BOF) Then
            .Find "TransactionItem = " & lngInventoryID
            If Not .EOF Then
                ADO_GetItemRank = .AbsolutePosition 'Not Zero based
            End If
        End If
    End With

    'Clean Up
    rst.Close

End Function
```

Using ADO's Seek **Method**

ADO's Seek method details are virtually identical to DAO's Seek method details. To summarize, the Seek searches an Index for a key value in a Recordset that is opened with the adCmdTableDirect option. The name of the Index for the Seek to use must be known and set. On success, the current record becomes the found record, while an unsuccessful Seek sets the current record to the EOF. The syntax of ADO's Seek method is

```
rst.Seek KeyValues, SeekOption
```

where *rst* is an ADO Recordset object, *KeyValues* is an array of values that each represent a key value from the Index in use, and *SeekOption* is a value from SeekEnum as listed in Table 19.17.

Table 19.17 Constants from SeekEnum

Constant	Description
adSeekFirstEQ	Seeks the first key equal to *KeyValues*
adSeekLastEQ	Seeks the last key equal to *KeyValues*
adSeekAfterEQ	Seeks either a key equal to *KeyValues* or just after where that match would have occurred
adSeekAfter	Seeks a key just after where a match with *KeyValues* would have occurred
adSeekBeforeEQ	Seeks either a key equal to *KeyValues* or just before where that match would have occurred
adSeekBefore	Seeks a key just before where a match with *KeyValues* would have occurred

19

Listing 19.15 demonstrates how to use the Seek method.

Listing 19.15   ADO_SeekTransaction

```
Public Sub ADO_SeekTransaction(lngTransactionID As Long)
'Seek the passed transaction id

    Dim rst As ADODB.Recordset

    'Open table
    Set rst = New ADODB.Recordset
    rst.CursorLocation = adUseServer
    rst.Open "tblTransactions", CurrentProject.Connection, _
            adOpenStatic, adLockReadOnly, adCmdTableDirect

    'Seek a record
    With rst

        'Set up and seek for the passed value
        .Index = "PrimaryKey"
        .Seek Array(lngTransactionID), adSeekFirstEQ

        'Indicate the result
        If .EOF Then
            MsgBox "Transaction not found!"
        Else
            MsgBox "Transaction found!"
        End If

    End With

End Sub
```

19

CAUTION

ADO's Seek method is supported only with server-side cursors. Seek is not supported when the Recordset object's CursorLocation property value is adUseClient.

Using ADO's Filter **Property**

As with DAO, the Filter property of an ADO Recordset can be used to identify a subset of records with in a Recordset. The Filter property is conceptually like a WHERE clause in a SQL statement without the keyword "WHERE." In ADO, the filtering of a Recordset is much more efficient than with DAO and is often used to identify a single record as well as a group of records. When filtering in ADO, there is no need to open a secondary Recordset; after the property has been set, the data provider will apply that filter with a process called *in-place filtering*. This means that all the records are still populated in the Recordset; however, records that do not match the criteria are inaccessible by the cursor. The properties of a filtered Recordset reflect the accessible records, so the Recordcount property of a filtered Recordset returns the number of records that meet the criteria, not the count of the complete Recordset. The syntax for the Filter property is

```
rst.Filter = criteria
```

where *rst* is an ADO `Recordset`, and *criteria* is any one of the following:

- A string expression made up of one or more individual clauses concatenated with AND or OR operators. Similar to a WHERE clause, without the keyword "WHERE."
- Array of bookmarks that point to records in the `Recordset`.
- A `FilterGroupEnum` value as listed in Table 19.18.

Table 19.18 Constants from `FilterGroupEnum`

Constant	Description
adFilterAffectedRecords	Filters for viewing only records affected by the last `Delete`, `Resync`, `UpdateBatch`, or `CancelBatch` call
adFilterConflictingRecords	Filters for viewing the records that failed the last batch update
adFilterFetchedRecords	Filters for viewing the records in the current cache
adFilterNone	Removes the current filter and restores all records for viewing
adFilterPendingRecords	Filters for viewing only records that have changed but have not yet been committed to the server (batch update mode only)

The ADO `Filter` property allows multicolumn criteria; however, there is no precedence between the AND and OR operators, so if precedence is required, it must be established with parentheses. Also keep in mind that logical operators are limited to <, >, <=, >=, <>, =, or `Like`. If `Like` is used, the valid wildcard characters are the asterisk (*) and the percent sign (%), and may only start or terminate the pattern being sought; for example:

```
rst.Filter = "FirstName Like '%Joe'"
rst.Filter = "FirstName Like 'Joe%'"
rst.Filter = "FirstName Like '%Joe%'"
```

Listing 19.16 contains the ADO version of Listing 19.13, which filters a `Recordset`.

Listing 19.16 ADO_FilterRecordset

```
Public Sub ADO_FilterRecordset()
'Displays the effect of applying a filter to a Recordset

    Dim rst As ADODB.Recordset
    Dim strSQL As String

    'Build the SQL statement
    strSQL = "SELECT * FROM tblTransactions"

    'Open a Recordset
    Set rst = New ADODB.Recordset
    rst.Open strSQL, CurrentProject.Connection, adOpenStatic, _
            adLockReadOnly, adCmdText
```

continues

Listing 19.16   Continued

```
If Not (rst.EOF And rst.BOF) Then

    'Display a message
    MsgBox "There are " & rst.RecordCount & " in the unfiltered Recordset"

    'Set the Filter
    rst.Filter = "Employee = 8"

    'Display message
    If Not (rst.EOF And rst.BOF) Then
        MsgBox "There are " & rst.RecordCount & _
                " records in the filtered recordset"
    End If

    'Clear the filter, just for illustration
    rst.Filter = adFilterNone

End If

'Clean up some more
rst.Close

End Sub
```

Updating Data

Updating data has already been discussed and illustrated in the "Inserting Data" section earlier in this chapter; we were just updating new data instead of existing data. Updating records, via code, in a table (or Recordset) can be accomplished in several ways, some of which are

- The Execute method as it applies to DAO's Database and QueryDef objects, as well as ADO's Connection and Command objects

- Modification of Field values of a record in an updatable DAO or ADO Recordset object

The Execute method is described in detail in the section "Inserting Data" earlier in the chapter. Please review that section if needed. Listings 19.6 and 19.7 utilize the Execute method for DAO and ADO, respectively, by building a SQL statement and then executing it. The SQL statement is the only modification necessary to utilize the core structure of those procedures for updating data. Listing 19.17 is a modification of Listing 19.6 to illustrate this concept.

Listing 19.17 DAO_UpdateRecordExec()

```
Public Sub DAO_UpdateRecordExec()
'Update a record in tblEmployees

    Dim strSQL As String

    'Build SQL command text
    strSQL = "UPDATE tblEmployees" & _
            " SET FirstName = 'Seth'," & _
            " LastName = 'Spalding'" & _
            " WHERE FirstName = 'Brent' And " & _
               " LastName = 'Spaulding'"

    'Execute the SQL command statement and display message
    With CurrentDb
        .Execute strSQL, dbFailOnError
        MsgBox "Updated " & .RecordsAffected & " record(s)."
    End With

End Sub
```

Along with the Execute method we can also navigate to a record (or limit the records returned by the SQL statement), and then modify the field values of that record. With DAO, you must invoke the Edit method of the DAO Recordset prior to the field updates to put the Recordset in the proper mode. To commit the changes to the modified record, we issue the Update method. Remember that with a DAO Recordset, an Update is required to save the changes, whereas with an ADO Recordset an Update occurs automatically when the modified record is no longer the current record; however, it is considered good practice to invoke the Update method with code. Listings 19.8 and 19.9 illustrate the insertion (or modification) of a new record with a DAO and ADO Recordset, respectively. Listing 19.18 illustrates the modification of an existing record. Listing 19.18 uses DAO, but an ADO counterpart would not be significantly different with respect to the logic or technique applied, and therefore is not shown.

19

Listing 19.18 DAO_UpdateRecord()

```
Public Sub DAO_UpdateRecord()
'Update a record from tblEmployees

    Dim rst As DAO.Recordset
    Dim strSQL As String

    'Build limiting SQL statement
    strSQL = "SELECT TOP 1 * FROM tblEmployees" & _
            " WHERE FirstName = 'Seth'" & _
               " And LastName = 'Spalding'"

    'Open the recordset
    Set rst = CurrentDb.OpenRecordset(strSQL, dbOpenDynaset, dbPessimistic)
```

continues

Listing 19.18   Continued

```
    With rst

        'Modify the record
        If Not (.EOF And .BOF) Then
            .Edit   'Not Required with ADO rst
            .Fields("FirstName") = "Rockwell"
            .Fields("LastName") = "Roland"
            .Update
        End If

        'Display message
        MsgBox "Modified employeeID: " & rst.Fields("EmployeeID") & vbCrLf & _
                " First Name: " & rst.Fields("FirstName") & vbCrLf & _
                " Last Name: " & rst.Fields("LastName")

    End With

    'Clean up
    rst.Close

End Sub
```

Deleting Data

Deleting data is not much different from modifying data. When deleting data with code, we basically have two options, just as with modifying data:

- The Execute method as it applies to DAO's Database and QueryDef objects, as well as ADO's Connection and Command objects

- The Delete method as it applies to an updatable DAO or ADO Recordset object

The Execute method, with both DAO and ADO, is virtually the same from a logic perspective, just as with the other action typed tasks required on the data. The primary element of using the Execute method is the construction of the SQL statement you want to have the database engine carry out. Listing 19.19 illustrates the execution of an action typed SQL statement that deletes a record. I chose DAO for this illustration simply because DAO is the default object model library for Access 2007.

Listing 19.19   DAO_DeleteRecordExec()

```
Public Sub DAO_DeleteRecordExec()
'Delete a record from tblEmployees

    Dim strSQL As String

    'Build SQL command text
    strSQL = "DELETE FROM tblEmployees" & _
            " WHERE LastName = 'Roland'" & _
                " And FirstName = 'Rockwell'"
```

```
'Execute the SQL command statement and display message
With CurrentDb
    .Execute strSQL, dbFailOnError
    MsgBox "Deleted " & .RecordsAffected & " records."
End With

End Sub
```

DAO'S Delete **Method for a** Recordset **Object**

The Delete method is self-explanatory: It deletes the current record in an updatable DAO Recordset object. The syntax for the Delete method is

`rst.Delete`

where *rst* is a DAO Recordset. Listing 19.20 illustrates of the Delete method in use.

Listing 19.20   DAO_DeleteRecord()

```
Public Sub DAO_DeleteRecord()
'Delete a record with the Delete method

    Dim rst As DAO.Recordset
    Dim strSQL As String

    'Build a limiting SQL statement
    strSQL = "SELECT * FROM tblEmployees" & _
            " WHERE Firstname = 'Brent'" & _
                " And LastName = 'Spaulding'"

    'Open the recordset and delete the record
    Set rst = CurrentDb.OpenRecordset(strSQL, dbOpenDynaset, dbPessimistic)

    'Delete the record, then move
    If Not (rst.EOF And rst.BOF) Then
        rst.Delete
    End If

    'Clean up
    rst.Close

End Sub
```

ADO's Delete **Method for a** Recordset **Object**

As with DAO, the Delete method is self-explanatory. The primary difference between the Delete methods from DAO and ADO is that with ADO, the Delete can affect more than one record. The syntax for the Delete method is

`rst.Delete AffectRecords`

where *rst* is a DAO Recordset and *AffectRecords* is a value from AffectEnum, which is detailed in Table 19.19. AffectEnum does contain more constants; however, they do not apply to the Delete method and therefore were not included to prevent confusion.

Table 19.19   Constants from AffectEnum

Constant	Description
adAffectCurrent	Default. Only the current record is affected.
adAffectGroup	Records that satisfy the Filter property setting are affected. The Filter property must be set to a value from FilterGroupEnum (refer to Table 19.18) or an array of Bookmarks to use this option.

For illustration, Listing 19.21 is the ADO version of Listing 19.20. Note that they are similar in construction.

Listing 19.21   ADO_DeleteRecord()

```
Public Sub ADO_DeleteRecord()
'Delete a record with the Delete method

    Dim rst As ADODB.Recordset
    Dim strSQL As String

    'Build a limiting SQL statement
    strSQL = "SELECT * FROM tblEmployees" & _
            " WHERE Firstname = 'Brent'" & _
                " And LastName = 'Spaulding'"

    'Open the recordset and delete the record
    Set rst = New ADODB.Recordset
    rst.Open strSQL, CurrentProject.Connection, _
            adOpenKeyset, adLockPessimistic, adCmdText

    'Delete the record, then move
    If Not (rst.EOF And rst.BOF) Then
        rst.Delete adAffectCurrent
    End If

    'Clean up
    rst.Close

End Sub
```

Case Study: Backing Up Data

As time goes on your database will accumulate many records. Generally, this is not a problem for the database; after all, an Access database can handle up to 2GB of information, which can translate into millions of records. With this much data, you begin to feel the need to keep a backup in the event of an unforseen issue.

That is where this exercise comes into play. The procedures in this case study do the following:

1. Create a database.
2. Update a log table to track actions.
3. Copy the data from the current database to the destination database.

Topics this case study covers are inserting/deleting data, creating a database, string manipulation, looping, and file manipulation.

The exercise in Listing 19.22 uses DAO to perform the primary task at hand; however, ADO is used to retrieve table names in the database with a technique showcased in the section, "Schema Recordsets" in Chapter 20, "Advanced Data Operations."

Listing 19.22 Case Study—Backing Up Data

```
Public Sub BackupLocalData()
'Backs up local data

    Const cStrBackupLog As String = "tblBackupLog"

    Dim rstLog As DAO.Recordset
    Dim rstSchema As ADODB.Recordset

    Dim strFilename As String
    Dim strExtension As String

    Dim blIsTable As Boolean
    Dim strSQL As String
    Dim tdf As DAO.TableDef

    'Determine if the log table exists, plus get the
    'table names in a recordset
    With CurrentProject.Connection

        'Status of log table
        blIsTable = Not .OpenSchema(adSchemaTables, _
                    Array(Empty, Empty, cStrBackupLog)).EOF

        'Get the table names
        Set rstSchema = .OpenSchema(adSchemaTables, _
                    Array(Empty, Empty, Empty, "TABLE"))
```

19

continues

Listing 19.22 Continued

```
End With

'Create the destination fileNAME
strFilename = CurrentDb.Name
strExtension = Mid(strFilename, InStrRev(strFilename, "."))
strFilename = Left(strFilename, InStrRev(strFilename, ".") - 1) & _
              "_" & Format(Date, "yyyymmdd") & strExtension

'KILL/Delete old file of same name in appropriate
If Len(Dir(strFilename)) > 0 Then Kill strFilename

'Create the destination database
DBEngine.CreateDatabase strFilename, dbLangGeneral

'Trasfer the data
With CurrentDb

    'Create or clean the log table
    If Not blIsTable Then

        'Create the table
        Set tdf = .CreateTableDef(cStrBackupLog)
        tdf.Fields.Append tdf.CreateField("DateTimeStamp", dbDate)
        tdf.Fields.Append tdf.CreateField("BackupAction", dbText, 255)
        .TableDefs.Append tdf
        RefreshDatabaseWindow

        'Insert log entry for creating db and the log table
        strSQL = "INSERT INTO " & cStrBackupLog & _
                " VALUES (#" & Now & "#,'Created:" & strFilename & "')"
        .Execute strSQL, dbFailOnError

        strSQL = "INSERT INTO " & cStrBackupLog & _
                " VALUES (#" & Now & "#,'Created log table')"
        .Execute strSQL, dbFailOnError

    Else

        'Build/Execute SQL to delete the records
        strSQL = "DELETE FROM " & cStrBackupLog
        .Execute strSQL, dbFailOnError

        'Insert log entry and the db creation
        'entry
        strSQL = "INSERT INTO " & cStrBackupLog & _
                " VALUES (#" & Now & "#,'Created:'" & strFilename & "')"
        .Execute strSQL, dbFailOnError

        strSQL = "INSERT INTO " & cStrBackupLog & _
                " VALUES (#" & Now & "#,'Cleaned log table')"
        .Execute strSQL, dbFailOnError

    End If
```

19

```
        'Point to the log table
        Set rstLog = .OpenRecordset(cStrBackupLog, dbOpenDynaset)

        'Loop the tables and push them to the destination
        'note that the SQL statment will Make the table
        'based on the source.
        Do Until rstSchema.EOF

            If Left(rstSchema!TABLE_NAME, 1) <> "~" Then
                'Create the SQL to make each table
                strSQL = "SELECT *" & _
                        " INTO [" & rstSchema!TABLE_NAME & "]" & _
                        " IN '" & strFilename & "'" & _
                        " FROM [" & rstSchema!TABLE_NAME & "]"

                'Execute the SQL statement and record the action
                .Execute strSQL, dbFailOnError

                'Record the action
                rstLog.AddNew
                rstLog!DateTimeStamp = Now()
                rstLog!BackupAction = "Inserted " & .RecordsAffected & _
                                    " into " & rstSchema.Fields(2)
                rstLog.Update
            End If

            'Move the the next table
            rstSchema.MoveNext

        Loop

    End With

    'Clean up
    rstSchema.Close
    rstLog.Close

End Sub
```

19

Advanced Data Operations

Creating Linked Tables

As you continue to develop your database you may find yourself in a challenging situation. The challenge I am referring to is created when you develop your user interface (UI) in one database file, and then you are faced with integrating those changes into your "released" application.

This challenge is overcome with the implementation of a *split configuration*. When implementing a split configuration, you create one database that stores all your tables and relationships (or your base data schema). The database with your tables is called the *back end* (BE). Then you create an application database to store all your forms, reports, queries, macros, and modules—everything except tables and relationships. The application database is called the *front end* (FE). After these two files exist, you link to your data in the BE by creating a *linked table* in the FE.

A linked table behaves in virtually the same manner as a local table. Plus, now that you have the application separate from the data, you can freely develop your application without affecting the front end in use.

Initially creating a split configuration can easily be done by using the Database Splitter tool in Access 2007. The splitter can be launched by clicking on the External Data ribbon, locating the Move Data group, and then choosing the Access Database icon. The wizard guides you through the splitting process.

After you have been in the split configuration for a while, you may find that you need to add a linked table to your application. Recall from Chapter 18, "Creating Schema," that the syntax for creating a table is

`expression.CreateTableDef([Name][, Attributes][, SourceTableName][, Connect])`

We use that same syntax while creating a linked table. Listing 20.1 shows an example of creating a linked table. Because I do not know where any other databases are on your system, the code links to the inventory application we have been using throughout this book. So, the FE and the BE are the same database.

Listing 20.1 Creating a Linked Table

```
Public Sub CreateLinkedTable()
'Create a linked table

    Dim tdf As DAO.TableDef
    Dim strFilename As String

    'Set the database name for the BE
    strFilename = CurrentDb.Name

    'Create the linked table
    With CurrentDb

        'Instantiate the table
        Set tdf = .CreateTableDef("x_tblTransactions")

        'Set the properties of importance
        tdf.Connect = ";DATABASE=" & strFilename
        tdf.SourceTableName = "tblTransactions"

        'Append the object to the collection
        .TableDefs.Append tdf

    End With

    'Refresh the navigation pane
    RefreshDatabaseWindow

End Sub
```

If you were to use this code in your own application you would simply substitute, or set, the proper values for the variable *strFilename*, the *Name* argument of `CreateTableDef`, as well as the `SourceTableName` property.

You can also use code similar to this if your BE location changes; see Listing 20.2 for an example of how to change the `Connect` property of an existing linked table.

Listing 20.2 `ReConnectLinkedTable`

```
Public Sub ReConnectLinkedTable()
'Create a linked table

    Dim tdf As DAO.TableDef
    Dim strFilename As String

    'Set the database name for the BE
    strFilename = CurrentDb.Name

    'Create the linked table
    With CurrentDb

        'Instantiate the table
        Set tdf = .TableDefs("x_tblTransactions")

        'Set the properties of importance
        tdf.Connect = ";DATABASE=" & strFilename
        tdf.RefreshLink

    End With

    'Refresh the navigation pane
    RefreshDatabaseWindow

End Sub
```

Data Definition Language

Data Definition Language (DDL) is the portion of SQL used to create schema. The Access 2007 help files are an excellent place to start learning more about DDL and *Data Modification Language* (DML). In the help files, to get the SQL Reference, click on the top level of the Table of Contents topic named "Microsoft Access SQL Reference."

When executing DDL statements I recommend that you always use an ADO `Connection`, or the `CurrentProject.Connection`. The reason for this recommendation is simple: ADO supports ACE SQL, which is virtually identical to the JET 4.0 SQL syntax. DAO does not support the new commands implemented in JET 4.0 SQL.

DDL uses many keywords; following are some of the main action keywords used within, or to begin, DDL statements:

- `CREATE TABLE`—Creates a table
- `CREATE INDEX`—Creates an index
- `ALTER TABLE`—Changes table and fields in a table
- `CONSTRAINT`—Creates relationships and other constraints

To illustrate the execution of DDL, see Listing 20.3, which performs the same tasks as in Listing 18.3 (`DAO_CreateTable`); Listing 18.5 (`DAO_AddField`); and Listing 18.9

(DAO_CreateRelation). As you may have gathered, Listing 20.3 is much smaller with respect to total lines required to perform the same operation. The procedure will create a table (tluSalaryRanges), add a field (SalaryRangeID) to a related table (tluJobTitles), and then create a relationship between the two tables.

> **NOTE**
> Note that Listing 20.3 creates a table and field that may be present in the database, assuming you implemented Listings 18.3, 18.5, and 18.9 in Chapter 18. An error will be raised if you run Listing 20.3 without deleting table tluSalaryRanges and the field SalaryRangeID from tluJobTitles.

Listing 20.3 CreateAndRelate

```
Public Sub CreateAndRelate()
'Create a table and a relationship

    Dim strSQL As String

    'Build the SQL to make the table
    strSQL = "CREATE TABLE tluSalaryRanges" & _
            " (SalaryRangeID COUNTER" & _
                " CONSTRAINT PrimaryKey PRIMARY KEY," & _
            " SalaryRange CHAR(50) NOT NULL," & _
            " Minimum MONEY NOT NULL," & _
            " Maximum MONEY NOT NULL)"

    'Execute the SQL against the database engine.
    CurrentProject.Connection.Execute strSQL, , adCmdText

    'Build the SQL to add the Foreign Key field to the foreign table
    strSQL = "ALTER TABLE tluJobTitles" & _
            " ADD COLUMN SalaryRangeID LONG"

    'Execute the SQL against the database engine
    CurrentProject.Connection.Execute strSQL, , adCmdText

    'Build the SQL to create the Relationship/Reference
    strSQL = "ALTER TABLE tluJobTitles" & _
            " ADD CONSTRAINT SalRange" & _
            " FOREIGN KEY (SalaryRangeID)" & _
            " REFERENCES tluSalaryRanges (SalaryRangeID)" & _
            " ON DELETE CASCADE"

    'Execute the SQL against the database engine.
    CurrentProject.Connection.Execute strSQL, , adCmdText

    'Refresh the navigation pane
    RefreshDatabaseWindow

End Sub
```

Schema Recordsets

Schema recordsets allow you to obtain `Database` schema information from the provider. You have seen a little of this in the Case Study in Chapter 19, "Data Manipulation." The syntax for opening a schema `Recordset` is

```
Set rst = cnn.OpenSchema(QueryType, Criteria, SchemaID)
```

where `rst` is an ADO `Recordset` object variable, `cnn` is an ADO `Connection` object, `QueryType` is a value from the list of constants from `SchemaEnum`, `criteria` (optional) is an array of values that must occur in the corresponding column, and `SchemaID` (required if `QueryType` is provider specific) is the GUID for a provider-schema query not defined by the OLE DB specification. The list of available constants to choose from is large. Table 20.1 lists the more common ones seen in use.

Table 20.1 `SchemaEnum` **Constants**

Constant	Description	Column Names
adSchemaColumns	The columns of tables	TABLE_CATALOG TABLE_SCHEMA TABLE_NAME COLUMN_NAME
adSchemaForeignKeys	The foreign key columns	PK_TABLE_CATALOG PK_TABLE_SCHEMA PK_TABLE_NAME FK_TABLE_CATALOG FK_TABLE_SCHEMA FK_TABLE_NAME
adSchemaIndexes	The indexes in a database (or catalog)	TABLE_CATALOG TABLE_SCHEMA INDEX_NAME TYPE TABLE_NAME
adSchemaPrimaryKeys	The primary key columns	PK_TABLE_CATALOG PK_TABLE_SCHEMA PK_TABLE_NAME
adSchemaProviderSpecific	Used by a provider to return nonstandard information	<Provider specific>
adSchemaTables	The tables and views in the catalog	TABLE_CATALOG TABLE_SCHEMA TABLE_NAME TABLE_TYPE
adSchemaViews	The views in the catalog	VIEW_CATALOG VIEW_SCHEMA VIEW_NAME

20

Listing 20.4 illustrates how to discover who is connected to a data file. The code lists the connections to the data file. If you run this code against a database that you link to in the application, you may see your computer in the list twice: one connection for the link your application is using and then another that was created when executing the code. I often run similar code from the Immediate window to see who is connected to the back-end database.

Listing 20.4 GetConnectedUsers

```
Public Function GetConnectedUsers(Optional strFilename As String) As String
'Get users connect to an Access database file

    Dim cn As ADODB.Connection
    Dim rst As ADODB.Recordset
    Dim strTemp As String, strUsers As String

    On Error GoTo Error_handler:

    'Connect to the data source, if strFilename is NOT
    'passed, then use the current application.
    If strFilename = "" Then
        strFilename = CurrentProject.FullName
        Set cn = CurrentProject.Connection
    Else
        Set cn = New ADODB.Connection
        cn.Provider = "Microsoft.ACE.OLEDB.12.0"
        cn.Open "MS Access;" & _
                "Data Source=" & strFilename
    End If

    'The user roster is a provider-specific schema rowset
    'from the ACE OLE DB provider.  You have to use a GUID to
    'reference the schema, as provider-specific schemas are not
    'listed in ADO's type library for schema rowsets. The GUID
    'in use was retreived from Microsofts knowledge base web site.
    Set rst = cn.OpenSchema(adSchemaProviderSpecific, , _
                "{947bb102-5d43-11d1-bdbf-00c04fb92675}")

    'Put all the records into a string, then massage the string
    'to remove trailing spaces and null characters.
    strUsers = rst.GetString(adClipString, , ",", vbCrLf, "<Null>")
    strUsers = Replace(strUsers, vbNullChar, "")
    Do Until strTemp = strUsers
        strTemp = strUsers
        strUsers = Replace(strUsers, " ,", ",")
    Loop

    'Add the field names to the string of users
    strUsers = "COMPUTER_NAME,LOGIN_NAME,CONNECTED,SUSPECT_STATE" & _
            vbCrLf & strUsers

    'Return the result
    GetConnectedUsers = strTemp

Error_handler:

    'Print out err message if appliable
```

```
    If err.Number <> 0 Then Debug.Print err.Description

    'Clean up
    On Error Resume Next
    rst.Close
    err.Clear

End Function
```

Other common uses of schema recordsets are to determine whether a particular object exists or to analyze the relationships of a table. Listing 20.5 is a simple function that can be used to determine whether a table exists.

Listing 20.5 `IsTable` **Function**

```
Public Function IsTable(strTableName As String) As Boolean
'Indicates if the passed string is a table or query
'in the current project
    With CurrentProject.Connection
        IsTable = Not .OpenSchema(adSchemaTables, _
                        Array(Empty, Empty, strTableName)).EOF
    End With
End Function
```

In Listing 20.5, notice the method in which I filtered the returned schema recordset. The `OpenSchema` method's second argument accepts an array; each element of the array is used as the filter for the corresponding column in the schema recordset. The third column of the `adSchemaTables` schema recordset is the name of the table or query in your schema, so I pass the value of the table or query you are looking for as the third column filter. If a match is found, a record is returned, thus preventing the `.EOF` property from being set.

> **NOTE**
>
> In ANSI standards, the term *base table* is used to describe what we know in MS Access as a `TableDef`. The ANSI term *derived table* is used to describe what we know in MS Access as a `QueryDef`. A *table*, according to ANSI, is either a *base table* or a *derived table*. ADO adheres to those definitions. This means that a `QueryDef` and a `TableDef` are considered *tables* (or sets of data in tabular form) to ADO and thus are both included in the `adSchemaTables` schema recordset.
>
> MS Access complies to the ANSI definition behind the scenes as evidenced by the fact that a `QueryDef` object and a `TableDef` object can be used interchangeably when retrieving records via code. Also, note that the name of a `TableDef` or a `QueryDef` must be unique among the combined set of query names and table names.

Subqueries

A *subquery* is a `SELECT` SQL statement embedded (or nested) inside another SQL statement. Subqueries are handy little tools to help solve some really tough situations.

Subqueries can be in the field list, WHERE clause, or HAVING clause of the main SQL statement. When a subquery is a form of criteria, the following syntax is used:

comparison [ANY ¦ ALL ¦ SOME] (*sqlstatement*)

expression [NOT] IN (*sqlstatement*)

[NOT] EXISTS (*sqlstatement*)

where *comparison* is an *expression* coupled with a logical operator, such as "x =" or "[field] <=]"; *expression* is a value or formula that returns a value; and *sqlstatement* is a valid SELECT type SQL statement.

The keywords in the subquery syntax are

- ANY or SOME—Indicate to return records in the main query that satisfy the comparison with ANY records returned by *sqlstatement*. Like this:
  ```
  SELECT * FROM tblTransactions
  WHERE Quantity >= ANY (SELECT TOP 5 Quantity
  FROM tblTransactions ORDER BY Quantity DESC)
  ```

- ALL—Similar to ANY or SOME, except the main query record needs to satisfy the comparison for ALL records returned by *sqlstatement*.

- IN—Indicates to return records from the main query if the value returned by *expression* is IN (or NOT IN, depending on your use of NOT) the set of records returned by *sqlstatement*.

- EXISTS—Indicates to return records from the main query if *sqlstatement* returns (or does not return, depending on the use of NOT) records.

CAUTION

You can also embed a SQL statement in the FROM clause of a SQL statement:

```
SELECT * FROM (SELECT * FROM tblTransactions) AS vTbl
```

However, by definition, that is not a subquery because the embedded SQL is not lower in scope with respect to the main SQL statement. In general, a subquery gets some sort of information from its parent.

A common use for subqueries is to discover duplicate records. Consider the following SQL statement:

```
SELECT * FROM tblEmployees
WHERE [FirstName] & [LastName] IN
    (SELECT [FirstName] & [LastName] As FullName
     FROM tblEmployees
     GROUP BY [FirstName] & [LastName]
     HAVING Count(*) >= 2)
```

Executing this SQL statement returns a recordset that contains all the employees that share a full name with someone else.

Advanced VBA

IV

Working with Other Data Files

21

Understanding File I/O

Access supports several different file types for import and export. However, sometimes you encounter a file that doesn't fit into a pattern that allows you to use the import/export process. For those instances, you may need to use file I/O. The *I/O* stands for *input and output functions*. These functions allow you to read and write data directly to a file, one line at a time.

Using VBA, the I/O process works like this:

- Use VBA's `Open` function to open a file.
- Use VBA's `Input` function to read in a line from the file.
- Use VBA's `Write` function to write a line to a file.
- Use VBA's `Print` function to write a series of values to an open file.

When you use the `Open` function, you assign it to a workspace which is an area of memory that Access assigns a number to keep track of where the data is. The number is used to refer to the workspace in subsequent code when dealing with the file. This number is called the *file handle*.

If you assign a file to a workspace that was previously used, you overwrite what was in that workspace. So, unless you are sure that a workspace is unused you want to find a free workspace before you make the assignment. The following two lines of code declare the handle as a `Long Integer` variable and assign the next unused file handle to it:

```
Dim lngWS As Long
lngWS = Freefile
```

Opening Files

We begin the process by opening a file with the VBA Open function using the syntax:

```
Open path For mode[Access access][lock] As [#]filenumber[Len=recordlength]
```

Table 21.1 lists the many arguments for the Open function.

Table 21.1   Open **Arguments**

Argument	Description
path	The full path and filename for the file you want to open
mode	One of the following values: Append, Binary, Input, Output, or Random (the default)
access	One of the following values: Read (the default), Write, or Read Write
lock	One of the following values: Shared (the default), Lock Read, Lock Write, or Lock Read Write
filenumber	The workspace number the file is opened within
recordlength	Either the length of the record, when using Random mode, or the number of buffered bytes, when using Append or Output mode

About mode

Windows uses the mode argument to decide how to handle the open file and what can be done with it using your code. The main actions that you can execute are

- If you want to just use the data within your application without writing back to the file, use Input mode. This opens the file with read-only access.
- If you need to add to the file or edit it, you use Append mode, which allows you to add values at the end of the file.
- If you need to replace the contents of the file, use Output mode.
- If you want to add or edit values byte by byte, open the file in Binary mode.
- If you need to add or edit values within a file that uses a fixed record length, use Random mode along with the recordlength argument, which specifies the record's size.

About access

The three values for this argument are Read, Write, and Read Write. Read allows you only to read from the file; conversely, Write allows only writing to the file. Read Write allows you to do both. You also need to remember that the ability to use the file depends on the user's system security settings. In other words, if the user has only read-only access, trying to open the file with Write or Read Write results in an error. Therefore, make sure you have error handling set up to account for this.

About `locking`

If your application is going to be used by only one user or even by only one user at a time, or if the file will only be opened by one user, locking won't be an issue. If you are working in a multiuser environment, however, locking becomes an issue. Because Access is designed as a multiuser application, the default locking is `Shared`. This allows other users to also use the file, even when another user has opened it. For a brief explanation of the locking settings see the following:

- `Shared`—Depending on the access setting and security permissions, the file can be opened and written to by multiple users.

- `Lock Read`—With the proper permissions, a user can write to the file but not retrieve values when previously opened by another user.

- `Lock Write`— With the proper permissions, a user can retrieve values but cannot write to the file, when previously opened by another user.

- `Lock Read Write`—If the file has been previously opened by another user, data can't be retrieved from or written to the file.

Demonstrating Opening a File

The following code demonstrates opening a file. It accepts a string that represents the full path and filename of the file.

```
Sub FileOpen(strFilename As String)
'opening a file using I/O
    Dim lngFile as Long
    lngFile = FreeFile
    Open strFilename For Input Access Read Shared as lngFile
    MsgBox lngFile & "-" & strFilename
    Close lngFile
End Sub
```

Enter this code into a standard module; then run it from the Immediate window with the following syntax:

```
FileOpen "c:\folder\filename"
```

Substitute the path and name of any file (preferably a text file). The result is a message box like the one shown in Figure 21.1.

21

Figure 21.1
A message box showing the opened file and its handle.

Of course this procedure doesn't do anything with the file after it is opened. I just wanted to illustrate the action of opening a file at this point. You see this put to more practical use as we go through this chapter.

Notice the Close statement at the end of the procedure. Make sure you always close each workspace after you are finished to prevent loss of data or access problems for other users.

> **NOTE**
> If your code requires opening multiple files using I/O you need to open a file using the number returned via the FreeFile function before you try to get the next open workspace. The FreeFile counter isn't incremented until a file is opened.

Reading from Files

As noted, opening a file does nothing without reading or writing to the file. The term *read*, actually means to retrieve data. If you are using the Input Output or Append modes to open your file, you would use the following read statements:

- Input
- Line Input #
- Input #

Using Input

After you open the file, retrieving data with the Input function uses the following syntax:

```
Input(number, [#]filenumber)
```

where *number* is the number of characters to return from the current line, and *filenumber* is any valid workspace. Input returns every character it reads in, including spaces, carriage returns, and line feeds.

Following is another simple example that uses Input to retrieve data from a text file. We use the CorpUpdate.csv file that was used in Chapter 8, "Object and Event-Driven Coding." Enter the following code into a standard module:

```
Sub ReadFile(strFilename As String)
    'Print the contents from specified file
```

21

```
      'in Immediate window
      Dim lngFile As Long
      lngFile = FreeFile
      Open strFilename For Input Access Read Shared As lngFile
      Debug.Print Input(LOF(lngFile), lngFile)
      Close lngFile
End Sub
```

Run this code by entering the following statement in the Immediate window:

```
ReadFile "path\CorpUpdate.csv"
```

You need to enter the actual path to where you stored the CorpUpdate.csv file (see Figure 21.2). The LOF(lngFile) argument indicates you want the entire contents of the file.

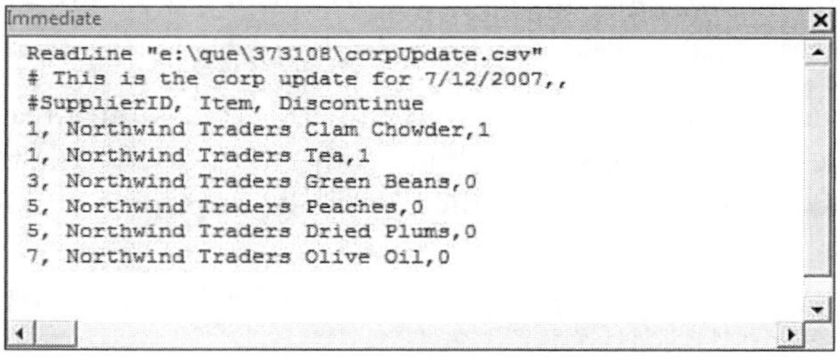

Figure 21.2
The contents of CorpUpdate.csv printed to the Immediate window.

```
Immediate
ReadLine "e:\que\373108\corpUpdate.csv"
# This is the corp update for 7/12/2007,,
#SupplierID, Item, Discontinue
1, Northwind Traders Clam Chowder,1
1, Northwind Traders Tea,1
3, Northwind Traders Green Beans,0
5, Northwind Traders Peaches,0
5, Northwind Traders Dried Plums,0
7, Northwind Traders Olive Oil,0
```

About EOF and LOF

We introduced the LOF function in the previous code example. It stands for Length of File, so it retrieves the entire file.

The EOF function returns a True value when the end of the file is reached. When you open the file, VBA internally creates and stores the current byte position. Each character is read in one at a time or byte by byte (because each character represents a byte). When the current byte is the end of the file, EOF will equal True.

Using Line Input

The Line Input # statement also retrieves data from the file. But it only retrieves one line at a time. The syntax for this statement is

```
Line Input #filenumber, varname
```

where *filenumber* is the number of the workspace you are retrieving the line from, and *varname* is the name of a variable you are storing the data into.

The following code retrieves the entire file but line by line. To show how effective this can be, we only print the actual lines of data.

```
Sub ReadLine(strFilename As String)
      'Read file line by line
      'print data lines to immediate window
      Dim lngFile As Long
      Dim strLine As String
```

21

```
lngFile = FreeFile
Open strFilename For Input Access Read Shared As lngFile
Do Until EOF(lngFile)
    Line Input #lngFile, strLine
    If Left(strLine, 1) <> "#" Then
        Debug.Print strLine
    End If
Loop
Close lngFile

End Sub
```

The heading lines in that file start with an octothorpe (#). We use an If statement to check whether the first character in the line is an octothorpe. If it isn't, the line gets printed.

In the Immediate window enter the following statement (see Figure 21.3):

```
ReadLine "path\CorpUpdate.csv"
```

(Be sure that you enter the correct *path*.) Because this code sample reads each line individually, we need the Do Loop to process each line; otherwise, only the first line is printed. The If statement then tests to see whether the line should be printed or skipped.

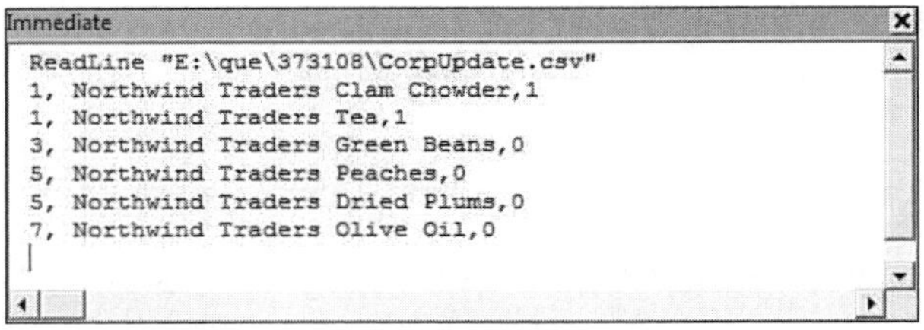

Figure 21.3
The data lines of CorpUpdate.csv printed to the Immediate window.

```
Immediate
ReadLine "E:\que\373108\CorpUpdate.csv"
1, Northwind Traders Clam Chowder,1
1, Northwind Traders Tea,1
3, Northwind Traders Green Beans,0
5, Northwind Traders Peaches,0
5, Northwind Traders Dried Plums,0
7, Northwind Traders Olive Oil,0
```

Using Input

Although Input # is similar to Line Input #, it has some more flexibility. The statement retrieves a line of data and assigns the data to a list of variables. The syntax for this statement is

```
Input #filenumber, varlist
```

where *varlist* is a comma-separated list of variables. Each data element of the retrieved line is then parsed out into the variables.

This time we open a modified version of CorpUpdate.csv included in the files for this chapter that has the header lines removed and read in the data, but into separate variables.

```
Sub ReadLineOct(strFilename As String)
    'Print data from file
    'to Immediate window
    Dim lngFile As Long
    Dim lngID As Long
    Dim strCo As String
```

21

```
    Dim intDisc As Integer
    Dim booDisc As Boolean

    lngFile = FreeFile

    Open strFilename For Input Access Read Shared As lngFile
    Do Until EOF(lngFile)
        Input #lngFile, lngID, strCo, intDisc
                booDisc = intDisc
                Debug.Print lngID & vbTab & strCo & vbTab & booDisc
        Loop
    Close lngFile
End Sub
```

The `Discontinue` value caused an overflow error when reading it into a Boolean field, so it became necessary to convert it after it was read into an integer data type. Running this procedure in the Immediate window produces the output shown in Figure 21.4.

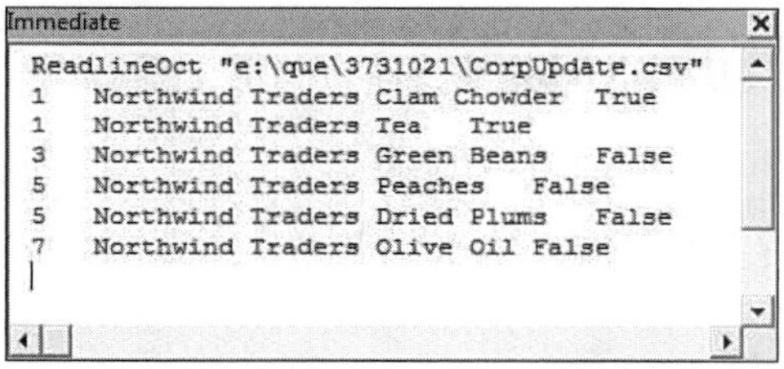

Figure 21.4
The data lines of CorpUpdate.csv printed to the Immediate window.

```
Immediate                                          ×
ReadlineOct "e:\que\3731021\CorpUpdate.csv"  ▲
1    Northwind Traders Clam Chowder   True
1    Northwind Traders Tea     True
3    Northwind Traders Green Beans    False
5    Northwind Traders Peaches     False
5    Northwind Traders Dried Plums    False
7    Northwind Traders Olive Oil False
|                                              ▼
◄                                           ►
```

Notice the spacing is different, and we were able to insert tabs between the elements.

Writing to Files

We can also add values to a file. If you use `Input`, `Output`, or `Append` modes when opening the file, you use the `Print #` or `Write #` statements. When opening using `Random` or `Binary` modes you would use the `Put` statement instead.

The `Write #` statement uses the following syntax:

```
Write #filenumber[, outputlist]
```

where *outputlist* represents one or several comma-delimited variables or literal values that are to be added to the file. These values need to be separated by commas, spaces, or semicolons. You can add a blank line by omitting the *outputlist* and just adding a comma after the *filenumber*.

Some things to watch out for when writing to a file are

- Any numeric value is written with the period decimal separator so that 12 would be written as 12. in the file.
- Any Boolean values are written as a string either #TRUE# or #FALSE#.

21

- Any dates are written using the universal date format.
- If *outputlist* is empty, nothing is written to the file.
- If *outputlist* is Null, the value #NULL# is written.
- Any error values are written as #ERROR errorcode#.

The next example adds a line to the file and then retrieves and prints the contents:

```
Sub Write1(strFilename As String, _
 lngID As Long, strCo As String, intDisc As Integer)

Dim lngFile As Long
lngFile = FreeFile

'Open file and write 1 line of data
Open strFilename For Append Access Write As lngFile
Write #lngFile, lngID, strCo, intDisc
Close lngFile

'open file and print contents
Open strFilename For Input Access Read Shared As lngFile
    Do Until EOF(lngFile)
        Input #lngFile, lngID, strCo, intDisc
        booDisc = intDisc
        Debug.Print lngID & vbTab & strCo & vbTab & booDisc
    Loop
Close lngFile

End Sub
```

We run this code by entering the following into the Immediate window:

```
Write1 "path\CorpUpdate2.csv", 4, "Northwind Traders Bananas",-1
```

This adds a new record for Supplier 4 of the item Northwind Traders Bananas, set as discontinued. As before, substitute the correct path for *path* in the statement. We use a copy of the CSV file named CorpUpdate2.csv. Figure 21.5 shows the statement and its results.

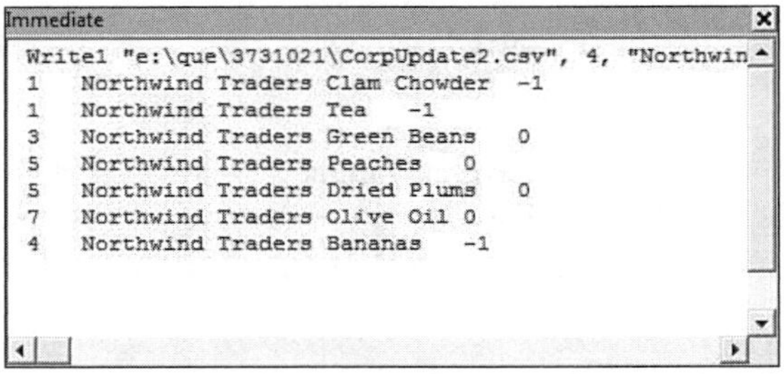

Figure 21.5
The data lines of CorpUpdate2.csv printed to the Immediate window.

Printing to Files

Finally, you use the `Print #` statement when you want to print data to a file. The `Print #` statement uses the following syntax:

```
Print #filenumber[, outputlist]
```

As you can see the syntax is the same as for the `Write #` statement. The difference between the two is that `Write #` adds data to an existing file, while `Print #` creates a new file.

Our last example opens a file and then creates a new file from the contents. The code follows:

```
Sub Print1(strFilename As String, strPrintfile As String)
Dim lngSourcefile As Long
Dim lngDestfile As Long
Dim strLine As String

'Read in and output a file
lngSourcefile = FreeFile
'open file for input
Open strFilename For Input Access Read Shared As lngSourcefile
lngDestfile = FreeFile
'open file for output
Open strPrintfile For Output Access Write As lngDestfile
'read each line and
'write to copy of file
Do Until EOF(lngSourcefile)
    Line Input #lngSourcefile, strLine
    Print #lngDestfile, strLine
Loop
Close lngSourcefile
Close lngDestfile

End Sub
```

Run this procedure from the Immediate window using the following statement:

```
Print1 "path\CorpUpdate2.csv", "path\CorpUpdate3.csv"
```

Make sure you substitute the correct paths. After the procedure executes, you can open the new file in Notepad and see it's a copy of the original. Figure 21.6 shows the new file.

Figure 21.6
The newly created CorpUpdate3.csv viewed in Notepad.

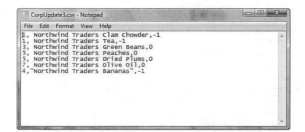

Case Study: Using `.ini` Files

You may be somewhat familiar with `.ini` files. These are files used by programs to grab some configuration information that allows the programs to be customized for the machine or user. Using file I/O Access can use the same concept.

You might remember, there is a company information table that contains information about the company using this application. But you may want to store that information outside the application for more security. You can use an `.ini` file for that and integrate it into your application. This case study sets up your application to check for the existence of the `.ini` file. If it doesn't exist, it makes sure the file is created. And then we show an example of reading it.

We first need to do make some changes to the setup of the Inventory sample application to accommodate this:

1. Select the Autoexec macro in the Navigation pane and right-click it. Select Rename and name it anything else such as ExecAuto. This causes it not to run automatically when the application opens.

2. Click the Office button and select Current Database. Change the Display form to `frmMainmenu`, so that that form opens when the database opens.

3. Open `frmMainMenu` in Design view and using the Code Builder add the following code to the end of the `On Load` event:

```
If IsNull(Dir("C:\windows\inventory.ini")) Then
    DoCmd.OpenForm "frmCoinfoUnbound"
End If
```

This code checks to see whether the `.ini` file for this application exists. If it doesn't, it opens a form to enter the data.

4. Open `frmCoInfoUnbound` in Design view.

5. Disable the wizard and add a command button to the form's header.

6. Set the caption for the button to `Save` and name the button `cmdSave`.

7. Using the Code Builder add the following code to the `On Click` event:

```
Private Sub cmdSave_Click()
Dim lngFile As Long
Dim strPath As String
Dim strLine As String

lngFile = FreeFile
strPath = CurrDBDir() & "\inventory.ini"

'open ini file for output
Open strPath For Output Access Write As lngFile

'create file contents
strLine = "Company: " & Me.txtCompanyName & vbCrLf
strLine = strLine & "Address: " & Me.txtStreetAddress & vbCrLf
strLine = strLine & "City: " & Me.txtCity & vbCrLf
strLine = strLine & "Province: " & Me.txtProvince & vbCrLf
strLine = strLine & "PostalCode: " & Me.txtPostalCode & vbCrLf
strLine = strLine & "Phone: " & Me.txtMainPhone & vbCrLf
```

```
strLine = strLine & "Fax: " & Me.txtFax & vbCrLf
strLine = strLine & "WebSite: " & Me.txtWebsite & vbCrLf

'Write info to file
Print #lngFile, strLine

Close lngFile
End Sub
```

This code, opens the file for output and writes the values from the controls to the .ini file as separate lines with each line prefaced by a label identifying the field type.

8. Finally, we add the following function to a standard module (use basUDFs):

```
Public Function GetCoInfo(strData As String) As String
Dim strPath As String, strLine As String
Dim lngFile As Long
Dim strCo As String, strAdd As String, strCity As String
Dim strProv As String, strPCode As String
Dim strPhone As String, strFax As String, strURL As String

strPath = CurrDBDir() & "\inventory.ini"

'get data from file
lngFile = FreeFile
Open strPath For Input Access Read Shared As lngFile
Do While Not EOF(lngFile)
    Line Input #lngFile, strLine
    'test if this line has the requested data
    If Left(strLine, Len(strData)) = strData Then
        GetCoInfo = Right(strLine, Len(strLine) - Len(strData) - 2)
        Exit Do
    End If
Loop
Close lngFile

End Function
```

The GetCoinfo() function can now be used to retrieve any element of the company information stored in the .ini file. The one caveat is that you need to supply the exact match for each line's label. So you would want to use this function in code and not make it open to the user, unless you make sure the user selects from a list of labels.

Working with Other Applications

22

Understanding Automation

Up to this point, we have shown you capabilities of Microsoft Access by itself. We can't forget, however, that Access is part of the Microsoft Office suite of programs. One of the main purposes of an integrated suite of applications is to allow the programs to work together, letting each program do what it does best. The term for this is *automation*. VBA provides a code structure that allows you to create applications that can control other applications within the suite from any one application. But automation is not limited to just Office components. Other vendors have bought into the VBA platform, and their programs can be controlled using automation code.

Working with automation requires two applications: a *client* and a *server*. The application executing the code is the client. Because this is an Access book, we use Access as the client. The server is the application being controlled by the code running from the client. The client-based code produces objects native to the server, and then uses those objects' properties and methods to perform some task.

An example you may use frequently is creating a new Microsoft Word document. You build the document (by generating a Word.Document object), manipulate the properties of the document, add and format text within the document, and then save it with a specified filename. The result is a Word file generated without your ever exiting Access.

Objects created through automation don't become part of the client application; instead, the client executes code that controls the objects supplied by the server application. This means that the user still needs to have the server application installed on his system for the automation code to work.

22

┌─ **CAUTION** ──┐
If a user has Access installed, it's likely the user also has Word, Excel, PowerPoint, and Outlook installed because all versions that include Access also include those programs. However, the possibility exists that Access was purchased separately, the user is using a runtime version, or the user just decided not to install other portions of Office. So make sure that you include error-trapping when using automation to prevent your code from terminating your application if the server application isn't installed.
└──┘

Setting Object References

For the automation client to be capable of using any objects from any automation server, there needs to be a mechanism to determine what objects are available. Such information is contained within files called *type libraries* that normally have a `.tlb` or `.olb` extension. Such type libraries contain information on the following items:

- Events
- Methods
- Objects
- Properties

It's to your advantage to use a type library if you plan to use objects from an automation server, even though it's not totally necessary. Using a type library gets you the benefits of Intellisense and the Object Browser when entering your code, so it is highly recommended that you use the available type libraries. Using a type library involves setting a reference to the library. The following steps set the references for the Word and Excel libraries that we use in this chapter's examples:

1. Open the Visual Basic Editor (press Ctrl+G or Alt+F11 or use the Visual Basic icon on the Database Tools ribbon).
2. Select Tools, References from the menu. This opens the References dialog shown in Figure 22.1.
3. Scroll down to the Microsoft Excel 12.0 Object Library and the Microsoft Word 12.0 Object Library among the listed references and check the box for each of them.
4. Click OK to add the type libraries to the current Access file.

Figure 22.1
The References
dialog box.

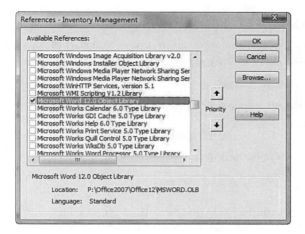

After you have added a type library reference, you can locate that type library's objects using the Object Browser. From the VBE press F2 to open the Object Browser. You can then choose which type library to explore from the Project/Library drop-down list. Figure 22.2 shows some of the objects from the Word type library. You can see these objects refer to documents and text, which is consistent with what Word does.

Figure 22.2
The Object Browser
showing the Word
type library.

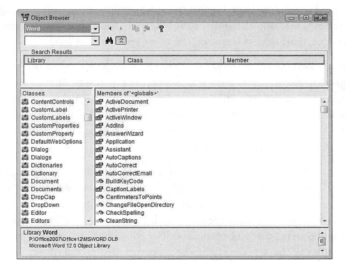

22

Creating Objects

Before you can use objects from automation servers, you start off by creating the objects within your Access code module. You have three options for doing this:

- With the `CreateObject` function
- With the `GetObject` function
- Using early binding

We discuss each of these options in the following sections.

Using `CreateObject`

The `CreateObject` function allows you to create an object by using the object's name, which then opens an instance of that object. A quick example follows:

```
Sub DemoCreateObject()
'With Word as automation server
'via CreateObject
Dim objWord As Object
Set objWord = CreateObject("Word.Application")
objWord.Visible = True
objWord.Quit
End Sub
```

VBA includes a special variable type of `Object` to indicate the object being created. You use `Object` to refer to any object from within VBA, whether it's a Word document, a PowerPoint chart, an Access form, or whatever you need to use.

By using the `CreateObject` function to assign an object type to an object variable you transform the generic variable into a particular object. The `CreateObject` function takes an argument referred to as a `ProgID`, which is a value that tells VBA the type of object being created. Most `ProgIDs` can be constructed from the name of the application and the object name within that application. In the example, `Word.Application` indicates the `Application` object from Microsoft Word as an automation server.

When the `CreateObject` function is executed in the sample code, it assigns an instance of the Word `Application` object to the variable `objWord`. The `Application` object represents all of the automation server program (just as the Access `Application` object represents an Access instance). After the instance is created, you won't see Word loaded anywhere. Typically, an automation server starts invisibly after being launched via an automation call. You then use the `Visible` property of the object to display the object on your screen.

The sample code ends with the `Quit` method of the Word `Application` object. This closes the instance of Word the same as if you selected File, Exit from the Word menu.

You might notice that, other than the `CreateObject` function, most of this code is similar to other code snippets we've used. After the automation object has been created, its methods and properties are available for your use the same as any other object within Access.

Using GetObject

Using the GetObject function is similar to the CreateObject function. The following code uses GetObject:

```
Sub DemoGetObject()
'With Word as automation server
'via GetObject
Dim objWord As Object
Set objWord = GetObject("", "Word.Application")
objWord.Visible = True
objWord.Quit
End Sub
```

This code performs the same as the CreateObject demo, but there are two differences between how CreateObject and GetObject work:

- CreateObject starts a new instance of the automation server when executed. GetObject uses an existing instance, if one is currently loaded on your system.

- GetObject has an optional parameter that allows you to open a specific file into the instance of the automation server that is opened. If you used GetObject("C:\myfolder\ mydoc.doc","Word.Application") the mydoc.doc file would open into the instance of Word being used.

  This makes GetObject useful when you need to work with a specific file, be it a document, spreadsheet, or whatever. It also is useful in conserving resources because it doesn't launch extra instances of the automation server unless necessary.

Using Early Binding

Early binding allows you to directly use the native variable types from the automation server within your VBA procedure. The first two methods we discussed, CreateObject and GetObject, use late binding where you declare a generic Object variable, and then assign the specific object type to that variable. With early binding you declare the specific object type.

> **TIP**
>
> You can use late binding regardless of whether you have set a reference for the type library for an automation server. Early binding, however, requires the reference to have been set. While there is a way to set a reference within VBA, we don't recommend its use because it hasn't shown itself to be stable, potentially resulting in file corruption.

Let's look at sample code modified for early binding:

```
Sub DemoEarlyBinding()
'With Word as automation server
'via early binding
Dim objWord As Word.Application
Set objWord = New Word.Application
objWord.Visible = True
objWord.Quit
End Sub
```

When declaring a variable, after you type the As keyword, Intellisense offers a list of object types from which to choose. This list includes any automation servers whose type library has been added as a reference to your application. So when typing in the sample code, you can scroll down to select Word as your Application server. From there you can choose from a list of objects available for that server. After you have declared the variable, you can assign the automation object using the same code you would with any Access object.

Our preference is toward using early binding for the following reasons:

- You can take advantage of Intellisense when typing your code, which makes for more error-free coding.

- You can use the same syntax as with Access objects so you don't have to remember different ones.

- Early binding performs better than using CreateObject or GetObject.

Working with Automation Servers

The syntax for using automation is not that difficult. After you set the type library reference you can use the objects from the automation server the same way you would with any native Access objects. The complexity comes into play with learning all the things you can do with automation servers. Depending on how much software is installed on your system you may have dozens of servers and hundreds of objects available to you.

It is way beyond the scope of this book to give you a comprehensive view of all the things you can do. We'll limit our discussion to a couple of examples using Word and Excel and suggest that you explore the Object Browser to learn more.

 TIP A good place to start is with the functions used by the other applications in the Microsoft Office suite—for example, Excel's more complex financial functions.

Talking To Excel

One common use of automation is to transfer data from one application to another so you can use the strengths of the other application in analysis of the data.

The following code takes the daily transactions for a specified date and transfers them to an Excel worksheet. Open a standard module (for example basAutomation) and enter the following code:

```
Sub Data2Excel(dteDate As Date)
'Transfer Daily Inventory Transactions
'to Excel for further use

Dim rsDailyTrans As ADODB.Recordset
```

```
Dim objExcel As Excel.Application
Dim objBook As Excel.Workbook
Dim objSheet As Excel.Worksheet
Dim fld As ADODB.Field
Dim intCol As Integer, intRow As Integer
Dim strSQL As String

'Define data to transfer
strSQL = "SELECT * FROM qryDailyInvTrans "
strSQL = strSQL & "WHERE TransDate = #" & dteDate & "#;"
Set rsDailyTrans = New ADODB.Recordset

'assign desired data into recordset
rsDailyTrans.Open strSQL, CurrentProject.Connection

'Open Excel
Set objExcel = New Excel.Application
'Add workbook
objExcel.Workbooks.Add
'open new worksheet
Set objSheet = objExcel.ActiveSheet

'Transfer data
'start with field names
For intCol = 0 To rsDailyTrans.Fields.Count - 1
    Set fld = rsDailyTrans.Fields(intCol)
    objSheet.Cells(1, intCol + 1) = fld.Name
Next intCol

'actual data
intRow = 2
Do Until rsDailyTrans.EOF
    For intCol = 0 To rsDailyTrans.Fields.Count - 1
        objSheet.Cells(intRow, intCol + 1) = _
        rsDailyTrans.Fields(intCol).Value
    Next intCol
    rsDailyTrans.MoveNext
    intRow = intRow + 1
Loop

objExcel.Visible = True

Set rsDailyTrans = Nothing
Set objExcel = Nothing
Set objBook = Nothing
Set objSheet = Nothing
End Sub
```

Although this code might seem a bit daunting, if you break it down, it can be easily understood. The complexity is due to manipulating ADO and Excel objects within the same procedure. The first section declares the variables. The next step is to define the data we want to transfer. This is done with a SQL statement that uses the supplied date to filter the records. We then open an ADODB recordset using the SQL statement. By not specifying a lock type or cursor type, the recordset opens as a forward-only, read-only recordset. Because all we need to do is read the data, this works fine, especially because this gives us the fastest performance.

Now we launch Excel and add a new workbook. When you open Excel directly it automatically opens a workbook with three worksheets. But when you open it via automation, you have to add the workbook in your code. From there you use the `ActiveSheet` property to reference the default worksheet.

Transferring the data takes two steps. In the first step, you loop through the `Fields` collection of the recordset assigning the field names as column headings for the worksheet. In the second step, the loop moves through the data of the recordset and transfers the values into the cells. The `intRow` and `intCol` variables are used to reference the rows and columns of the spreadsheet.

The final piece is to make the instance of Excel visible. You don't want to do this until after the data has been transferred so that the screen refreshes don't slow down the process. After the spreadsheet is made visible, you need to run your cleanup code, setting your variables to `Nothing`. Figure 22.3 shows the completed spreadsheet.

Figure 22.3
The completed spreadsheet.

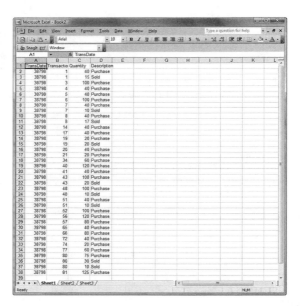

Talking to Word

The report writing capability of Access is powerful. Even with the new Rich Text Format memo fields, doing reports with highly formatted text is better done in Word than Access. Using automation you can create form letters and reports that would be more difficult in Access. To illustrate this, we will build a form that allows you to create and populate a Word document through the form. Following are detailed steps:

1. Open a new form in Form Design mode from the Create ribbon.

2. Set the Navigation Buttons and Record Selector properties to both, and set the Scroll Bars property to Neither.

22

3. Add a form header.

4. Set the Recordsource for the form to **qryEmployeesExtended**.

5. Use the Combo Box Wizard to add a Search combo box (third option) to the form header. Select the LastName and FirstName fields for the combo box.

6. Open the RowSource for the combo and add a column with the following expression:
FullName: LastName & ", " & FirstName

7. Move this added column to the second column and set Ascending sorts on the LastName and FirstName columns; then uncheck the Show boxes for both columns.

8. Name this combo box **cboSelEmp**.

9. Add another combo box to the main form and set the Row Source Type to Field List and the RowSource to qryEmployeesExtended. Name it **cboFields**.

10. Add a text box control and name it **txtAddText**.

11. Add a text box control and name it **txtFilename**.

12. Add a command button (without the wizard), name it **cmdCreate**, and set the Caption to Create Document.

13. Using the Code Builder add the following code snippet:

```
Private Sub cmdCreate_Click()
'Open new document
Set objWord = New Word.Application
'add document and save as specifed name
objWord.Documents.Add
objWord.ActiveDocument.SaveAs (Me.txtFilename)
objWord.Visible = True
End Sub
```

14. Scroll up to the Declarations area and add the following declaration:

```
Dim objWord As Word.Application
```

This sets the scope of the variable to the form module so you can use the document throughout the form.

15. Add another button and name it **cmdClose**; set the Caption to Close Document.

16. Using the Code Builder enter the following code:

```
Private Sub cmdClose_Click()
objWord.ActiveDocument.Save
objWord.Quit
End Sub
```

17. Add another button and name it **cmdAddText**; set the Caption to Add Text.

18. Use the Code Builder to add the following code:

```
Private Sub cmdAddText_Click()
'Add entered text
objWord.ActiveDocument.Range.InsertAfter (Me.txtAddText)
'Clear text box
Me.txtAddText = Null
End Sub
```

19. Select the Field List combo box. Use the Code Builder to add the following code to the `After Update` event:

```
Private Sub cboField_Click()
Dim varField As Variant
varField = " " & DLookup(Me.cboField, "tblEmployees", _
  "[EmployeeID] = " & Me.cboSelEmp)
objWord.ActiveDocument.Range.InsertAfter (varField)
End Sub
```

20. Save the form and name it **frmWordDoc**.

The form should now look like the one shown in Figure 22.4.

Figure 22.4
The completed form for creating a Word document.

To test the form, enter a path and filename in the Filename text box and click the Create Document button. This opens an instance of Word and names the document. In the Document Text box enter **Dear** and click the Add Text button. From the Field combo box select FirstName. Return to the Document Text box and type:

```
I'm pleased to inform you that, effective 9/16/07, you have been promoted to
```

Then click the Add Text button. From the Field combo box select JobTitle. Finally, go back to the Document Text box and type in:

```
. Congratulations!
```

```
Sincerely,
```

Then enter your name. Click the Add Text button and the document should look like the one shown in Figure 22.5.

Figure 22.5
The completed Word document.

The code to open the document is similar to opening a workbook. The key part of this code is in adding text to the document. With Word documents you need to use the `Range` object. This object represents the currently selected text. The `Range` object includes a number of methods, such as `InsertAfter` and `InsertBefore`, that can be used to add text. Because a newly created document has no text in it, the `Range` object would point to the beginning of the document, so that using `InsertAfter` inserts the text right at the start.

With this form we allow the user to enter her own text, which is added to the document. In addition, the user can select a field from the query and insert the value of that field at the current position to build a letter. This is a somewhat simplistic example, but it can be easily expanded on to construct letters from within Access.

CASE STUDY

Case Study: Using Excel Charts

This case study demonstrates creating a chart in Excel using data from Access. We will create a pie chart showing the breakdown of sales by category.

The first step is to add a query that summarizes sales by category. Open Query Design view and add three tables: `tblTransactions`, `tblInventory`, and `tluCategory`. Join `tblTransactions` to `tblInventory` on `InventoryID` and `tblInventory` to `tluCategory` on `CategoryID`. Add the `Category` field from `tluCategory` and the `Quantity` field from `tblTransactions`. Then click the Totals icon on the Design ribbon. Set the Category column to Group and the Quantity column to Sum. The resulting query should look like that shown in Figure 22.6.

Figure 22.6
The query shows total sales for each category.

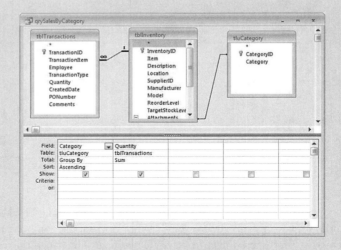

Next open a standard module (such as `basAutomation`) and add the following code:

```
Sub ExcelChart()
'Send the sales by Category to Excel
'for charting

Dim rsSales As ADODB.Recordset
Dim objExcel As Excel.Application
Dim objSheet As Excel.Worksheet
Dim objChart As Excel.Chart

Dim fld As ADODB.Field
Dim intCol As Integer
Dim intRow As Integer

'Define and populate recordset
Set rsSales = New ADODB.Recordset
rsSales.Open "qrySalesbyCategory", CurrentProject.Connection

'Launch Excel and create WorkSheet
Set objExcel = New Excel.Application
objExcel.Workbooks.Add
Set objSheet = objExcel.ActiveSheet

'Transfer the data
For intCol = 0 To rsSales.Fields.Count - 1
    Set fld = rsSales.Fields(intCol)
    objSheet.Cells(1, intCol + 1) = fld.Name
Next intCol
intRow = 2
Do Until rsSales.EOF
    For intCol = 0 To rsSales.Fields.Count - 1
        objSheet.Cells(intRow, intCol + 1) = _
        rsSales.Fields(intCol).Value
    Next intCol
    rsSales.MoveNext
```

```
        intRow = intRow + 1
Loop

'Add a new chart
objExcel.Charts.Add
Set objChart = objExcel.ActiveChart

'set up the chart
objChart.ChartType = xl3DPie
objChart.SetSourceData _
 Source:=objSheet.Range("A1:B" & CStr(intRow - 1)), _
 PlotBy:=xlColumns
objChart.Location xlLocationAsNewSheet
objChart.HasTitle = True
objChart.ChartTitle.Characters.Text = "Sales By Category"

objExcel.Visible = True

End Sub
```

Most of this code is similar to the Excel example we used earlier in his chapter. It opens a recordset from the `qrySalesbyCategory` query and transfers that data to Excel. The differences appear where we call the `Add` method of the `Charts` collection to create a new chart in the workbook.

While there are many methods and properties for the `Chart` object, we've kept it pretty simple here. We've chosen a basic 3D Pie chart with a simple title.

Run this code from the Immediate window; Figure 22.7 shows the results.

Figure 22.7
The resulting chart.

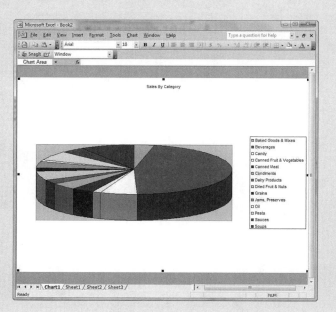

Working with XML Files

Understanding XML

A universal format for data has been sort of a holy grail. Both software developers and end users have long sought some standard way of identifying data to different applications and for different uses. Extensible Markup Language (XML) comes close to becoming this standard. Officially XML is a platform-independent markup language used for structured documents. This means that the structure of the document is defined by tags that identify the different elements of the document. Similar to HTML, XML uses tags to bracket the data. These tags define what the specific data represents and how it fits in with the rest of the data.

This chapter deals with automating the use of XML files in Access, so we won't go into a lot of detail about how to create and structure XML documents. The important thing for the purposes of this book is that XML makes it easy to share data without concern for the original format. As long as the application that has the data you want to use can export the data as an XML file, you can use Access to import it.

Access began supporting XML with version 2002. Office 2007 makes the most extensive use of XML yet. The following XML file types are supported:

- **XML**—A formatting standard used for structured data files. It uses formatting tags to organize the actual data into identifiable blocks of data.

- **XSL**—A standard used for altering imported or exported data. The XSL file is used to format the XML file. These two files may be combined by embedding the XSL data within the XML file.

23

■ **XSD**—This standard describes the database structure in XML terms. Referred to as *schema definition* files, they contain constraint and data type information for the tags in the corresponding XML file.

This chapter shows you how to use all three of these file types. You'll learn how XML holds the data, XSL formats the data, and XSD defines the structure of the data.

> **NOTE**
> We define a structured file as a text file that contains formatting tags to identify the parts of the file and how they are used. For example, a file that stores data about employees would be likely to contains tags such as `<EmpFName>`, `<EmpLName>`, and so on. Access interprets these tags as field names. Tags are paired to indicate the beginning and end of the data. A tag pair might look like this: `<EmpFName>Scott</EmpFName>`, with the closing tag prefaced with a slash (/).

Access can also create an HTML file ready for adding to a website or page as part of the XML-based features. We detail that later in this chapter in the section "Exporting a Web-Ready File."

Using `ExportXML`

Data can be exported to an XML file from within a code procedure using VBA's `ExportXML` method, which uses the following syntax:

```
Application.ExportXML objecttype, datasource[, datatarget] _
[, schematarget], [presentationtarget] _
[, imagetarget][, encoding][, otherflags] _
[, filtercriteria][, additionaldata]
```

where *application* refers to the Access model. Table 23.1 details this method's several arguments. Although the trio of arguments *datatarget*, *schematarget*, and *presentation-target* are all optional, at least one of them must be specified. Tables 23.2 and 23.3 further detail the constants that can be used with some of `ExportXML`'s arguments.

Table 23.1   `ExportXML` Arguments

Argument	Explanation
objecttype	An intrinsic constant that specifies the type of object you are exporting (see Table 23.2).
datasource	A `String` value that provides the name of the object being exported.
datatarget	The full path and filename for the destination XML file being exported to.
schematarget	The full path and filename for the schema data (XSD file) being exported.
presentationtarget	The full path and filename for the presentation information (XSL file) being exported.

Argument	Explanation
imagetarget	The path for any graphics or image files being exported.
encoding	Either of two constants, acUTF16 or acUTF8, that specifies the text encoding.
otherflags	A bit mask value (see Table 23.3). You can add values together to specify multiple options.
filtercriteria	A String value that limits the records being exported by applying a filter.
additionaldata	Allows you to specify multiple tables for export. It is ignored when *otherflags* is set to acLiveReportSource.

Table 23.2 Object Constants

Object	Constant
Form	acExportForm
Function	acExportFunction
Query	acExportQuery
Report	acExportReport
View	acExportServerView
Stored Procedure	acExportStoredProcedure
Table	acExportTable

Table 23.3 Values for the *otherflags* Argument

Value	Constant	Description
1	acEmbedSchema	Embed schema information within the XML document specified by *datatarget*.
2	acExcludePrimaryKeyAndIndexes	Do not export primary key and indexes to the schema document.
4	acRunFromServer	Generate an Active Server Page (ASP) wrapper for the exported report.
8	acLiveReportSource	Create a live link to a remote SQL Server database for the exported report.
16	acPersistReportML	Persist the exported object as ReportML, a special type of XML specifically designed for Access reports.

23

> **CAUTION**
>
> When you use VBA's ExportXML it overwrites any existing files without warning. If you don't want that to happen, make sure that the filename exists and warn the user to change the name if she doesn't want to lose the existing file.

An Example of Exporting

In its simplest form ExportXML generates a single XML file. Enter the following code into a standard module (such as basAutomation):

```
Sub ExportQuery(strSource As String, strPath As String, _
 strTarget As String)
'Export to XML
Access.Application.ExportXML acExportQuery, strSource, _
 strPath & strTarget
End Sub
```

To use this code you pass the name of the query you want to export, the folder where you want to store it, and the name you want to store it as. For instance, in the Immediate window enter code such as the following:

```
ExportQuery "qryEmployeesExtended", "path", "employees.xml"
```

You need to substitute the actual path for *path* according to your system's folder structure, and include the .xml extension to make sure other programs can recognize it as an XML file. Figure 23.1 shows the exported XML file opened in Microsoft Word, which is one of many applications that can display XML files.

Figure 23.1
The XML file containing the tags and data. However, it's not very readable in this form.

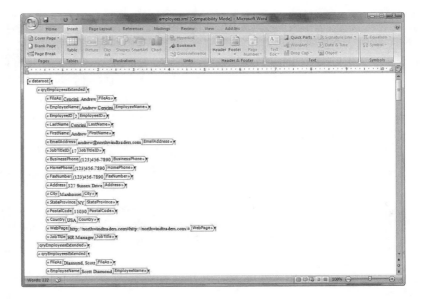

As you can see from the figure, the actual XML native format is not very readable. This is not a way that you normally use an XML file. We do, however, want to point out some parts of the structure. Notice that each record is surrounded by tags that refer to the name of the exported query. Within those tags, each field has an opening and closing tag with each field name. This structure is repeated for each record.

Exporting a Web-Ready File

You can also use the same ExportQuery procedure to create an HTML file that can be uploaded to your website. Just change the extension for the file listed in the strTarget argument from .xml to .html. When the file is opened in a browser, just the data displays, without the tags.

Try this by changing the previous statement we used in the Immediate window to the following:

```
ExportQuery "qryEmployeesExtended", "path", "employees.html"
```

Now open the file in your browser by finding the file using Windows Explorer and then double-clicking the file. The result should be similar to Figure 23.2.

Figure 23.2
The exported HTML file viewed in a browser.

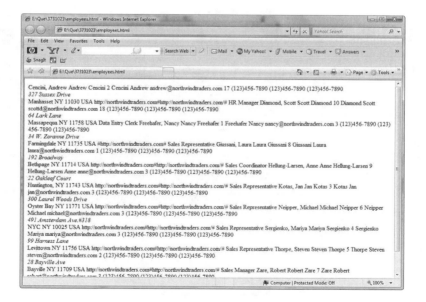

Exporting Related Data

Although the user interface makes exporting related data a simple task, automating the process is more complex. You can use ExportXML's *additionaldata* argument to specify additional tables to include in the export. But it's not as simple as just adding the table name. You need to use the AdditionalData object to append the table.

The process involves defining an `AdditionalData` object and then using that object's `Add` method to append the table to the collection. The following code illustrates how this works:

```
Sub ExportMultiples(strSource As String, strpath As String, _
 strTarget As String, strAddlTbls As String)
'export related tables to XML
Dim objAddlTable As AdditionalData
Set objAddlTable = Application.CreateAdditionalData
objAddlTable.Add (strAddlTbls)
Access.Application.ExportXML acExportTable, strSource, _
 strpath & strTarget, , , , , , objAddlTable
 End Sub
```

To test this code enter the following statement in the Immediate window (remember to use the correct path):

```
ExportMultiples "tblSuppliers", "e:\que\3731023\", "suppliers.html", _
"tblInventory"
```

Figure 23.3 shows the resulting HTML file as viewed through your browser. As you can see, the format leaves something to be desired in terms of readability. But the data is all shown.

Figure 23.3
The exported HTML file with related tables as viewed in a browser.

Using `ImportXML`

It would be nice if all your data was in one place using one database format. But unless you are a very small business, that's not likely to be the case. There will be times when you have to use data from other databases or programs. If the other program has the capability to export to XML, you can automate the import by using the `ImportXML` method within your VBA code to import the XML data and schema information. The syntax for the `ImportXML` method follows:

```
Application.ImportXML datasource[, importoptions]
```

where *datasource* is a required string value that contains the full path and filename for the XML file you want to import, and *importoptions* is one of the three optional intrinsic constants shown in Table 23.4.

Table 23.4   `ImportXML` Constants

Constant	Integer Value	Explanation
acStructureOnly	0	Only the table's structure is imported.
acStructureAndData	1	Both the structure and data are imported (the default option).
acAppendData	2	Data is appended to an existing table.

As you can see the arguments for the `ImportXML` method are much fewer, so importing is not as complex as exporting. Sometimes you may need to copy the structure or append the data to an existing table. For the most part, though, you indicate the file and import the data into a new table.

An Import Example

We'll look at how the three constants affect the results of importing the employee data exported earlier in this chapter. We'll start by entering the following code in a standard module (or use the `basAutomation` module from Chapter 22, "Working with Other Applications"):

```
Sub DemoImportXML(strSource As String, _
 Optional varimpopt As Variant)
'import an XML file
If IsMissing(varimpopt) Then
    varimpopt = acStructureAndData
End If
Access.Application.ImportXML strSource, varimpopt
End Sub
```

To use this procedure, you pass the full path and filename of the XML file you are importing as the source, and then you can specify the constant either with its integer value or the actual text description. If you omit the second argument, the procedure checks and deals with that by supplying the default constant.

> **CAUTION**
>
> Before you use the `ImportXML` method, you need to close all applications (Word, browsers, and so on) that have an open XML file. If an `.xml` file is open it can return an error in some instances.

From the Immediate window run the following statement:

```
DemoImportXML "path\employees.xml"
```

Don't forget to substitute the actual path for *path*. Figure 23.4 shows the imported table listed in the Navigation pane and the opened table in Datasheet mode.

Figure 23.4
The imported table shown in the Navigation pane and opened for viewing.

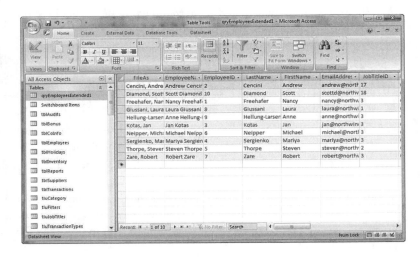

Notice that the new table was created using the name of the query that was exported. Also notice that a "1" was added to the name because there is an existing object with the same name. If you open the table in Design view you also see that no primary key or index was created.

If we tried using the `acAppendData` constant we would encounter an error. Because the exported data contains the `EmployeeID` primary key field, when you try to append the records to the existing table you encounter a key violation because you can't have duplicate `EmployeeID`s. If, for some reason you need to duplicate these records, you would have to edit the `EmployeeID`s to prevent duplicates, so we will skip demonstrating that constant.

To import just the structure of the table, change the statement in the Immediate window to

```
DemoImportXML "path\employees.xml", acStructureOnly
```

Again, remember to enter the correct path. Now open the imported table in Datasheet view, and it should look like Figure 23.5.

Figure 23.5
The imported structure shown opened in Datasheet view.

Notice the new name is qryEmployeesExtended2 because qryEmployeesExtended and qryEmployeesExtended1 already exist.

> **CAUTION**
>
> Importing only the structure of the XML file doesn't create any primary key or indexes.

The ImportXML method also recognizes that related tables were exported using the AdditionalData argument. So, when importing tables related within the XML file, Access does all the work for you, making the process much simpler. To demonstrate this, run the import again, but specify the related files (suppliers.html) that you exported. The statement to run from the Immediate window is

```
DemoImportXML "path\supplier.html"
```

Figure 23.6 shows the result of this import. You see the "1" concatenated to tblSuppliers and tblInventory. Notice that you specified a .html file to import. The ImportXML has the flexibility to handle XML-formatted HTML files.

Figure 23.6
The related tables imported back into Access.

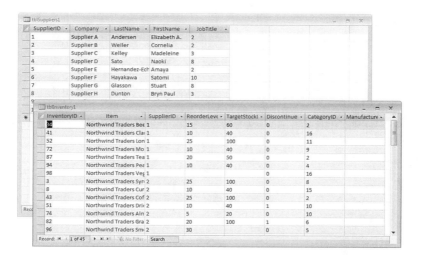

> **CAUTION**
>
> Although `ImportXML` can import related tables and parse the data correctly into the separate tables, it cannot create a formal relationship with referential integrity. You need to create that relationship yourself.

23

Using the Windows API

24

Declaring API Calls

One function of an operating system such as Windows is to act as an interface between productivity applications, such as Microsoft Office, and the system hardware. Windows makes the programmer's job easier because she doesn't have to write code to control the printer or to control how the screen displays what she needs the user to see. Instead, the programmer just needs to tell Windows what she wants Windows to do, and Windows handles the translation to the hardware.

This means a programmer can use any one of several programming languages such as C++, Visual Basic, .Net, and several others to develop programs. These programs can then use a special software layer that sits between the code and the hardware. This layer is called the *Windows Application Programming Interface* or *Windows API*. The Windows API includes thousands of functions that automate the tasks of drawing windows, selecting files, sending output to the printer, and so on.

VBA provides a mechanism for you to call procedures of the Windows API, referred to as *API calls*. This chapter demonstrates how to use this mechanism to provide more direct control of Windows.

To use a Windows API involves a two-step process. The first step requires a declaration of the API call that you want to use. This creates a connection between your VBA code and the Windows software. After the API call is declared, the second step is to use the declared function as you would use any other VBA procedure.

To illustrate this, we'll show you how to retrieve the name assigned to the local PC using the API. You use the Declarations section of any VBA module like so:

```
Declare Function GetComputerName _
 Lib "kernel32" Alias "GetComputerNameA" _
 (ByVal lpBuffer As String, nSize As Long) As Long
```

This declaration provides several pieces of information to VBA:

- The name of the function for VBA to use is GetComputerName.
- The actual function is part of a Windows library named kernel32.
- The name of the function within that library is GetComputernameA.
- The function uses two arguments, a String value and a Long value.
- The function returns a single Long value.

> **TIP**
>
> Because API calls are a Windows function, the VBA help files don't have any information on them. Microsoft provides the Windows Platform Software Developers Kit, usually referred to as the Platform SDK. The Platform SDK can be found online. For example, you can find documentation on GetComputerName at http://msdn2.microsoft.com/en-us/library/ms724295.aspx.

Using API Calls

After you declare an API call using the Declare keyword, it can be used just like any function or procedure you create in your VBA code (with the Sub or Function keywords). Following is a code snippet that uses the declared function:

```
Function GetPCName() As String
'Retrieve the name of the lcoal PC
'using the Windows API

Dim strName As String
Dim lngChars As Long
Dim lngRet As Long

strName = Space(255)
lngChars = 255

lngRet = GetComputerName(strName, lngChars - 1)
If lngRet > 0 Then
    GetPCName = Left(strName, lngChars)
Else
    GetPCName = "Name unavailable"
End If
End Function
```

You do need to be aware of some factors when using API calls. Because the API definition of a string differs from the VBA definition, you need to exercise some care when passing string arguments to the API call. This is an issue because API strings are a fixed length, and VBA strings are of variable length. This means that you have to initialize any string passed to an API call to a fixed length and a variable to tell the function what that length is. The API call returns, as the second variable, the actual number of characters used by the fixed-length string.

> **TIP**
>
> The sample code uses the VBA `Space()` function to initialize the fixed-length string. It's ideal for that purpose because it returns a string containing the specified number of spaces.

The string used by the API needs to reserve one character to use as its end of string marker. This means you have to tell the API that it will be working with one less character than the string was initialized for. That's why, even though you set `lngChars` to 255, you subtract one from the value actually passed. The VBA `Left` function is used to trim the returned string back to the fixed length passed to the API call.

The second factor you need to be concerned with is that API calls generally return a nonzero value if the call worked properly and a zero if an error occurred. The returned value is captured in the `lngRet` variable, which is then tested to make sure the call was successful.

Figure 24.1 shows what happens when you run this function from the Immediate window. Of course, your system will return a different name.

Figure 24.1
Running the `GetPCName` function in the Immediate window.

API Calls You Can Use from Access

As mentioned earlier the API includes thousands of functions that can be called. If you want to learn more about what you can do, check out the MSDN area of Microsoft's website at http://msdn2.microsoft.com/en-us/library/aa383750.aspx.

We want to give you an idea of some of the things you can do, so we'll demonstrate the following functionalities:

- Check to see whether an application is loaded into memory.
- Capture the network login ID of the current user.
- Retrieve the name of the program associated with a data file.

Check Whether an Application Is Loaded

There may be an occasion when you need to check whether an application is currently running on your user's computer. For example, you might need to determine whether Excel is loaded before making an automation call to Excel. You can use the `FindWindow` API call to do this:

```
Declare Function FindWindow Lib "user32" _
 Alias "FindWindowA" (ByVal lpClassname As String, _
 ByVal lpWindowName As String) As Long

Function IsAppLoaded(strClassname As String, _
 strWindowname As String) As Boolean
 'Check whether app is running
 'using class name or title bar text

 If strClassname = "" Then
    IsAppLoaded = (FindWindow(vbNullString, _
      strWindowname) <> 0)
 Else
    IsAppLoaded = (FindWindow(strClassname, _
      vbNullString) <> 0)
 End If
End Function
```

The `FindWindow` API call can use either a class name or the window caption to determine whether the application is loaded. If a match is found, the window handle is returned. *Window handles* are numbers that the operating system uses to keep track of objects. The thing to note is that a window handle can never be a zero value because you will get an error.

Any open window is identified by a class name. The class name is assigned by the developers of the application. For example, Excel uses the class name x1Main, and Word uses the class name OpusApp (Opus, the penguin from the *Bloom County* comic strip, was the mascot of the original development team for Word). Because you might not always know the class name of an application, an alternative method is to use the title bar text. Just make sure you match that text exactly. If you open Microsoft Word 2007 to a new blank document, the actual title is *Document1 – Microsoft Word*. So, if you are checking for an instance of Word, you might get the following results:

```
? IsAppLoaded("","Word")
False
? IsAppLoaded("","Document1 - Microsoft Word")
True
```

You need to pass a null string for the argument that you aren't going to use. Because VBA doesn't use null strings, it provides the vbNullString constant for just such an occasion.

Capture the Network Login ID

One way I secure my applications is to capture the Network Login ID for the current user. I use this in conjunction with a user table that stores the role of each user (for example, reader, editor, or admin). For this I use the following API call and function:

```
Declare Function GetUserName Lib "advapi32.dll" _
  Alias "GetUserNameA" (ByVal lpBuffer As String, _
  nSize As Long) As Long

Function GetOSUsername() As String
 'Capture network login ID using
 'windows API

 Dim strUsername As String
 Dim lngChars As Long
 Dim lngRet As Long

 strUsername = Space(255)
 lngChars = 255

 lngRet = GetUserName(strUsername, lngChars - 1)
 If lngRet > 0 Then
    GetOSUsername = Left(strUsername, lngChars)
 Else
    GetOSUsername = "Name unavailable"
 End If
End Function
```

If this looks familiar, it should; it's similar to the code for capturing the computer name. The difference is the API being called and which library it's contained in. The rest of the pattern involves setting up the string, passing its length, and determining whether the valid returned string remains the same. So you can use this pattern to capture a lot of system information just by changing the API call.

> **TIP**
>
> You might have noticed that all the functions names we've used end in an A. There really are two versions of each of these functions: one ending in an A, the other ending in a W. The A version uses ANSI characters, and the W version uses Unicode characters. Because VBA uses only ANSI characters, you need to use the A version.

24

Retrieving the Name of the Program Associated with a Data File

What program opens .doc files? Is it Microsoft Word, WordPad, or some other program? What image viewer is set to open .jpg or .bmp files? What browser displays .html files? These questions and similar ones can be answered with the FindExecutable API call, which returns the executable program file associated with a particular type of data file.

```
Declare Function FindExecutable Lib "shell32.dll" _
  Alias "FindExecutableA" (ByVal lpFile As String, _
  ByVal lpDirectory As String, ByVal lpResult As String) _
  As Long

Function GetExecutable(strDataFile As String, _
  strDir As String) As String
  'Retrieve the executable for the
  'specified data file

  Dim strApp As String
  Dim lngRet As Long

  strApp = Space(260)
  lngRet = FindExecutable(strDataFile, strDir, strApp)

  If lngRet > 32 Then
      GetExecutable = strApp
  Else
      GetExecutable = "No associated application found"
  End If
End Function
```

Let's test this function by checking what application opens .jpg files. You need to supply the full name and path of the data file and the working directory it's in. On my system I used this expression, and following that is what was returned:

```
? GetExecutable("C:\temp\mycomp.jpg","c:\temp")
C:\Program Files\Windows Photo Gallery\PhotoViewer.dll
```

With this function the string length is 260. This is the maximum length for a path and filename under Windows. Another point to note is FindExecutable breaks the rule of returning zero for failure; instead it returns some number less than 32.

Knowing When to Use the Windows API

The following points can help you know when to use the Windows API:

- Only when there is no VBA alternative
- To manipulate applications other than those that support VBA automation
- To retrieve information from Windows
- To interact with functions (such as network messages) that are inaccessible using VBA

If you want to learn more about this advanced topic several books are available. I would recommend *Windows 2000 API SuperBible* by Richard Simon, Sams Publishing.

Case Study: Capturing a Filename to Use for Processing

You learned how to import files at different points in this book. In those cases the user typed in the full path and filename. But often, the user might not know exactly where a file is or what it's named. At times like that, you might want users to open the standard File, Open dialog to browse the system and locate the file they need. This case study will show you how to do just that.

> **NOTE** This case study uses an example from a fellow MVP, Doug Steele, who has graciously given me permission to use it. The code and examples were originally published in the December 2006 issue of *Advisor Guide to Microsoft Access*.

This code is fairly complex and involves several different modules and code snippets. In addition, it introduces some concepts we haven't covered before. One of those is the `Type...End Type` statement, which creates a user-defined type that contains variables used by the library containing the API. The set of functions to open the File, Open dialog and to capture the full path and filename follows. I recommend placing it in a new standard module.

```
Private Type OPENFILENAME
      lStructSize        As Long
      hWndOwner          As Long
      hInstance          As Long
      lpstrFilter        As String
      lpstrCustomFilter  As String
      nMaxCustFilter     As Long
      nFilterIndex       As Long
      lpstrFile          As String
      nMaxFile           As Long
      lpstrFileTitle     As String
      nMaxFileTitle      As Long
      lpstrInitialDir    As String
      lpstrTitle         As String
      Flags              As Long
      nFileOffset        As Integer
      nFileExtension     As Integer
      lpstrDefExt        As String
      nCustData          As Long
      lpfnHook           As Long
      sTemplateName      As String
      pvReserved         As Long
      dwReserved         As Long
      FlagsEx            As Long
End Type
```

24

The preceding code creates a user-defined type that contains a variable that will be used by the rest of this code. Following are the three API functions that must be declared:

```
Declare Function GetOpenFileName Lib "comdlg32.dll" _
    Alias "GetOpenFileNameA" (OFN As OPENFILENAME) As Boolean
```

The following section declares and populates a number of global constants that the rest of the code needs:

```
Public Const OFN_ALLOWMULTISELECT  As Long = &H200
Public Const OFN_CREATEPROMPT As Long = &H2000
Public Const OFN_ENABLEHOOK As Long = &H20
Public Const OFN_ENABLESIZING As Long = &H800000
Public Const OFN_ENABLETEMPLATE As Long = &H40
Public Const OFN_ENABLETEMPLATEHANDLE As Long = &H80
Public Const OFN_EXPLORER As Long = &H80000
Public Const OFN_EXTENSIONDIFFERENT As Long = &H400
Public Const OFN_FILEMUSTEXIST As Long = &H1000
Public Const OFN_FORCESHOWHIDDEN As Long = &H10000000
Public Const OFN_HIDEREADONLY As Long = &H4
Public Const OFN_LONGNAMES As Long = &H200000
Public Const OFN_NOCHANGEDIR As Long = &H8
Public Const OFN_NODEREFERENCELINKS As Long = &H100000
Public Const OFN_NOLONGNAMES As Long = &H40000
Public Const OFN_NONETWORKBUTTON As Long = &H20000
Public Const OFN_NOREADONLYRETURN As Long = &H8000
Public Const OFN_NOTESTFILECREATE As Long = &H10000
Public Const OFN_NOVALIDATE As Long = &H100
Public Const OFN_OVERWRITEPROMPT As Long = &H2
Public Const OFN_PATHMUSTEXIST As Long = &H800
Public Const OFN_READONLY As Long = &H1
Public Const OFN_SHAREAWARE As Long = &H4000
Public Const OFN_SHAREFALLTHROUGH As Long = 2
Public Const OFN_SHAREWARN As Long = 0
Public Const OFN_SHARENOWARN As Long = 1
Public Const OFN_SHOWHELP As Long = &H10
Public Const OFN_EX_NOPLACESBAR As Long = &H1
```

The following function is the main procedure that actually opens the dialog and returns the selected file:

```
Function GetFileOpen( _
    Optional ByVal hWnd As Variant, _
    Optional ByVal Filter As String = vbNullString, _
    Optional ByVal FilterIndex As Long = 1, _
    Optional ByVal FileName As String = vbNullString, _
    Optional ByVal InitialDir As Variant, _
    Optional ByVal DialogTitle As String = vbNullString, _
    Optional ByRef Flags As Long = 0, _
    Optional ByVal DefaultExt As String = vbNullString, _
    Optional ByVal ExtendedFlags As Long = 0 _
) As Variant

' This code was originally written by
' Doug Steele, MVP  AccessHelp@rogers.com
' http://I.Am/DougSteele
' You are free to use it in any application
' provided the copyright notice is left unchanged.
'
```

```
' Description:  Provides a means of calling the GetOpenFileName
'               API function.
'
'Inputs: hWnd        Variant (Optional)  Handle of Parent window.
'                                        Defaults to handle of
'                                        Access application.
'        Filter      String  (Optional)  A set of "patterns" designating what
'                                        types of files can be selected.
'                                        Defaults to a blank string
'                                        (i.e.: no pattern).
'        FilterIndex Long    (Optional)  1-based integer indicating
'                                        which filter to use initially.
'                                        Defaults to 1.
'        FileName    String  (Optional)  Default file name to use.
'                                        Defaults to a blank string.
'        InitialDir  String  (Optional)  Directory in which to start
'                                        looking for files.
'                                        Defaults to current directory.
'        DialogTitle String (Optional)   Title to use for the dialog box.
'                                        Defaults to a blank string.
'        Flags       Long    (Optional)  A set of bit flags (OFN_*)
'                                        used to initialize the dialog box.
'                                        Defaults to 0.
'        DefaultExt  String  (Optional)  Extension to use if the user
'                                        doesn't enter one.
'                                        Defaults to a blank string.
'        ExtendedFlags String (Optional) An additional set of bit flags
'                                        (OFN_EX_*) used to initialize
'                                        the dialog box.
'                                        Defaults to 0.
'                                        (only applicable to machines running
'                                          Windows 2000 or newer)
'
' Returns:     A variant value. If on

Dim OFN As OPENFILENAME
Dim lngBufferSize As Long
Dim lngExtendedError As Long
Dim lngLoop As Long
Dim lngReturn As Long
Dim lngNull As Long
Dim strExtendedError As String
Dim strFileName As String
Dim strPath As String
Dim varFiles As Variant

    If IsMissing(hWnd) Then hWnd = Application.hWndAccessApp
    If IsMissing(InitialDir) Then InitialDir = CurDir

' Allocate string space for the returned strings.
' Normally, 256 bytes is adequate.
' However, if you're typically allowing multiple files
' to be selected, you may find that 256 bytes isn't enough.
```

24

```
' Let's start by allocating 512 bytes.
' (If it's not enough, increase it...)

    lngBufferSize = 512

    strFileName = Left(FileName & String(lngBufferSize, 0), lngBufferSize)

' Set up the data structure before you call the function.
    With OFN
' Define the size of the structure.
        .lStructSize = Len(OFN)
' Set the window that owns the dialog.
        .hWndOwner = hWnd
' Set the allowable file types (patterns).
        .lpstrFilter = Filter
' Set the default file type for which to search.
        .nFilterIndex = FilterIndex
' Pass the buffer.
' Note that the buffer may contain a
' default file name at the beginning, then
' contains a large number of null characters.
        .lpstrFile = strFileName
' Pass the size of the buffer/
        .nMaxFile = Len(strFileName)
' Pass a buffer for just the filename.
' (Will only work if only a single selection is made).
        .lpstrFileTitle = strFileTitle
' Pass the size of the buffer.
        .nMaxFileTitle = Len(strFileTitle)
' Set the title for the dialog
        .lpstrTitle = DialogTitle
' Pass the appropriate flags to control how the
' dialog functions
        .Flags = Flags
' Set the default extension (to be used if no extension provided)
        .lpstrDefExt = DefaultExt
' Set the starting folder
        .lpstrInitialDir = InitialDir
' Pass the Extended flags
        .FlagsEx = ExtendedFlags
    End With

    lngReturn = GetOpenFileName(OFN)

    If lngReturn > 0 Then
' Since the value of Flags may get reset to reflect
' certain information about what was selected, you
' may wish to pass back what was returned for Flags.
' Note, of course, that you can't do that unless
' a variable was passed for Flags.
        If Not IsMissing(Flags) Then Flags = OFN.Flags
' Assume that there's at least 2 Null character at the very end of the string...
        lngNull = InStr(OFN.lpstrFile, vbNullChar & vbNullChar)
        If lngNull > 0 Then
```

```
' If the dialog was opened in Explorer view, the file names will be delimited
' with Null characters.
' If the dialog wasn't opened in Explorer view, they'll be delimited with spaces.
            If (Flags And OFN_EXPLORER) = OFN_EXPLORER Then
                varFiles = Split(Left$(OFN.lpstrFile, lngNull - 1), vbNullChar)
            Else
                varFiles = Split(Left$(OFN.lpstrFile, lngNull - 1), " ")
            End If
            If UBound(varFiles) > 0 Then
                strPath = varFiles(0)
                If Right$(strPath, 1) <> "\" Then
                    strPath = strPath & "\"
                End If
                For lngLoop = 1 To UBound(varFiles)
                    varFiles(lngLoop - 1) = strPath & varFiles(lngLoop)
                Next lngLoop
                ReDim Preserve varFiles(0 To (UBound(varFiles) - 1))
                GetFileOpen = varFiles
            Else
                GetFileOpen = varFiles
            End If
        Else
            GetFileOpen = vbNullString
        End If
    Else
' If the user selected the Cancel button, GetOpenFileName returns 0,
' and CommDlgExtendedError returns 0.
' I'm going to ignore errors of 0.
        strExtendedError = GetExtendedError()
' GetExtendedError returns errornumber: errordescription.
' Strip out the ErrorNumber from the beginning.
        lngExtendedError = Val(strExtendedError)
        If lngExtendedError <> 0 Then
            MsgBox "Your call to GetOpenFileName failed." & vbCrLf & _
                "The error returned was " & strExtendedError, _
                vbOKOnly + vbCritical
        End If
        GetFileOpen = Null
    End If

End Function
```

This next function enables you to add extensions that can restrict the type of files that appear in the File, Open dialog:

```
Function CreateFilterItem( _
    Description As String, _
    Pattern As String _
) As String
' This code was originally written by
' Doug Steele, MVP  AccessHelp@rogers.com
' http://I.Am/DougSteele
' You are free to use it in any application
' provided the copyright notice is left unchanged.
'
```

```
' Description:   Formats the filter parameter as required for the
'                GetOpenFileName API function.
'
'     Note that no validation is done that what was passed for Pattern is valid.
'
'     Note, too, that it's necessary to add an additional Null character at the
'                end of the final pattern.
'
' Inputs: Description   String  Name to associate with the pattern for
'                                display purposes.
'         Pattern       String  Filter pattern to use. (Like *.txt).
'                                To specify multiple filter patterns
'                                for a single display string, use a semicolon
'                                to separate the patterns (for example,
'                                "*.TXT;*.DOC;*.BAK").
'                                A pattern string can be a combination of
'                                valid file name characters and the asterisk
'                                (*) wildcard character.
'                                Do not include spaces in the pattern string.
'
' Returns:      A string consisting of what was passed for Description,
'               followed by a Null character,followed by what was
'               passed for Pattern, followed by another Null character.

    CreateFilterItem = Description & vbNullChar & Pattern & vbNullChar

End Function
```

To demonstrate this code, two forms are provided; frmBasic and frmDetails. The first form enables you to set parameters for the dialog box. Figure 24.2 shows the options you have to configure the File, Open dialog.

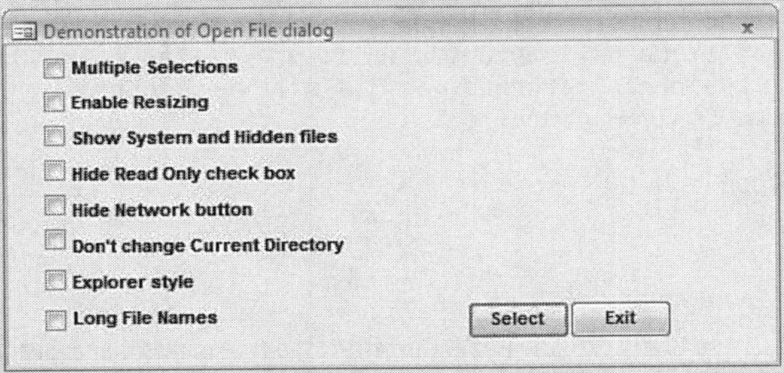

Figure 24.2
Use frmBasic to configure and open the File, Open dialog.

Behind the Select button is the following code, which uses the parameters and returns the selected files. These results are then displayed in frmDetails.

```
Private Sub cmdSelect_Click()

' Call our GetOpenFile function. (sort of the whole point of this database....!)
'
' I'm arbitrarily setting the Filter property, just to illustrate how it's done.
' I'm not setting FileName (the name of the default file).
' I'm setting InitialDir to the same directory as this database is in.

On Error GoTo Err_cmdSelect_Click
```

```
Dim lngExtendedFlags As Long
Dim lngFlags As Long
Dim lngLoop As Long
Dim lngSelected As Long
Dim strFilter As String
Dim strInitialDir As String
Dim strMessage As String
Dim varResponse As Variant

' Arbitrarily set some filters...
    strFilter = strFilter & CreateFilterItem("All Files (*.*)", "*.*")
    strFilter = strFilter & CreateFilterItem("Access Files (*.mda, *.mdb,_
                *.mde)", "*.MDA;*.MDB;*.MDE")
    strFilter = strFilter & CreateFilterItem("Excel Files (*.xls)", "*.XLS")
    strFilter = strFilter & CreateFilterItem("Text Files (*.txt)", "*.TXT")

' Set the flags, based on what options were selected
    lngFlags = SetFlags()
    lngExtendedFlags = SetExtendedFlags

' Set the initial directory
    strInitialDir = Left$(CurrentDb.Name, Len(CurrentDb.Name) - _
    Len(Dir(CurrentDb.Name)))

' Open frmDetails (hidden) to save the values
    DoCmd.OpenForm "frmDetails", windowmode:=acHidden
    With Forms("frmDetails")
        .txtInitialDirBefore = strInitialDir
        .txtFlagsBefore = lngFlags
    End With

    varResponse = GetFileOpen(Filter:=strFilter, _
        FilterIndex:=1, _
        InitialDir:=strInitialDir, _
        DialogTitle:="Hello! Open Me!", _
        Flags:=lngFlags, _
        ExtendedFlags:=lngExtendedFlags _
    )

    If IsNull(varResponse) Then
        strMessage = strMessage & "Null returned." & vbCrLf
    Else
        lngSelected = UBound(varResponse) - LBound(varResponse) + 1
        Select Case lngSelected
            Case 0
                strMessage = strMessage & "No files selected." & vbCrLf
            Case 1
                strMessage = strMessage & "1 file selected:" & vbCrLf
                strMessage = strMessage & varResponse(0) & vbCrLf
            Case Else
                strMessage = lngSelected & " files selected:" & vbCrLf
                For lngLoop = LBound(varResponse) To UBound(varResponse)
                    strMessage = strMessage & varResponse(lngLoop) & vbCrLf
                Next lngLoop
        End Select
    End If
```

24

```
        With Forms("frmDetails")
            .txtFilesSelected = strMessage
            .txtInitialDirAfter = strInitialDir
            .txtFlagsAfter = lngFlags
            .Visible = True
        End With

End_cmdSelect_Click:
    Exit Sub

Err_cmdSelect_Click:
    MsgBox Err.Number & ": " & Err.Description & _
        " occurred in " & Me.Name & ".cmdSelect_Click", _
        vbOKOnly + vbCritical
    Resume End_cmdSelect_Click

End Sub
```

To test all this, use frmBasic, select the parameters you want, and click the Select button. You will then see frmDetails with the results of the selection, as shown in Figure 24.4.

Figure 24.3
The File, Open dialog opened from frmBasic.

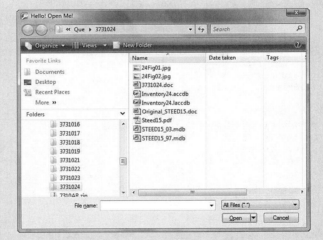

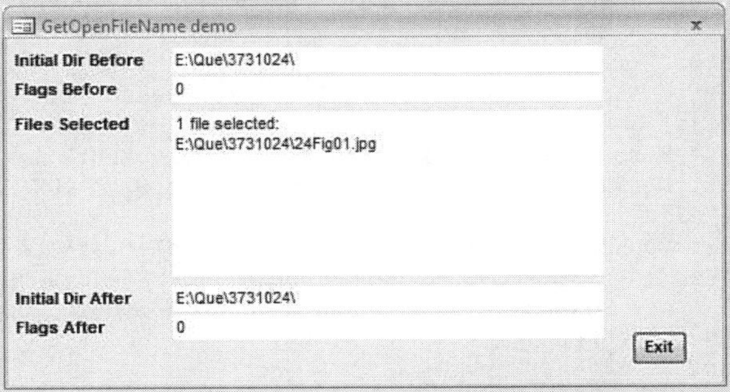

Figure 24.4
The results of the selected file appear in frmDetails.

A Review of Access SQL

Introduction to SQL

In addition to VBA, Access understands another computer language—Structured Query Language (SQL). SQL (pronounced *sequel* or *S-Q-L*) is the standard for working with relational databases, so it makes sense for Access to understand it. Although SQL is the standard, SQL itself has a number of dialects, each with its own keywords, syntax, and features. The dialect Access uses is, appropriately, called Access SQL. It follows the ANSI-SQL 92 standard pretty closely but does include some proprietary extensions.

You will probably use SQL within your VBA modules (as we have in some of the examples) to generate recordsets or manage the data in your tables. So we've included this appendix to give you some background on building SQL queries. This isn't meant to be a comprehensive tutorial on SQL, but it does give you the basics.

A

NOTE

The American National Standard Institute (ANSI) is responsible for adopting, maintaining, and coordinating many standards, of which SQL is one. For more information about SQL standards see www.ansi.org.

CAUTION

Because of the differences in dialects, SQL statements that work in Access might need to be modified to work in other dialects. For example, T-SQL, used by SQL Server, requires strings to be surrounded by single quotes only.

SQL keywords fall into two categories:

- **Data Manipulation Language (DML)**—Used to manipulate the data in your tables. It can retrieve, modify, delete, or append data.
- **Data Definition Language (DDL)**—Deals with the objects in your database. It can create and drop tables, modify the structure of tables, and more.

➜ We discuss DDL briefly in "Data Definition Language" **p. 315**.

CAUTION

This section contains a number of examples of SQL statements for demonstration purposes. If you want to test these statements we suggest making a copy of one of the versions of the sample database. Running these statements may affect the outcome of other examples from earlier in the book.

SQL Structure and Syntax

SQL was designed to be almost a natural English language. The basic SQL statement of SELECT...FROM...WHERE looks almost like a regular English sentence. SQL has specific *keywords*, such as the three just mentioned, that have specific meanings. Just like your functions and procedures, keywords have arguments. The combination of keywords and arguments constitutes a *clause*.

Clauses are combined together to create a SQL *statement*. The statement makes a request of the database engine to retrieve or modify the data. Statements can contain one or more clauses, but usually more than one.

In its most basic form a statement would follow syntax such as the following:

`action fieldlist FROM datasource`

where `action` is one of several keywords that indicate the purpose of the statement, `field-list` identifies what fields are to be acted on by the statement, and `datasource` identifies the table (or tables) where the data is stored.

A further keyword that is often used is WHERE. This keyword is used to limit what records are acted on by the query. A WHERE clause uses the following syntax:

`WHERE condition`

Table A.1 lists the most common action keywords used by DML. Table A.2 lists more keywords that are used to modify the actions being performed by the statement.

Table A.1 Common SQL Action Keywords

Keyword	Purpose	Syntax
SELECT	Retrieve data	SELECT *fieldlist* FROM *datasource*
UPDATE...SET	Modify existing data	UPDATE *datasource* SET *field* = *expression*
DELETE	Delete whole records	DELETE FROM *datasource*
INSERT INTO	Add records to an existing table	INSERT INTO *table (fieldlist)* SELECT *source* INSERT INTO *table (fieldlist)* VALUES*(list)*
SELECT INTO	Copy an existing table (data and structure) into a new table	SELECT *fieldlist* INTO *newtable* FROM *datasource*

Table A.2 Additional Keywords

Keyword	Purpose	Syntax
ALL	Returns or acts on all records (default)	SELECT ALL FROM *datasource*
DISTINCT	Returns unique values for specified fields	SELECT DISTINCT *fieldlist* FROM *datasource*
DISTINCTROW	Returns unique records	SELECT DISTINCTROW *fieldlist* FROM *datasource*
FROM	Identifies the data source	FROM *datasource*
JOIN	Connects to another table using a key field	FROM table [INNER/OUTER] JOIN table ON field1 = field2
TOP	Limits the number or percentage of records returned	TOP *value*
WHERE	Identifies an expression that limits the returned records	WHERE *conditionalexpression*
GROUP BY	Arranges records that have similar values	GROUP BY *fieldlist*
ORDER BY	Defines how the returned records are sorted	ORDER BY *fieldlist*
HAVING	Defines which records make it within a group	HAVING *condition*

A

The SELECT Statement

The statement you are going to use most often is the SELECT statement, which is used to retrieve a set of data from a table or tables. The SELECT statement doesn't make any changes to the data; it simply retrieves the specified data for display or assignment to a recordset object. The SELECT statement is flexible, which makes its structure complex:

```
SELECT [ALL ¦ DISTINCT ¦ TOP] fieldlist ¦ *
FROM datasource
[WHERE condition]
[GROUP BY col1[, col2...]]
[HAVING condition]
[ORDER BY col1 [ASC ¦ DESC] [, col2... [ASC¦DESC]]
```

The ALL¦DISTINCT keywords are optional. If omitted SQL assumes ALL. Also, ASC (ascending) is assumed in your ORDER BY clause, so it can be omitted. You can either use a specific fieldlist or the asterisk (*), which indicates that you want all fields included. You should retrieve only the fields you actually need for performance reasons. The more data being called from the tables, the longer the process takes. Retrieving a lot of data across a wide area network can be painful. The only required clause is the FROM clause to identify the datasource. Everything else is optional.

The simplest SQL statement uses none of the optional keywords or clauses. It takes the following form:

```
SELECT *
FROM datasource;
```

Access SQL requires the semicolon to indicate the end of the statement. Normally, you will use a specified fieldlist argument, which represents the fields within the datasource that you want to display, separated by a comma as follows:

```
SELECT col1 [AS alias][, col2 [AS alias]...]
```

Within your query you refer to columns not fields. This is because a column can be represented by a calculation not only by a field. The AS keyword can be used to change or assign a column heading, referred to an Alias. When using calculations within your column, the AS keyword is required. To illustrate this consider the following statement:

```
SELECT LastName & ", " FirstName AS Fullname
FROM tblEmployees;
```

The LastName and FirstName fields are concatenated around a comma and assigned a heading of Fullname. This is a common usage.

The SQL Predicates

The ALL, DISTINCT, DISTINCTROW, and TOP predicates tell the SELECT statement what records to return. ALL is the default and returns all the records in the datasource. DISTINCT returns only records that are unique for the fieldlist specified. For example, the following statement would return only one record for each unique combination of first and last names:

```
SELECT DISTINCT Lastname, Firstname
FROM tblEmployees;
```

If there were two employees named Jack Jones, only one record for them both would be returned.

> **CAUTION**
>
> Using the DISTINCT predicate results in an uneditable recordset, so you can't use this predicate if you need to modify data.

Use DISTINCTROW when you want to return records that are unique in all fields. The DISTINCT predicate checks for uniqueness only among the fields requested. Because almost all tables require a unique primary key, using DISTINCTROW on such a table really doesn't do anything.

Use SQL's TOP predicate when you want to restrict the returned records to a specific number or percentage of records. The syntax is

```
SELECT TOP n [PERCENT] col1[, col2...]
```

where *n* is a number indicating the amount of records you want to return. Let's look at the following examples:

```
SELECT TOP 5 Company FROM tblSuppliers;
SELECT TOP 10 * PERCENT FROM qryInventoryTransactionsExtended;
```

In the first statement you retrieve five records. These will be the first five suppliers depending on the sort order. In the second statement you retrieve 11 records, because there are 101 transaction records and 10% rounds up to 11.

The SQL FROM Clause

You have to include a FROM clause; otherwise, the statement does not know what data sources to pull the records from. The full syntax for the clause looks like this:

```
FROM datasource ¦ parenttable JOIN childtable ON parenttable.primarykey =
  childtable.foreignkey
```

where *parenttable* refers to the parent or one side of the relation, and *childtable* refers to the child or many side of the relation. The clause to the right of the vertical line allows you to retrieve data from multiple tables by setting a relationship between the key field of one table and a key field of the other. The JOIN argument comes in two flavors: INNER and OUTER. For Access SQL this takes on three forms: INNER JOIN, RIGHT JOIN, or LEFT JOIN. An INNER JOIN retrieves only those records where the two key fields match. A RIGHT JOIN retrieves all records from the right side of the join and only matching records from the left side, while the LEFT JOIN works conversely.

Let's say you want to show sales by employee. But you want to include all employees regardless of whether they had made a sale. The SQL would look like this:

```
SELECT tblEmployees.LastName, tblEmployees.FirstName, tblTransactions.Quantity
FROM tblEmployees LEFT JOIN tblTransactions ON tblEmployees.EmployeeID =
    tblTransactions.Employee
ORDER BY tblEmployees.LastName, tblEmployees.FirstName;
```

If you used an INNER JOIN, only employees with sales transactions would be listed, but with a LEFT JOIN, you get all the employees because that table is on the left side of the join and matching transactions. Where there isn't a match, the opposite side of the join contains a Null. So, in our example, the *Quantity* column for employees without matching transactions would be Null.

The SQL WHERE Clause

One of the main purposes of using SQL is to retrieve subsets of data that satisfy certain conditions. These conditions are supplied via criteria included within the WHERE clause. This clause uses the following syntax:

```
WHERE condtionalexpression
```

where *conditionalexpression* can be as simple as a comparison between a field and a specific value, or a complex series of comparisons. The main substance here is that the value in a specific field must meet some criteria to be included in the results. A WHERE clause can be as simple as

```
SELECT * FROM tblEmployees
WHERE EmployeeID = 1;
```

which returns only one record, where the value of the EmployeeID = 1. Conversely, a WHERE clause can be a complex set of criteria using the AND and OR operators. For example, assume you want to show all transactions for a specific item, sold by a specific employee within a specific range of dates. Such a WHERE clause might look like this:

```
SELECT * FROM tblTransactions
WHERE TransactionItem = 8 AND Employee = 6 AND
    CreatedDate BETWEEN #3/21/06# AND #4/5/06#;
```

In this example we are retrieving all the columns, but it should be noted that the WHERE clause can include columns not listed in the field list. So we could use a statement like this:

```
SELECT TransactionItem, Employee, Quantity FROM tblTransactions
WHERE TransactionItem = 8 AND Employee = 6 AND
    CreatedDate BETWEEN #3/21/06# AND #4/5/06#;
```

Even though the CreatedDate is not one of the returned columns, we can still set criteria on it.

Now this query doesn't tell us a lot because it uses the foreign keys for TransactionItem and EmployeeID. To make this query truly useful, you would want to include some joins. The SQL statement may look like this:

```
SELECT tblEmployees.LastName, tblEmployees.FirstName, tblInventory.Item,
tblTransactions.Quantity
```

```
FROM tblInventory INNER JOIN (tblEmployees INNER JOIN tblTransactions ON
tblEmployees.EmployeeID = tblTransactions.Employee) ON tblInventory.InventoryID =
tblTransactions.TransactionItem
WHERE (((tblEmployees.EmployeeID)=6) AND ((tblTransactions.TransactionItem)=8) AND
((tblTransactions.CreatedDate) Between #3/21/2006# And #4/5/2006#));
```

With this statement we can get the employee's names from `tblEmployees` and the item name from `tblInventory` while still restricting the results by the indicated criteria.

The SQL ORDER BY **Clause**

More often than not you will want to see the returned records in a specific order. For that you use the ORDER BY clause to sort text, number, or date/time values. The syntax for the ORDER BY clause is

```
ORDER BY col1 [ASC|DESC][, col2 [ASC|DESC],...]
```

The ASC|DESC argument tells Access whether to sort in ascending or descending order, where ascending is the default and can be omitted. For instance the following SQL statement returns employee records sorted by employee names:

```
SELECT LastName & ", " & FirstName AS Fullname
FROM tblEmployees
ORDER BY LastName, FirstName;
```

As with the WHERE clause, sorting can be done on fields not in the field list. Sorting is done in the order the columns are listed. So in the preceding sample the records are sorted first by `LastName`, and then by `FirstName` within `LastName`.

The SQL GROUP BY **Clause**

The GROUP BY clause allows you to organize the returned records into groups. The groups are most often accompanied by some sort of calculation that summarizes some value (or values) attributable to the group. Let's go back and review the statement we used to illustrate the FROM clause. We can now add a GROUP BY clause to group on employee:

```
SELECT tblEmployees.LastName, tblEmployees.FirstName,
    Sum(tblTransactions.Quantity) AS SumOfQuantity
FROM tblEmployees INNER JOIN tblTransactions ON
    tblEmployees.EmployeeID = tblTransactions.Employee
GROUP BY tblEmployees.LastName, tblEmployees.FirstName;
```

This statement returns one record for each employee with a total of the quantity column.

Each column in the SELECT statement must be used to either define the group or evaluate the group. This means that each column in the field list must either be listed in the GROUP BY clause or be part of an aggregate function (such as Sum, Count, Avg, and so on). Columns in the GROUP BY clause are evaluated left to right just as in the ORDER BY clause.

A

The SQL HAVING **Clause**

You use the HAVING clause in concert with a GROUP BY clause. You can't have a HAVING clause without a GROUP BY, although a HAVING clause isn't necessary for the GROUP BY. The HAVING clause is similar to the WHERE clause in that it limits the returned record based on some criteria. The difference is that the HAVING clause is evaluated after the grouping. This gives you the ability use the results of your aggregate functions to limit the returned records. The HAVING clause uses the syntax:

```
HAVING condition
```

The `condition` argument would be an expression (or expressions) used to provide criteria in the following syntax:

```
HAVING expression1 AND¦OR expression2...
```

For example, in the previous example of sales by employee, you might want to restrict the returned records to those where the sales are greater than 500 units. The new statement now looks like this:

```
SELECT tblEmployees.LastName, tblEmployees.FirstName,
    Sum(tblTransactions.Quantity) AS SumOfQuantity
FROM tblEmployees INNER JOIN tblTransactions ON
    tblEmployees.EmployeeID = tblTransactions.Employee
GROUP BY tblEmployees.LastName, tblEmployees.FirstName
HAVING (((Sum(tblTransactions.Quantity))>500));
```

Notice that the HAVING clause uses the aggregate function as its argument, not the alias.

> **TIP**
>
> The WHERE and HAVING clauses are used to limit the returned records. Although they perform similar functions and you can often get the same results using either, they aren't interchangeable.

The INSERT **Statement**

Adding new records to a table is a common task for SQL statements generated and run within VBA. The INSERT INTO statement can be used to add records to a table or copy records from one table to another. When copying records you would use the syntax:

```
INSERT INTO target
SELECT source
```

where `target` is the destination table that the records will be copied to, and `source` is the table you are copying records from. The SELECT part of this statement supports WHERE and ORDER BY clauses. The target must exist before executing the statement; otherwise, an error occurs.

If you are adding data to a table you would use a second form of the INSERT INTO statement with the following syntax:

```
INSERT INTO target (col1[, col2,...])
VALUES(val1[, val2,...]);
```

There are some rules to follow when using this form of the INSERT INTO statement:

- Column references are optional. If you omit them, the VALUES clause must include a value for each field in the *target*.
- There must be an expression in the VALUES clause for each column in the target list, and they must be in the same order. The order in the target list does not have to match the order of fields in the table.

One place where this would be often used is in unbound forms. An example might be a new employee entry form where you just enter the basic information. Such code might look like this:

```
Dim strSQL As String
strSQL = "INSERT INTO tblEmployees ([Firstname], [Lastname]) "
strSQL = strSQL & "VALUES ('" & Me.txtFirst & "', '" & Me.txtLast & "');"
CurrentDb.Execute strSQL
```

Another thing this example points out is that, when generating SQL statements within your VBA code, you generally assign the statement to a string variable and then use that variable as the argument when executing the statement.

> **NOTE**
> When executing SQL statements within your VBA code, you can use either DoCmd.RunSQL or CurrentDB.Execute. The main difference between the two is that the RunSQL method generates warning messages that you will be performing an action query and if there are some problems running it.

> **CAUTION**
> When executing SQL statements within your VBA you can only execute action queries (Append, Update, Delete). Trying to execute a SELECT statement results in an error.

Notice also, that the values being drawn from controls on a form need to have single quotes concatenated around them, just as date/time values would need the octothorpe (#) character.

One last caveat: When appending records to a table with an Autonumber primary key (which would be almost every table if you follow my recommendations), you have to leave the Autonumber out of the target column list. An error results if you don't.

A

The UPDATE **Statement**

The SQL UPDATE statement is used to change values in specified fields within a table. This statement uses the following syntax:

```
UPDATE datasource
SET col1 = expression[, col2 = expression, ...]
[WHERE condition]
```

Because each SET clause in an UPDATE statement deals with one field in each individual record, the GROUP BY, ORDER BY, and HAVING clauses are not applicable to this statement. Another difference with the UPDATE statement is that it doesn't return a result set. It just updates the records involved.

For an example, let's assume we had a price field in tblInventory (which we don't), and we wanted to increase prices across the board by 10%. The UPDATE statement would look like this:

```
UPDATE tblInventory
SET Price = Price * 1.1;
```

Let's take this a step further and assume you only wanted to update items from a specific supplier. The UPDATE statement would look like this:

```
UPDATE tblInventory
SET Price = Price * 1.1
WHERE SupplierID = 4;
```

Now, it will update items only from Supplier D.

> **TIP**
>
> Before you run an UPDATE query with a WHERE clause, you should test it as a SELECT query first. Make sure the affected records are what you want. Alternatively, you can make a copy of the table first so that you can restore the table to its previous state if the modifications aren't correct.

Any changes you make have to respect the properties of the field and any validation rules in place; otherwise, errors will occur. So your code should include error trapping for those potential problems.

The SELECT INTO **Statement**

The SELECT INTO statement allows you to add records into a new table. The syntax for this statement is

```
SELECT INTO * ¦ col1[, col2, >>>] INTO newtable
FROM source
```

The SELECT INTO statement can use WHERE, GROUP BY, ORDER BY, and HAVING clauses to limit the records copied to the new table.

If you just need to copy the table structure, you can use the syntax:

```
SELECT * INTO newtable
FROM source
WHERE False
```

Because no record matches the criteria `False`, no data is copied, but the table is still created. Remember that the primary key and indexes are not copied.

> **CAUTION**
>
> If the table specified in *newtable* already exists, `SELECT INTO` overwrites the existing table with the copied structure and/or data. So, be sure that this is what you want to do. You might want to use code to check for the table before you run the statement.

The DELETE Statement

The `DELETE` statement is straightforward. It deletes entire records that meet the criteria supplied in a `WHERE` clause. The statement uses the syntax:

```
DELETE
FROM datasource
[WHERE condition]
```

Like the `UPDATE` statement, the nature of the `DELETE` statement makes the `GROUP BY`, `ORDER BY`, and `HAVING` clauses inapplicable. The following statement deletes all records where the value in the Quantity field is Null or zero, because any such records are probably mistakes:

```
DELETE
FROM tblTransactions
WHERE Quantity Is Null OR Quantity = 0;
```

Crosstabs

A *crosstab query* is a great way to present normalized data in a non-normalized summary. These queries allow you to summarize data based on two or more attributes and use an aggregate function to do the summarization.

Crosstab queries use the SQL `TRANSFORM` statement to convert the data into a row-by-column format. It uses the following syntax:

```
TRANSFORM aggregate
SELECT statement
PIVOT column
```

Where *aggregate* is one of the several aggregate functions used on one field in the table, *statement* is any valid SQL statement, and *column* identifies the column headings. The `HAVING` clause is not support by the `TRANSFORM` statement.

A

The following example can produce a crosstab that summarizes sales by employee and supplier. To illustrate this example we will use a query set up for this example named `qryXTabBase`. Figure A.1 shows the results of that query.

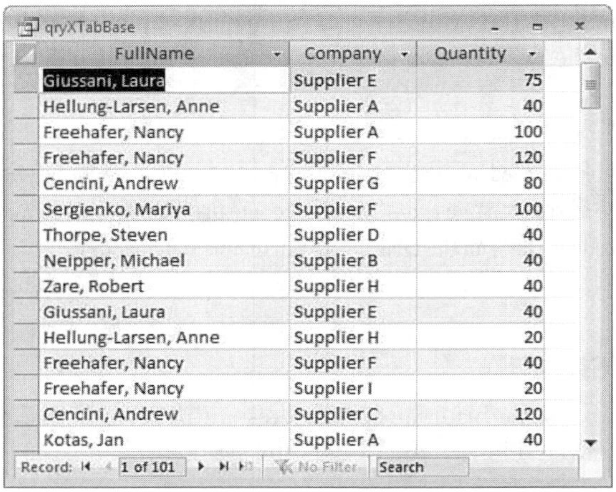

qryXTabBase

FullName	Company	Quantity
Giussani, Laura	Supplier E	75
Hellung-Larsen, Anne	Supplier A	40
Freehafer, Nancy	Supplier A	100
Freehafer, Nancy	Supplier F	120
Cencini, Andrew	Supplier G	80
Sergienko, Mariya	Supplier F	100
Thorpe, Steven	Supplier D	40
Neipper, Michael	Supplier B	40
Zare, Robert	Supplier H	40
Giussani, Laura	Supplier E	40
Hellung-Larsen, Anne	Supplier H	20
Freehafer, Nancy	Supplier F	40
Freehafer, Nancy	Supplier I	20
Cencini, Andrew	Supplier C	120
Kotas, Jan	Supplier A	40

Record: 1 of 101 No Filter Search

Figure A.1
The query that will be used to create the crosstab query.

A

The following statement performs the crosstab:

```
TRANSFORM Sum(qryXTabBase.[Quantity]) AS SumOfQuantity
SELECT qryXTabBase.[FullName], Sum(qryXTabBase.[Quantity]) AS [Total Of Quantity]
FROM qryXTabBase
GROUP BY qryXTabBase.[FullName]
PIVOT qryXTabBase.[Company];
```

As you can see the `TRANSFORM` clause specifies a `Sum` (aggregate) of the `Quantity` field. The `SELECT` statement selects the three columns including the `Sum` of `Quantity`. The `GROUP BY` clause sets up a grouping on the employee name, and the `PIVOT` clause indicates which field defines the columns. Figure A.2 shows the results of the crosstab query.

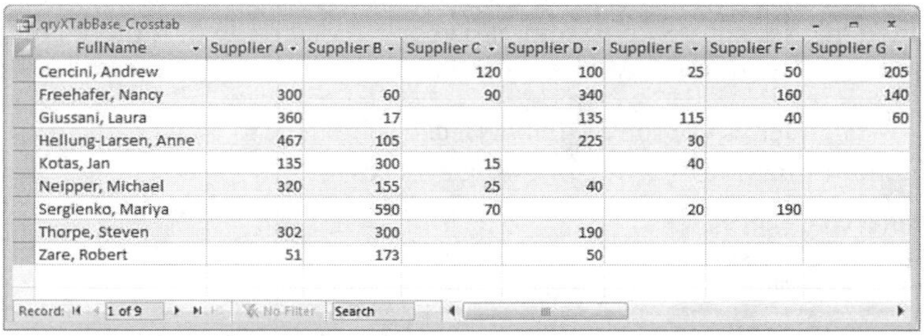

qryXTabBase_Crosstab

FullName	Supplier A	Supplier B	Supplier C	Supplier D	Supplier E	Supplier F	Supplier G
Cencini, Andrew			120	100	25	50	205
Freehafer, Nancy	300	60	90	340		160	140
Giussani, Laura	360	17		135	115	40	60
Hellung-Larsen, Anne	467	105		225	30		
Kotas, Jan	135	300	15		40		
Neipper, Michael	320	155	25	40			
Sergienko, Mariya		590	70		20	190	
Thorpe, Steven	302	300		190			
Zare, Robert	51	173		50			

Record: 1 of 9 No Filter Search

Figure A.2
The results of the crosstab query.

> **TIP** Although you need to include the actual SQL statements in your VBA code, a shortcut to creating the statements is to use Query Design mode. You can build your query using the interactive interface, switch to SQL view, and then copy and paste the generated statement into your VBA module.

INDEX